The Insider's Complete Guide to

AP US History

A STRATEGIC REVIEW

Second Edition

by LARRY KRIEGER

The Insider's Complete Guide to

AP US History

A Strategic Review

Second Edition

LARRY KRIEGER

ISBN: 978-0-9852912-6-6

An INSIDER TEST PREP publication of Larry Prep LLC

Art Direction & Design by Station16 (Station16 LLC)

For more Insider resources visit
www.InsiderTestPrep.com

LETTER FROM THE AUTHOR

The new *AP US History Course and Exam Description* (CED) book is a formidable 264-page document providing students with a challenging opportunity to study American history. The course contains nine chronological units that extend from 1491 to the present era. Learning the required content and using the key history reasoning skills will be a challenging but rewarding task.

The second edition of AP US History: A Strategic Review does not attempt to cover every topic in the CED. It doesn't have to. The APUSH scoring guide is surprisingly generous. You can earn a five by correctly answering 76 percent of the 140 exam points, a four by answering 64 percent, and a 3 by answering 51 percent.

I have used the scale and a careful study of the CED and released College Board materials to devise a strategic review to guide your preparation for the APUSH exam. Part I provides a careful review of the key topics in Periods 1 – 3 (1491 to 1800). Taken together, these periods will generate between 20 and 31 percent of your exam points. Parts II and III provide comprehensive coverage of African American and women's history. These two topics always generate a significant number of APUSH questions. Part IV provides 5 chapters on key topics including Native American history, the Populist Movement, the Cold War, Immigration and Nativism. A concluding chapter covers the modern Conservative revival, the Reagan presidency, the end of the Cold War, the digital revolution, and globalization. Our strategic review then presents eight Mini-Chapters. This very popular feature allows you to quickly review 18 topics ranging from the Second Great Awakening to the Vietnam War and the modern environmental movement.

Our 25 content chapters present the key information you will need to achieve a high score. However, the APUSH exam does more than test your knowledge of content; it also tests your ability to use historical reasoning skills. Part VI of our book contains four chapters that will help you master multiple-choice, short-answer, DBQ, and long-essay questions. *AP US History: A Strategic Review* provides you with an opportunity to test your knowledge and skills on 190 multiple-choice questions, 27 short-answer questions, two DBQs, and two long-essay questions.

AP US History: A Strategic Review concludes with a unique Glossary. Unlike textbooks and prep books, our Glossary does not contain an exhaustive (and exhausting) list of every conceivable term that could appear on the APUSH exam. Instead, it focuses on the 64 key terms that appear in the CED and on released exams. The Glossary provides clear definitions for each of these terms.

In addition, it lists key understandings and historic generalizations associated with each term.

AP US History: A Strategic Review contains insights learned from many years of teaching AP US History. Students and teachers praised the book's first edition. I am confident that the second edition will provide you with an efficient, effective, and rewarding guide to achieving a high score on your APUSH exam.

TABLE OF CONTENTS

PART I
THE COLONIAL PERIOD

PART II
AFRICAN AMERICAN HISTORY

PART III
WOMEN'S HISTORY

PART IV
KEY TOPICS, MOVEMENTS, AND EVENTS

PART V
MINI CHAPTERS ON KEY TOPICS

PART VI
TEST-TAKING STRATEGIES

PART IV
GLOSSARY

ABOUT THE AUTHOR

Larry Krieger earned his B.A. and M.A.T. from the University of North Carolina at Chapel Hill and his M.A. from Wake Forest University. In a career spanning more than four decades, Mr. Krieger taught in urban, rural, and suburban public high schools in North Carolina and New Jersey. He taught a variety of AP subjects including U.S. History, Art History, European History, and American Government. Mr. Krieger has published popular books in all of these subjects.

Mr. Krieger's AP US History courses were renowned for their energetic presentations, commitment to scholarship, and dedication to helping students achieve high AP exam scores. Over 90 percent of Mr. Krieger's APUSH students have scored fives, with the remainder scoring fours. Mr. Krieger has never had an AP student score a one or two.

ACKNOWLEDGEMENTS

Books do not write or publish themselves. They require the work of a number of dedicated and creative people.

The typed manuscript must be proofed and assembled into an attractive, well-designed book. As always, Station16 more than met this challenge. Brenton played a key leadership role. He created a distinctive design, offered valuable advice, and managed the project to a successful conclusion. Jesh shaped the manuscript into flowing layouts, and Margo supervised the entire project.

I would like to thank my students for their support, encouragement, and constructive suggestions. Special thanks to Vikram and Mukund Srikishan. They attended every class and read every chapter. Their insights and suggestions helped strengthen the book.

I would especially like to thank my wife Susan for her indefatigable dedication to this project. As "Editor-in-Chief," Susan read, critiqued, and proofed every page of this book. Her "close reads" spotted misplaced modifiers, passive voice verbs, and unconnected thoughts. Susan gave each chapter a grade and always encouraged me to be "clear, concise, and interesting!" Susan's frequent questions and curiosity encouraged me to do additional research to find fascinating details to enliven the text.

INTRODUCTION

BASIC QUESTIONS AND ANSWERS

AP US History: A Strategic Approach offers unique materials designed to help you achieve a high score on your APUSH exam. Before explaining why this book is unique let me begin with two fundamental questions. First, how many points are on the APUSH exam? And second, how many points do you need to earn a 5, 4, or 3?

Most students do not know the answers to these two questions. Many students assume that the APUSH exam contains 100 points and that they need 90 points for a 5, 80 points for a 4, and 70 points for a 3. These answers are all incorrect. The APUSH exam actually contains a total of 140 points. On the 2019 exam students needed 106 points for a 5, 90 points for a 4, and 72 points for a 3. Here is the official APUSH score conversion chart for the 2019 exam:

SCORE RANGE	AP SCORE	MINIMUM PERCENT CORRECT
106–140	5	76 percent
90–105	4	64 percent
72–89	3	51 percent
53–71	2	38 percent
0–52	1	0–37 percent

This chart is not a misprint. You can earn a 3 by correctly answering just 52 percent of the questions, a 4 by correctly answering 65 percent of the questions, and a 5 by correctly answering 77 percent of the questions.

A NEW STRATEGIC APPROACH

A grand total of 496,573 students took the 2019 APUSH exam. Of this group 11.8 percent scored a 5, 18.4 percent scored a 4, and 23.4 percent scored a 3. The remaining 46.3 percent scored 1's and 2's.

These results underscore the fact that the APUSH exam will present you with a challenging test of your level of preparation. Given this formidable challenge, what is the best strategy for achieving a 3, 4, or 5 and avoiding a 1 or 2?

Teachers traditionally use a chronological approach. That is, they begin their course in 1491 and then teach a series of chronological units. Although their intent is to reach the twenty-first century, most fall short of this goal.

APUSH prep books mirror this chronological approach. They present thousands of facts in a condensed version of a college textbook. This attempt to cover everything turns reviewing into a tedious and boring exercise in memorization.

AP US History: A Strategic Approach offers a very different plan for helping you successfully prepare for the APUSH exam. Instead of providing you with yet another chronological review, this book takes a strategic approach designed to identify the core material you need to study in order to earn a 3, 4, or 5.

Our strategic approach is based on three central facts. First and foremost, the APUSH exam does not test students on a random group of questions. Instead, exam questions cluster around key historic topics clearly identified in the APUSH Course Framework. Second, these central topics can be identified by carefully studying the Framework and released exams. And finally, the core topics can be organized into chapters that make history interesting and memorable.

A STRATEGIC ORGANIZATION

AP US History: A Strategic Approach is divided into seven distinct parts. Each part plays a specific role in helping you build a winning coalition of points.

PART I
A REVIEW OF PERIODS 1 - 3 (1491 - 1800)

Recent changes in the APUSH exam have dramatically increased the strategic importance of Periods 1 – 3 (1491 – 1800). The new College Board Course and Exam Description (CED) book states that these three periods will generate between 20 and 31 percent of the total number of exam points. This translates into between 28 and 42 of the 140 exam points. Remember, you only need 109 points for a 5, 91 for a 4, and 73 for a 3.

Why are the first three time periods receiving so much weight? All three time periods will continue to generate several sets of multiple-choice questions. However, the real reason can be found in the distribution of short-answer and long-answer essay questions. The College Board exam format now calls for two short-answer questions between periods 3 and 8 and another short-answer question between Periods 1 and 5. So there is a good chance that your exam will contain a short-answer question from Periods 1 – 3. At the same time, the College Board test format now states that you will only have to answer one of three long-essay questions. The first of these three questions will be from

Periods 1 – 3! Remember, each long-essay question is worth 21 exam points or 15 percent of your total score.

From a strategic point of view, Periods 1 – 3 have another important advantage. The density of events during the years between 1491 and 1800 is much less than the density of events in the 19th century and especially the 20th century. Why is this true? The answer is very straightforward – a combination of fewer people and slower communications reduced the number of events. The important events that occurred between 1491 and 1800 can be easily identified and efficiently reviewed.

Part I is designed to help you prepare for the key events and trends between 1491 and 1800. Chapter 1 provides a comprehensive narrative review of Period 1. Chapters 2 – 6 provide detailed mini-chapters of the key points about New World empires (Chapter 2), colonial regions (Chapter 3), main currents in colonial thought (Chapter 4), the causes of the American Revolution (Chapter 5) and the debate between the Federalists and the Anti-Federalists (Chapter 6). Taken together these 6 chapters will help you build a strong foundation of points that will put you in position to achieve a very high score.

PART II
A REVIEW OF AFRICAN AMERICAN HISTORY

African American history has always generated a number of questions on the APUSH exam. Chapters 7 – 10 provide a comprehensive review of key trends, developments, and leaders from the origins of slavery to the modern Civil Rights Movement. Each chapter is followed by 15 multiple-choice questions and two short-answer questions. These carefully written questions are designed to help you evaluate your knowledge of African American history and your test-taking skills.

PART III
A REVIEW OF WOMEN'S HISTORY

Women's history is rapidly becoming a key topic on recent APUSH exams. Chapters 11 and 12 provide a comprehensive review of key trends, developments, and leaders from Anne Hutchinson to Betty Friedan. Each chapter is followed by 15 multiple-choice questions and two short-answer questions. These carefully written questions are designed to help you evaluate your knowledge of women's history and your test-taking skills.

PART IV

KEY TOPICS, MOVEMENTS, AND EVENTS

Chapters 13 – 17 are based upon a careful analysis of APUSH exams since 2015. Chapter 13 focuses on Native American history from the Columbian Exchange to the modern Red Power Movement. Chapter 14 examines the causes and consequences of the Populist Movement. Chapter 15 describes the origins and early history of the Cold War. Chapter 16 explores patterns of immigration and nativism. And finally, Chapter 17 provides detailed coverage of the modern conservative revival, the Reagan revolution, the end of the Cold War, the digital revolution and the emergence of globalization. Each chapter is followed by 15 multiple-choice questions and two short-answer questions. These carefully written questions are designed to help you evaluate your knowledge of the topics covered in Chapters 13 – 17.

PART V

MINI–CHAPTERS ON KEY TOPICS

This section contains eight mini-chapters. Each of these two-to-four page "minis" is devoted to a point-by-point comparison of key APUSH topics. The mini-chapters cover a wide range of topics that begin with the Second Great Awakening and conclude with the Korean and Vietnam wars and environmental movements since 1900.

The eight mini-chapters are short but mighty! In fact, I often call them the "Great Eight." The mini-chapters are easy to read, understand, and remember. However, at the same time they cover topics that have generated a significant number of multiple-choice and short-answer questions. The combined information in our narrative chapters and the mini-chapters should be sufficient to enable you to score a 5!

PART VI

TEST–TAKING STRATEGIES

The APUSH exam contains four distinctive types of questions. Each type tests a specific range of historic reasoning skills. *AP US History: A Strategic Approach* provides a comprehensive chapter devoted to each of the four types of APUSH questions.

A. MASTERING THE MULTIPLE-CHOICE QUESTIONS

Your APUSH exam will begin with a 55-minute period devoted to 55 multiple-choice questions. The questions are grouped into sets containing 2 to 4 questions. Each set of questions is based upon a stimulus prompt. Most prompts are brief passages taken from primary and secondary sources. In addition, a few prompts contain a graph, map, or political cartoon. Taken together, the multiple-choice questions are worth 55 points or 40 percent of your APUSH exam score.

Chapter 26, Mastering the Multiple-Choice Questions, provides a detailed discussion of the multiple-choice questions. The chapter devotes special attention to how APUSH test writers use history reasoning skills such as contextualization, causation, comparison, and continuity and change over time to design their multiple-choice questions. The chapter concludes with 10 practice questions. Taken together, *AP US History: A Strategic Approach* contains 190 practice multiple-choice questions.

B. MASTERING THE SHORT-ANSWER QUESTIONS

After completing the multiple-choice section you will be given 40 minutes to answer 3 short-answer questions. The short-answer questions ask you to respond to prompts such as a debate between two historians, a map, or a political cartoon. In addition, there is a question asking you to compare the similarities and differences between two important historic movements, trends, or eras. Each short-answer question will ask you to provide 2 to 4 sentence answers to three very specific questions. Taken together, the 3 short-answer questions are worth 28 exam points or 20 percent of your total exam score.

Chapter 27, Mastering the Short-Answer Questions, provides a detailed discussion of this type of question. The chapter includes detailed annotated examples that guide you through the do's and don'ts of answering short-answer questions. Taken together, *AP US History: A Strategic Approach* contains 27 practice short-answer questions.

C. MASTERING THE DOCUMENT-BASED QUESTION (DBQ)

The DBQ is an essay question that requires you to interpret and analyze 7 brief primary source documents. The documents typically include excerpts from diaries, speeches, letters, and official decrees. In addition, DBQ's often include a graph, map, or political cartoon. The DBQ begins with a recommended 15-minute reading and planning period. You will then have 45 minutes to write your essay. Your DBQ will be scored on a scale that includes 7 specific points. Each point is worth 5 exam points. Taken together, the DBQ is worth a maximum of 35 points or 25 percent of your total score.

Chapter 28, Mastering the Document-Based Question, provides a detailed discussion of the DBQ. The chapter devotes particular attention to explaining each of the 7 points in the DBQ rubric. Thus far, DBQ questions have asked students to apply the history reasoning skills of causation and continuity and change over time to major historic developments. Our chapter provides a model DBQ for each of these two skills. The model DBQs devote particular attention to explaining and illustrating how to write a sophisticated thesis and how to incorporate complexity into your essay.

D. MASTERING THE LONG-ESSAY QUESTION (LEQ)

Your APUSH exam concludes with a 40-minute time period devoted to a long-essay question. You will be given three long-essay questions. Although the three questions will be taken from different time periods, they will be related by a common theme and history reasoning skill. You will be asked to select and write about just one long-essay question. Your essay will be scored on a scale that includes 6 specific points. Each point is worth 3.5 exam points. The long-essay question is thus worth 21 exam points or 15 percent of your total exam score.

Chapter 29, Mastering the Long-Essay Question, provides a detailed discussion of the LEQ. The chapter devotes particular attention to explaining each of the 6 rubric points. Two model LEQs explain and illustrate how to write a sophisticated thesis and how to incorporate complexity into your essay.

PART VII
GLOSSARY OF KEY TERMS

APUSH textbooks and prep books conclude with extensive glossaries containing hundreds of terms. Do you really need to memorize the definitions of all these terms? Fortunately, the answer is a definitive no! A careful analysis of the APUSH CED and released exams reveals that there are 64 key terms you absolutely, positively have to know. Needless to say, the Glossary includes all 64 of these terms.

Glossaries traditionally provide terms and definitions. However, this traditional approach will only provide limited help on your APUSH exam. Test writers do not compose multiple-choice questions that ask students to choose the best definition of the Columbian Exchange. Instead, they provide a stimulus prompt that identifies an aspect of the Columbian Exchange. They then ask questions about the context, causes, and consequences of this complex exchange of people, goods, animals, plants, and germs.

The Glossary in this book does more than provide definitions. Most terms are followed by brief statements summarizing key understandings about the how the concept affected historic events. A careful review of the Glossary will reward you with a substantial number of exam points!

"WE CAN DO IT"

The new APUSH Framework and exam first appeared during the 2014-2015 school year. The Framework and exam marked a significant departure from the previous course. I have devoted the past 5 years to carefully studying all the relevant College Board materials. I am pleased and proud to report that about 90 percent of my students have scored 5s with the remainder scoring 4s.

These high scores did not happen by accident. I have worked very hard to provide my students with the best possible review strategies and materials. *AP US History: A Strategic Approach* shares these strategies and materials with you.

During our review sessions my students always adopt an inspirational slogan. Most choose the "We Can Do It" slogan from the famous World War II Rosie the Riveter poster. This is a particularly apt slogan. The APUSH exam presents a formidable challenge. However, this book provides you with a strategic approach that will enable you to "Do It!" Good luck!

PART I

THE COLONIAL PERIOD
1491 – 1789

CHAPTER 1
FROM COLUMBUS TO JAMESTOWN
1491–1607

STRATEGIC IMPORTANCE

According to the College Board, Period 1 will account for 5 percent of your total APUSH score. Five percent equals 7 of the 140 available points. This total is derived from at least one set of multiple-choice questions and a short-answer question that includes information from both Period 1 and Period 2.

At first glance, this doesn't seem like a significant number of points. But looks are deceiving. Remember, you only need about 75 points to score a 3. Period 1 thus accounts for about 10 percent of the points you need to earn a 3!

Period 1 covers a small group of easily mastered topics. For example, College Board test writers place special emphasis on the *encomienda* system and the Columbian Exchange. It is important to remember that Period 1 will NOT generate either a DBQ or a long essay question.

KEY POINTS AND HISTORIC GENERALIZATIONS

- Native American populations settled across the vast expanse of North America. Over time, they developed distinct and increasingly complex societies by adapting to and transforming their diverse environments.

- The European exploration, conquest, and colonization of North and South America caused immense changes in both the Old and New Worlds.

- The *encomienda* system allowed Spanish colonial economies to marshal Native American labor to support plantation-based agriculture and extract precious metals.

- European traders partnered with West African groups who practiced slavery to forcibly extract slave labor for the Americas. The Spanish imported enslaved Africans to labor in plantation agriculture and mining.

- New Spain's high rate of intermarriage produced a racially diverse population of Europeans, Africans, and Native Americans.

- The COLUMBIAN EXCHANGE set in motion a series of profound changes that brought catastrophic population losses to Native Americans, immense suffering to West Africans, and unprecedented prosperity to West Europeans.

TOPIC 1.1
THE FIRST AMERICANS

A. ARRIVAL AND DISPERSAL

The first Americans crossed a land bridge connecting Siberia and Alaska. Multiple crossings took place between 15,000 and 30,000 years ago. Over time, migrating bands of hunters spread across North and South America. They may have reached the tip of South America about 11,000 years ago.

B. THE PACIFIC NORTHWEST

The Pacific Northwest stretches from northern California to southeastern Alaska. The region is blessed with a mild climate, generous rainfall, and abundant natural resources. The seacoast offered a seemingly inexhaustible supply of sea otters, seals, whales and other sea mammals while rivers teemed with salmon. Dense forests provided cedar trees that could be used to carve canoes and build homes.

Nature's plentiful resources enabled tribes such as the Haida and Kwakiutl to build settled communities and use their leisure time to create elaborate works of art. For example, skilled craftsmen carved towering totem poles decorated with figures honoring dead chiefs, powerful animals, and supernatural beings.

The region's natural bounty also enabled chiefs to accumulate vast stores of material possessions. In a special ceremony called a *potlatch*, chiefs gave away huge supplies of valuable furs, food, and prized artworks to cement alliances and demonstrate their status.

C. THE SOUTHWEST

The Southwest confronted Native American settlers with a demanding and at times harsh environment. The intense morning sun quickly heated the air. Nightfall then brought plunging temperatures that often dropped 30 degrees before dawn. Life-giving summer rains and winter snowfall produced an average annual rainfall of about 16 to 18 inches of moisture.

Despite these drawbacks, the Southwestern environment did provide its early settlers with several advantages. A long growing season and the careful use of irrigation supported agriculture. In addition, forests of pinon (small pine trees with edible seeds) and juniper trees supplied building materials, firewood, and edible roots and berries.

The Hopi built their settlements on high ground that could be more easily defended. They collected rainwater in rock cisterns and carefully parceled it out to fields where they grew maize, beans, melons, and squash. The Hopi constructed apartment-like dwellings of adobe that the early Spanish explorers called *pueblos* meaning "towns." Clusters of Hopi homes typically faced a central plaza where many religious celebrations took place.

D. THE GREAT PLAINS

The Great Plains stretch from the Rocky Mountains to the Mississippi River. The climate features cold, snowy winters followed by hot, dry summers. When they first ventured into this vast region, awestruck Spaniards reported seeing huge herds of buffalo roaming across the open grasslands.

Hollywood movies and television westerns depicted Native American warriors wearing elaborate feather headdresses as they hunted buffalo from horseback. In reality, the horse-and-buffalo culture of the Plains Indians did not emerge until the eighteenth and nineteenth centuries.

Tribes such as the Pawnee drifted into the Great Plains from eastern Texas around 1300 C.E. They settled along the Platte River and its many tributaries. Like other tribes living in the Great Plains, the Pawnee developed a mobile lifestyle based upon both farming and hunting. In the spring, families planted corn, squash, and beans. Once the plants were strong enough to survive, the entire tribe packed up for the buffalo hunt. While on the hunt, the Pawnee lived in portable tepees made of buffalo skins.

E. THE EASTERN WOODLANDS

The Eastern Woodlands extended from the Mississippi River to the Atlantic Coast. Dense hardwood forests dominated the landscape. It was said that a squirrel could travel from Tennessee to New York without ever touching the ground.

About 7,000 years ago, farmers living on the plains of western Mexico crossbred wild grasses and created maize, or corn. The new food had many advantages. It was high in caloric content and could be easily stored and dried. Corn cultivation soon spread north into the Ohio River Valley. By about 1000 C.E., corn became a staple food among Native Americans living in the Eastern Woodlands.

The spread of corn brought population growth and the emergence of mixed agriculture and hunter-gatherer economies that supported the development of permanent villages. For example, Iroquois-speaking people in upstate New York built bark longhouses that sheltered families related through their female line. Iroquois tribes successfully formed a powerful alliance known as the Iroquois Confederation. The alliance ended generations of warfare. It formed the most important Native American organization to confront the European colonists.

F. COMMON CHARACTERISTICS

The diverse Native American societies of North America shared three key characteristics. First, they all believed that sacred spirits resided in both living and inanimate things. They relied upon religious leaders to conduct ceremonies designed to influence these supernatural powers. Second, the Native Americans viewed land as a common resource that could not be bought or sold. And finally, many Native Americans lived in matrilineal societies in which children traced their descent through their mother's line.

No Native American society north of Mexico developed a written language. The North American tribes also lacked large domesticated animals, wheeled vehicles and gunpowder.

TOPIC 1.2
PORTUGAL AND SPAIN LAUNCH A NEW AGE

A. PORTUGAL AND PRINCE HENRY

In 1434, no European vessel had ever sailed beyond Cape Bojador, a treacherous cape located 1,000 miles southwest of Portugal. Superstitious Europeans believed that boiling seas filled with monsters awaited any mariner foolish enough to venture into these dangerous waters. However, Portugal's Prince Henry the Navigator ignored these false beliefs and ordered a series of expeditions to explore the West African coastline.

During the 1440s, Portuguese caravels systematically pushed farther and farther down Africa's western coast. They quickly established a series of trading posts that did a thriving business in gold, ivory, and slaves.

The Portuguese also colonized the Canary Islands and the Azores. They soon learned the secret of growing sugar cane and manufacturing sugar. Their lucrative sugar plantations imported thousands of enslaved Africans. The system of using slave labor on sugar plantations provided a model for producing vast wealth and great human suffering.

B. SPAIN AND CHRISTOPHER COLUMBUS

Christopher Columbus successfully persuaded the Spanish monarchs King Ferdinand and Queen Isabella that he could reach the fabled riches of the East Indies by "attempting a great leap over the sea." Intrigued by Columbus' novel idea, the Spanish monarchs approved his bold plan. On August 3, 1492, Columbus left Spain and sailed into the uncharted waters of the Atlantic Ocean.

On October 12th, a lookout on the Pinta cried out the words everyone on Columbus's three ships yearned to hear – "Tierra! Tierra!" Within a short time, San Salvadore's astonished inhabitants came out to welcome the Spaniards. Convinced that he had found a shortcut to the Indies, Columbus called the people Indians.

During the next few weeks, Columbus cruised the northern coasts of Cuba and Hispaniola. Although he did not find spices or gold, he did taste pineapples, eat sweet potatoes, and observe people smoking tobacco.

Columbus received a hero's welcome when he returned to Spain. The royal court marveled at the parrots and captive Indians he brought back. Neither Columbus nor the Spanish monarchs saw any reason to respect Native American culture. Instead, they proposed to Christianize the indigenous peoples, seize their mineral wealth, and exploit their labor.

C. THE SPANISH CONQUISTADORES

The Spanish conquistador Hernan Cortes arrived in the Aztec capital of Tenochtitlan on November 8, 1519. Cortes did not come as a tourist. His letters to the Spanish monarch Charles V reveal an all-consuming desire for power and status. Within a short time, Cortes toppled the Aztec empire. His metal swords, guns, horses, and ruthless tactics all played an important role in terrifying the Aztec armies. However, his greatest ally proved to be diseases such as smallpox, influenza, and measles that decimated the Aztec population.

Soon other ambitious Spanish conquistadores followed in Cortes's footsteps.

In 1532, Francisco Pizarro successfully invaded and conquered the Inka empire in Peru. Like Cortes, he used guile and superior weapons to defeat the Inka armies while deadly European diseases devastated the Inka people.

TOPIC 1.3
NEW SPAIN

A. INTRODUCTION

The conquest of the Aztec and Inka empires enabled the Spanish to establish a vast New World empire. They used the empire to spread Catholicism and enrich themselves.

Spain created a rigid and highly centralized empire controlled by the crown in Madrid. The Spanish tried to exercise complete control over New Spain. By 1635, the Crown and the Council of the Indies enacted over 400,000 laws to regulate each detail of daily life. A reform program in 1681 reduced this number to "only" 64,000 laws.

B. THE *ENCOMIENDA* SYSTEM

An *encomienda* was a license granted by the Spanish crown to royal officials to extract labor and tribute from native peoples living in specified areas. For example, Cortes appropriated tribute from 23,000 families living in the fertile Oaxaca Valley.

The *encomienda* system began in the Caribbean and then spread to Mexico. It enabled Spanish colonial administrators to organize and regulate native labor to support sugar plantations and mining operations. In exchange, the *encomenderos* were responsible for converting the native peoples under their protection to Catholicism.

Although the native peoples were legally not slaves, ruthless *encomenderos* nevertheless created a brutal system of forced labor that led to many abuses. The inhumanity of the *encomienda* system appalled the Dominican priest Bartolome de las Casas. In a scathing critique he denounced the system of forced labor as "the harshest, fiercest, most terrible servitude and captivity."

C. A NEW SOCIETY

European diseases caused an unprecedented demographic catastrophe. Smallpox and other diseases claimed the lives of as many as 90 percent of Mexico's original 20 million native inhabitants.

It soon became clear that the native population could not meet New Spain's growing demand for labor. In the early 1500s, the Spanish began to import enslaved Africans to labor on sugar plantations and in silver mines. About 300,000 enslaved Africans arrived in New Spain between 1500 and 1650.

During the 150 years between 1500 and 1650, about 350,000 Spaniards emigrated to the Caribbean, Mexico, and Andes. Young, single males comprised the majority of these migrants. The ensuing high rate of intermarriage produced a diverse mixture of Europeans, Africans, and indigenous peoples.

TOPIC 1.4
THE PUEBLO REVOLT

A. INTRODUCTION

Visitors to Statuary Hall in Washington, D. C. are greeted by 100 statues, two from each state in the Union. Most of the statues commemorate the contributions of presidents, senators, and governors. However, a statue from New Mexico is very different from the others. It is dedicated to a proud Pueblo religious leader named Pope'.

B. THE CAUSES OF THE PUEBLO REVOLT

During the 17th century, Spanish officials and settlers gradually gained control over New Mexico and the Pueblo people. At the same time Franciscan friars forcibly converted the people to Catholicism. The Spanish further disrupted the Puebloan's traditional way of life by forcing them to labor on *encomiendas*. By 1680, the Pueblos faced an unrelenting assault on their beliefs and cultural identity.

C. POPE' LEADS A REVOLT

Contemporaries described Pope' as "a fierce and dynamic" leader who deeply resented the Spanish rulers. As his world began to collapse, Pope' secretly organized a rebellion to expel the Spanish and return to the traditional ways that had brought the Pueblo peace, prosperity, and independence.

The Pueblo Revolt began on August 10, 1680. The sudden uprising caught the Spaniards completely by surprise. By the end of the month, the insurgents killed over 400 Spanish civilians and 21 of the 33 Franciscan friars.

D. SHORT- AND LONG-TERM CONSEQUENCES

The Pueblo Revolt did not bring peace and prosperity to the people of New Mexico. A drought destroyed their crops and internal divisions weakened their ability to resist both the Spanish and other nearby tribes, In addition, Pope's death in 1685 deprived the Pueblo of their most inspirational leader. Just four years later, the Spanish began a successful reconquest of the Pueblos.

Although their independence from Spanish rule proved to be short-lived, the Pueblo Revolt had important enduring consequences. The Spanish no longer tried to eradicate the Pueblo's culture and religion. Over the next centuries, New Mexico became a blend of both Spanish and Pueblo cultures. Today, the Puebloans view their ancestors revolt as a key reason for their survival as a distinct people.

TOPIC 1.5
NEW FRANCE

A. INTRODUCTION

The Spanish carved out a vast New World empire that stretched from what is today New Mexico to Peru. They built impressive cathedrals in Mexico City and Lima and even opened universities in both of these cities. As the seventeenth century opened, France had yet to establish permanent colonies in North America.

B. CHARACTERISTICS OF NEW FRANCE

French explorers initially searched for a Northwest Passage to Asia. Although this search proved futile, the French did explore and claim the Great Lakes, Mississippi River, and Louisiana.

Within a short time, French traders dominated the lucrative fur trade. Beaver skins quickly became France's major "money crop." In the best years, traders bought and sold over 100,000 beaver skins. In 1693, a fleet of 400 Indian canoes brought furs to Montreal. The fur trade produced great profits that played a role in Western Europe's ongoing shift from feudalism to capitalism.

The French fur traders developed a generally cooperative relationship with the Native American tribes. The trappers lived and worked in widely scattered trading posts. Unlike the English settlers, they did not build plantations or farms on lands claimed by Native American tribes.

TOPIC 1.6
THE COLUMBIAN EXCHANGE

A. DEFINITION

In 1491 no one in Ireland had ever seen a potato, no one in Italy had ever tasted a tomato, and no one in Switzerland had ever eaten chocolate. At the same time, no one in the Americas had ever ridden a horse, roasted a chicken, or enjoyed the sweet taste of sugar. Columbus's voyages launched a momentous but unplanned process that forever altered diets and life in the New and Old Worlds. The COLUMBIAN EXCHANGE refers to the exchange of plants, animals, peoples, and diseases between the New World, Europe, and Africa.

The Columbian Exchange began during Columbus' second voyage. He introduced sugar cane, horses, cows, chickens, and pigs to the Caribbean islands. At the same time, his sailors also carried invisible but deadly viruses and microbes. Within a short time, small pox, measles, and cholera decimated once thriving island populations. For example, the Taino on the island of Hispaniola became extinct within 50 years.

The process of exchange initiated by Columbus continued during the sixteenth and seventeenth centuries. European vessels brought wheat, rice, apples, oranges, and other Old World crops. They returned with New World crops that included maize, potatoes, peanuts, tomatoes, and chili peppers. In addition, New World mines provided a steady stream of gold and silver. For example, the fabulously rich Potosi mine in what is today Bolivia produced 200 tons of silver a year for two centuries.

B. IMPACT ON EUROPEANS

New World foods and precious metals had a dramatic and long-lasting impact on Europe. Nutritious American crops fueled a surge in European population. At the same time, the influx of gold and silver facilitated economic growth. These powerful forces stimulated the rising prosperity of the merchant class in Western Europe. This facilitated a historic shift from a stagnant feudal economy to a new and more energetic capitalist economy.

C. IMPACT ON NATIVE AMERICANS

Old World diseases decimated the Native American population. Demographers estimate that 40 to 100 million people lived in the Americas in 1491. This figure plummeted to an estimated 8 million people in 1600. The sudden collapse of entire New World communities enabled European colonists to more easily gain control over Native American lands.

Diseases also had a severe psychological impact upon Native Americans. Resistance against seemingly invincible invaders seemed futile. Birth rates plummeted as demoralized New World survivors saw no future for their children.

D. IMPACT ON AFRICANS

The Spanish quickly discovered that coffee and sugar flourished in New World soils and climates. These highly prized crops produced great profits but required a large labor force. The severe drop in the New World population forced the Spanish to look to Africa for a source of labor. Between the sixteenth and nineteenth centuries, European slave traders forcibly transported over 12 million Africans to the Americas. The ATLANTIC SLAVE TRADE marked the largest involuntary migration of people in human history.

CHAPTER 1
PRACTICE QUESTIONS

MULTIPLE-CHOICE QUESTIONS

Questions 1–4 refer to the excerpt below:

"The city has many squares, in which are situated the markets and other places for buying and selling. There is one square twice as large as that of the city of Salamanca (in Spain), surrounded by porticoes, where are daily assembled more than sixty thousand souls, engaged in buying and selling; and where are found all kinds of merchandise that the world affords, embracing the necessities of life, as for instance articles of food, as well as jewels of gold and silver, lead, brass, copper, tin, precious stones, bones, shells, snails, and feathers."

Hernan Cortes, from Second Letter to Charles V, 1520

1. The excerpt best reflects which of the following?

A. The presence of a plantation-based economy focused on cash crops and luxury items

B. The presence of a complex society with a mixed economy based on agriculture and trade

C. The presence of a rigid racial hierarchy dominated by the Aztecs

D. The presence of deadly epidemics brought to the Americas by the Spaniards

2. By the end of the sixteenth century the "articles of food" referenced in the excerpt became part of the

A. Columbian Exchange

B. First Great Awakening

C. Atlantic slave trade

D. Protestant Reformation

3. Cortes's description of Tenochtitlan is most consistent with

A. Coronado's account of the Seven Cities of Gold

B. De Soto's account of settlements in the Mississippi River Valley

C. Ponce de Leon's account of his travels in Florida

D. Pizarro's account of the Inka capital at Cuzco

4. **The description in this excerpt most directly challenged the prevailing seventeenth-century English view that Native Americans**
    A. made no distinction between men's work and women's work
    B. inhabited a thinly populated wilderness
    C. were a cosmopolitan people with advanced technology
    D. were immune to European diseases

Questions 5–6 refer to the excerpt below:

"If ten thousand years ago, you had been asked to guess which area of the world would be the seat of the greatest future civilizations, you would probably have settled on some part of Central or South America on the basis of the amazing things they were doing with food there…Mesoamericans were the greatest cultivators in history, but of all their many horticultural innovations none was more lastingly important or unexpected than the creation of maize…"

Bill Bryson, historian, *At Home*, 2010

5. **The "amazing things" developed in pre-Columbian Mesoamericaa included all of the following EXCEPT:**
    A. the creation of a mathematically based calendar
    B. the construction of complex irrigation systems
    C. the building of cities inhabited by 50,000 or more people
    D. the use of wheeled vehicles

6. **Maize and other New World crops directly impacted European societies by**
    A. spreading New World diseases and triggering a short-term decline in population
    B. causing a devastating famine in Ireland
    C. contributing to widespread economic inflation that began in Spain and spread throughout Western Europe
    D. improving diets, boosting birth rates, and extending life expectancies

Questions 7–8 refer to the excerpt below:

"The Europeans who peopled America in Columbus's wake believed the land had never been settled, much less civilized…When whites first penetrated the fertile Ohio Valley, they found many mounds but few Indians. The Southwest also seemed vacant when the French came to stay around 1700. As they moved into lands that abounded in natural resources, the settlers kept wondering where the Indians had gone."

Lewis Lord with Sarah Burke, historians, "America Before Columbus," 1991

7. **Modern historians believe that the catastrophic decline in the population of Native Americans was caused by**

    A. generations of tribal warfare
    B. a prolonged drought
    C. epidemics triggered by European diseases
    D. armed conflicts with the English and Spanish

8. **European explorers typically explained the absence of Native Americans as**

    A. proof that America was an "empty continent" open to settlement
    B. evidence of the effectiveness of germ warfare
    C. a sign that they should avoid Native American agricultural practices
    D. an opportunity to adopt the Native American belief that land was to be shared, not owned

Questions 9–11 refer to the excerpt below:

"We are informed that because of the...liberty enjoyed by the said Indians, they avoid contact...with the Spaniards to such an extent that they will not even work for wages, but wander about idle, and cannot be had by the Christians to convert to the Holy Catholic Faith.... I command you, our said Governor...that you will compel and force the said Indians to associate with the Christians... and to work on their buildings...and mine the gold...and to till the fields and produce food for the Christians.... This the Indians shall perform as free people, which they are, and not as slaves."

Instructions from the Spanish Crown to the governor of Hispaniola, 1503

9. **The instructions in this excerpt most clearly provide evidence for which of the following?**

    A. The beginning of competition between Spain and France for control of the New World
    B. The beginning of the *encomienda* system that developed in New Spain
    C. The beginning of deadly epidemics that devastated native populations
    D. The beginning of joint-stock companies to develop gold and silver mines

10. **Which type of activity ultimately dominated economic activity in Hispaniola and the West Indies?**

    A. Tobacco plantations
    B. Sugar plantations
    C. Shipbuilding and fishing
    D. Textile factories

11. **Which of the following was a direct consequence of the widespread death of Native Americans in the West Indies?**

    A. The migration of English Puritans to the West Indies
    B. The decision by Spain to abandon the West Indies and focus on Mexico and Peru
    C. The forcible importation of slaves from West Africa
    D. The Spanish decision to shift from a feudal to a capitalist economy

Questions 12–13 refer to the excerpt below:

"They are among the least robust of human beings: their delicate constitutions make them unable to withstand hard work or suffering and render them liable to succumb to almost any illness, no matter how mild…. It was upon these gentle lambs…that from the very first day they clapped eyes on them the Spanish fell like ravening wolves…. The pattern established at the outset has remained unchanged to this day, and the Spaniards still do nothing save tear the natives to shreds, murder them and inflict upon them untold misery…"

Bartolomé de Las Casas, *A Short Account of the Destruction of the Indies*, 1552

12. **The inability of Native Americans "to withstand hard work" and tendency to "succumb to almost any illness" prompted the Spaniards to**

    A. recruit indentured servants from Portugal
    B. import slave labor from Africa
    C. abandon plans to develop sugar plantations
    D. partner with the Aztec and Inka rulers

13. **All of the following would become key parts of "the pattern" referenced in this excerpt EXCEPT:**

    A. Autonomous farming communities
    B. Extensive mining of silver
    C. A racially mixed population
    D. The *encomienda* system

Questions 14–15 refer to the excerpt below:

"The discovery of America, and that of a passage to the East Indies by the Cape of Good Hope, are the two greatest and most important events recorded in the history of mankind. Their consequences have already been very great; but, in the short period of between two and three centuries which have elapsed since these discoveries were made, it is impossible that the whole extent of their consequences can have been seen. What benefits, or what misfortunes to mankind may hereafter result from those great events, no human wisdom can foresee. By uniting, in some measure, the most distant parts of the world, by enabling them to relieve one another's wants, to increase one another's enjoyments, and to encourage one another's industry, their general tendency would seem to be beneficial."

Adam Smith, economist, *The Wealth of Nations*, 1776

14. **Which of the following social changes provides one of the "benefits...to Europe" that resulted from the discovery of America?**

    A. The increased importance placed upon extended family relationships
    B. The adoption of new ideas about the proper roles of husbands and wives
    C. The decline in income gap between the mercantile class and those working in agriculture
    D. The introduction of new foods that supported a rising population

15. **Which of the following would best support Smith's contention that the discovery of America led to a "general tendency [that] would seem to be beneficial?"**

    A. The use of the *encomienda* system to organize and regulate Native American labor
    B. The creation of extensive and peaceful trade relations with the Pueblos
    C. The large-scale slave rebellions on Hispaniola
    D. The creation of a trans-Atlantic trading network

MULTIPLE-CHOICE ANSWERS

1. B	5. D	9. B	13. A
2. A	6. D	10. B	14. D
3. D	7. C	11. C	15. D
4. B	8. A	12. B	

SHORT-ANSWER QUESTIONS

Question 1
Answer A, B, and C.

A. Briefly explain ONE example of how geographic conditions influenced life in Native American societies in the Pacific Northwest.

B. Briefly explain ONE example of how geographic conditions influenced life in Native American societies in the Four Corners region of the Southwest.

C. Briefly explain ONE example of how geographic conditions influenced life in Eastern Woodlands of North America.

Question 2
Answer A, B, and C.

A. Briefly explain ONE example of how the Columbian Exchange brought changes to Native American societies in the period 1492 to 1607.

B. Briefly explain a SECOND example of how the Columbian Exchange brought changes to Native American societies in the period 1492 to 1607.

C. Briefly explain ONE example of how the Columbian Exchange brought changes to Western European societies in the period 1492 to 1607.

SHORT-ANSWER ANSWERS

Question 1

A. The Pacific Northwest is blessed with a mild climate, generous rainfall, and abundant natural resources. These environmental advantages enabled the Haida and other Native American tribes to build settled communities and use their leisure time to create elaborate works of art. Chiefs accumulated vast stores of possessions, which they gave away in a special *potlatch* ceremony.

B. The Four Corners region of the Southwest confronted the Hopi and other Native Americans with a demanding and at times harsh environment. Nonetheless, the Hopi took advantage of the long growing season and used irrigation to compensate for the sparse rainfall. The Hopi lived in apartment-like dwellings of adobe that the early Spanish explorers called *pueblos*.

C. The Eastern Woodlands contained dense forests and fertile land. Iroquois-speaking peoples cultivated corn and built permanent villages that included bark longhouses. They formed a powerful alliance known as the Iroquois Confederation.

Question 2

A. The Columbian Exchange brought Old World diseases such as smallpox and measles that decimated the Native American population. Demographers estimate that the Native American population plummeted by at least 80 percent.

B. The sudden collapse of entire New World communities enabled European colonists to more easily gain control over Native American lands. Birth rates collapsed as demoralized New World survivors saw no future for their children.

C. Nutritious New World foods fueled a surge in European population and stimulated economic growth. This facilitated a shift from a stagnant feudal economy to a new and more energetic capitalist economy.

CHAPTER 2
THREE NEW
WORLD EMPIRES

LOCATION AND STRATEGIC IMPORTANCE

The Spanish, French, and English New World empires overlap Period 1 (1491–1607) and Period 2 (1607–1754). This chapter can stand alone as part of a topical review. Another option would be to use it after Chapter 1 as part of a chronological review of Periods 1 and 2.

The information in Chapter 2 has generated a significant number of points on multiple-choice and short-answer questions. Focus particular attention on the consequences of the Columbian Exchange and the characteristics of the *encomienda* labor system. A recent short-answer question asked students to identify similarities and differences between the goals of the Spanish and English colonies.

TOPIC 2.1
CHARACTERISTICS OF NEW SPAIN

1. Columbus and other Spanish sea captains hoped to chart a new ocean route to Asia. Instead, they discovered vast new continents.

2. Ruthless and often brutal Spanish conquistadores conquered immense new lands for the Spanish crown. For example, Hernan Cortes used superior weapons and shrewd diplomacy to topple the Aztec empire.

3. Jesuit and Franciscan priests waged a vigorous campaign to convert Native Americans to the Catholic faith.

4. Spanish colonists were devout Catholics. They did not leave Spain to seek greater religious freedom.

5. Spanish authorities attempted to exercise a significant degree of administrative control over New Spain. The royal council in Madrid divided their American empire into two immense regions known as viceroyalties. The king appointed a viceroy to govern each region. However, the great

distance between Madrid and New Spain enabled colonial authorities to delay, frustrate, and sometimes evade royal orders.

6. The Spanish created the *encomienda* system to organize and exploit Native American labor. The labor system began in the Caribbean and spread to Mexico. For example, the Spanish crown rewarded Cortes with a huge *encomienda* in the fertile Oaxaca Valley in southern Mexico.

7. Small pox, measles, and other virulent diseases decimated the Native American population. Demographers estimate that epidemics claimed the lives of as many as 90 percent of Mexico's original inhabitants. The Spanish then began to import enslaved Africans as a new source of labor for their Caribbean sugar plantations.

8. The Spanish began the Columbian Exchange of plants, animals, people, and diseases between Europe and the Americas.

9. The Spanish forced Native Americans and enslaved Africans to extract precious metals from hazardous mines. Between 1500 and 1650, the Spanish shipped about 180 tons of gold and 16,000 tons of silver to Europe.

10. Women comprised less than one-third of the total number of Spaniards who settled in the New World. As a result, many male emigrants married Native American women. Their racially mixed offspring became known as *mestizos*.

TOPIC 2.2
CHARACTERISTICS OF NEW FRANCE

1. French explorers initially searched for a Northwest Passage that would connect the Atlantic and Pacific oceans. Although their search proved to be futile, the French did explore and claim a vast territory. New France included the St. Lawrence River valley, the Great Lakes, the Mississippi and Ohio river valleys, and Louisiana.

2. French traders dominated the lucrative fur trade. Profits from this trade played a role in Western Europe's ongoing shift from feudalism to capitalism.

3. French fur traders lived and worked in widely scattered trading posts. They generally developed cooperative relationships with nearby Native American tribes. The French developed stronger alliances with Native American tribes than did either the Spanish or the English.

4. Jesuit missionaries lived among Native Americans and attempted to convert them to Catholicism. Although many Native Americans converted, they never fully embraced Jesuit teachings.

5. The people of New France had no elected assemblies. Decisions were made by local magistrates on behalf of the French king.

6. The lack of civil liberties and Canada's cold winter weather discouraged most French citizens from moving to New France. In 1700, the French territory contained just 19,000 white settlers. During the entire colonial period only about 250 French families settled in New France. As a result, French males often intermarried with Native Americans.

TOPIC 2.3
CHARACTERISTICS OF THE ENGLISH COLONIES

1. The English founded thirteen colonies along the Atlantic coast of North America.

2. English kings allowed private individuals and joint-stock companies to found colonies. While many colonies were established for economic profit, others were started by people fleeing religious and political persecution.

3. The English kings were unable to exert a high degree of royal control over their North American colonies. As a result, the colonists developed a tradition of local assemblies, town meetings, and an independent spirit.

4. Native Americans played an indispensible role in the early success of the English colonies. They provided supplies of desperately needed food and taught the colonists how to hunt and fish in the strange new environments.

5. Families typically settled the English colonies. They rarely intermarried with local Native Americans. As a result, English interaction with Native Americans often promoted separation between the two groups.

6. The English colonies developed diverse labor systems that included the use of indentured servants and enslaved Africans.

7. A landed aristocracy did not take root in the English colonies. This allowed ambitious planters and merchants to become prosperous and influential.

8. Emigrants from Great Britain dominated colonial life. However, the thirteen colonies included a rich diversity of peoples such as Scotch-Irish, Germans, Dutch, and French Huguenots.

9. The English colonists failed to discover deposits of gold and silver. However, they did develop lucrative cash crops. As a result, colonial ports participated in the trans-Atlantic economy.

10. The British colonies became steadily more populous and prosperous. By the mid-1700s, they emerged as the strongest colonial presence in North America.

CHAPTER 3
THE ENGLISH NORTH AMERICAN COLONIES

LOCATION AND STRATEGIC IMPORTANCE

The historic development of the Chesapeake, New England, and Middle Atlantic colonies occurred during Period 2 (1607 – 1756). This chapter can stand alone or as part of a topical review. Another option would be to use it after Chapters 1 and 2 as part of a chronological review of Periods 1 and 2.

The information in Chapter 3 has generated a significant number of multiple-choice and short-answer questions. The APUSH exam committee has written a number of short-answer questions asking students to compare the similarities and differences between British colonies in the Chesapeake, New England, and Middle Atlantic colonies. Devote particular attention to the Chesapeake colonies. This region has been an integral part of three recent short-answer questions.

TOPIC 3.1
CHARACTERISTICS OF THE CHESAPEAKE COLONIES

1. The Chesapeake colonies included Virginia and Maryland. These two colonies bordered the Chesapeake Bay. This body of water was about 300 miles long and 20 miles wide. The Virginia Tidewater region featured fertile land, a long growing season, abundant rainfall, and wide, navigable rivers.

2. Jamestown was founded in 1607 by the Virginia Company, a joint-stock company launched to make a profit for its investors. Despite the company's enormous financial investment, the Jamestown colony teetered on the brink of collapse. During the first 15 years, disease, malnutrition, and starvation claimed the lives of as many as 80 percent of Jamestown's first 10,000 colonists.

3. The Jamestown colonists wasted valuable time in a futile search for gold and silver. John Rolfe saved the colony when he learned how to raise a

sweet form of tobacco that thrived in Virginia's rich Tidewater soil. Tobacco quickly found a lucrative market in England where it sold for about 5 to 10 times as much as it cost planters to produce. As a result, tobacco production soared from 200,000 pounds in 1624 to 10,000,000 pounds in 1670.

4. The Jamestown settlers did not colonize an uninhabited land. Virginia's broad coastal plain sustained about 24,000 Native Americans divided into 30 tribes under the loose authority of a paramount chief named Powhatan. The Indians lived in small agricultural villages supplemented by fishing the tidewater basin and hunting for deer and other wildlife. The Native Americans lacked guns, metal armor, and professional armies.

5. Convinced of their own cultural superiority, ethnocentric English settlers viewed Native Americans as scantily clad savages who worshipped unfamiliar gods and spirits. Virginia's tobacco planters valued land more than Indian friendship. Sensing an ever-mounting threat to their way of life, Native Americans launched well-coordinated surprise attacks in 1622 and again in 1644. Although these uprisings badly damaged the Virginia colony, they inflicted even more damage on the Native Americans. War and disease reduced Virginia's Native American population from 24,000 in 1607 to just 2,000 by 1669. During the same time, the colony's population surged to 41,00.

6. Tobacco required a large supply of inexpensive labor. At first, Virginia planters relied upon indentured servants from England. Pushed by high rates of unemployment and poverty, homeless young men and women became indentured servants. They comprised about three-fourths of the 120,000 people who emigrated to the Chesapeake during the seventeenth century.

7. The tobacco boom of the 1640s and 50s enabled a small group of Tidewater planters to accumulate wealth and power. As a result, they dominated Virginia's economy and political institutions such as the House of Burgesses.

8. Indentured servants hoped for a better life after working without wages for 4 to 7 years. However, a combination of falling tobacco prices, rising taxes, and dwindling opportunities to purchase fertile land caused bitter feelings of frustration and resentment. Long-simmering grievances sparked a rebellion against the arbitrary rule of Governor Berkeley and the arrogant class of wealthy planters he represented. Led by a disgruntled and ambitious young planter named Nathaniel Bacon, the rebels successfully captured and burned down Jamestown. However, when Bacon suddenly died, Governor Berkeley quickly crushed the rebellion.

9. Bacon's Rebellion marked a significant turning point in the development of slavery in Virginia. Frightened planters began to replace troublesome indentured servants with more easily controlled enslaved Africans. As a result, the number of slaves in Virginia soared from 300 in 1650 to 16,000 in 1700 and over 100,000 in 1750.

10. In 1705, the Virginia General Assembly enacted a series of laws codifying slavery as a system of race-based, inherited, and perpetual bondage. Virginia thus developed a rigid racial system that contrasted with the racially mixed society that evolved in New Spain.

TOPIC 3.2
THE NEW ENGLAND COLONIES

1. The New England colonies included Massachusetts Bay, New Hampshire, Connecticut, and Rhode Island.

2. The New England colonies were founded by a relatively homogenous group of Puritan settlers who fled religious persecution in England.

3. The Puritans had a powerful sense of mission. In his famous "City Upon a Hill" sermon, John Winthrop expressed the Puritan belief that they had a special pact with God to build a "city upon a hill" that would serve as an ideal Christian commonwealth. Winthrop's sermon is often cited as the first example of American exceptionalism, the belief that America has a mission to be a beacon of democracy and freedom.

4. Although Puritans fled to escape religious persecution, they did not tolerate religious dissenters. For example, they banished both Anne Hutchinson and Roger Williams to Rhode Island.

5. The Puritans settled in families and rarely intermarried with Native Americans. They typically lived in small tightly knit communities centered around a meetinghouse. As New England's population grew, the region became dotted with a number of small towns.

6. The Puritans established a patriarchal society in which women played a subordinate role. New England's small towns and congregational churches nonetheless promoted a tradition of self-government. Male property owners attended town meetings where they resolved local issues. At the same time, each congregation chose its own ministers rather than being assigned one by a distance official.

7. The environment in New England featured long, cold winters, stony soils, and relatively brief growing seasons. The region contained short rivers with

narrow flood plains that did not allow for the creation of large agricultural plantations.

8. New England's rocky soils rewarded hard labor. Family farms produced a healthy mix of crops that included wheat, rye, maize, potatoes, and beans. Ambitious farmers could export small but profitable surpluses to sugar plantations in the Caribbean.

9. New England's dense forests produced fine lumber for ships. By 1700, Boston contained 15 shipyards that built more vessels than the rest of the English colonies combined. By the mid-1700s, New England merchants played a leading role in the lucrative network of transatlantic trade routes.

10. Native Americans originally welcomed the Puritans. They provided the English settlers with food and taught them how to hunt and fish in the new environment. But as in Virginia, tensions quickly developed over differing attitudes towards land. King Philip's War left the Native Americans a broken and defeated people.

TOPIC 3.3
THE MIDDLE ATLANTIC COLONIES

1. The Middle Atlantic colonies consisted of New York, New Jersey, Pennsylvania, and Delaware.

2. The region boasted fertile farmland and a temperate climate that permitted a long 180-day growing season. As a result, Middle Atlantic farmers could grow abundant crops of wheat and other grains. However, killing fall frosts meant they would not be tempted to raise tobacco.

3. The Susquehanna, Delaware, and Hudson formed a trio of broad, navigable rivers that enabled enterprising merchants to tap into the lucrative interior fur trade. For example, ships could ascent the Hudson 160 miles to Albany, a greater distance than was possible on any other river on the Atlantic seaboard.

4. Geography also blessed the region with deep natural harbors. As a result, New York City and Philadelphia experienced rapid growth and economic prosperity.

5. William Penn founded Pennsylvania in 1682 as a "Holy Experiment" that would serve as a refuge for Quakers. Penn created an unusually liberal colony that granted freedom of religion and included a representative assembly elected by the landowners.

6. Quakers believed that God communicated directly with an individual through a "Light within" or "inner light." Quakers favored simple services that excluded formal prayers, sermons, and rituals.

7. Quaker religious beliefs led to radical social conclusions. Insisting on the equality of all persons before God, Quakers permitted women to openly participate in their religious services. Quakers opposed slavery and became the first people in North America to urge the abolition of human bondage.

8. William Penn established amiable relations with the local Native American tribes by purchasing rather than seizing their lands. His farsighted policy enabled Pennsylvania to enjoy a prolonged period of peace with the Native Americans thus avoiding the destructive wars that devastated the New England and Virginia colonies.

9. William Penn employed paid agents who distributed pamphlets that promoted Pennsylvania's numerous advantages. Penn's promise of generous land sales, equal rights, and religious toleration attracted a diverse range of settlers that included Anglicans, Lutherans, Irish Catholics, and Jews from the Netherlands.

10. During the early years, the Middle Atlantic colonies included a number of African slaves. At one time, Philadelphia served as the region's main port for the importation of enslaved Africans. Estate records from 1682 to 1705 reveal that less than 7 percent of families in Philadelphia owned slaves. The moral opposition of Quakers and the absence of large plantations prevented slavery from becoming a defining feature of life in Pennsylvania.

CHAPTER 4
MAIN CURRENTS IN COLONIAL THOUGHT

LOCATION AND STRATEGIC IMPORTANCE

The three currents of intellectual thought covered in Chapter 4 occurred in Period 2 (1607 – 1754) and Period 3 (1754 – 1800). Puritanism and the First Great Awakening played important roles in Period 2 while the Enlightenment dominated thought in Period 3. This chapter can stand alone as part of a topical review. Another option would be to use it after Chapter 3 as part of a chronological review of Periods 2 and 3.

The information in Chapter 4 has generated a significant number of multiple-choice and short-answer questions. For example, a recent short-answer question asked students to compare and contrast the differences and similarities between the First Great Awakening and the Enlightenment.

TOPIC 4.1
PURITANISM

1. The Puritans were English Protestants who wanted to reform or "purify" the Church of England. They renounced elaborate rituals and ornate artistic decorations such as stain-glass windows and statues of saints. Puritans opposed the Anglican Church's hierarchy of bishops appointed by the Crown. Instead, they formed independent self-governing congregations.

2. The Puritan exodus from England began in 1630 with the departure of a fleet of 11 ships carrying 900 migrants. Led by John Winthrop, the Puritans sought a new home where they could escape political repression, religious restrictions, and an economic recession. During the next decade 14,000 more Puritans settled in Massachusetts Bay.

3. The Puritans believed in the teachings of John Calvin. According to Calvin, God is all-powerful and all-knowing. Through his inscrutable will, God has chosen a small group of the "Elect" to be saved while denying his grace

to everyone else. According to this doctrine of predestination, nothing an individual can say or do will change his or her predetermined fate.

4. The doctrine of predestination did not induce a sense of helplessness or despair. Instead, it prompted Puritans to prove they were part of the Elect by working hard, avoiding idleness, and living unpretentious lives. Their devotion to hard work, self-discipline, and frugal lifestyles embodied a set of values known as the Puritan work ethic. The commitment to these values helped the Massachusetts Bay colony thrive. Puritans interpreted their worldly prosperity as a sign of divine favor.

5. The Puritans were determined to create a society that would serve as an ideal Christian commonwealth. John Winthrop expressed this guiding vision when he urged his fellow settlers to remember. "We shall be as a city upon a hill, the eyes of all people are upon us." This image of America as what President Reagan later called "a shining city" became an enduring part of American exceptionalism, the belief that America has a mission to become a beacon of freedom and democracy.

6. The Puritans typically migrated in family groups rather than as single individuals. A combination of a nutritious diet, clean water, and cold temperatures that retarded virulent microbes extended lifespans and encouraged a high birth rate. Longevity contributed to family stability. Many Puritan families included grandparents. This intergenerational continuity helped created strong family ties and a stable social structure.

7. The Puritans lived in small tightly knit communities that encouraged a tradition of self-rule. Puritans worshipped in independent churches that elected their own ministers. Villagers gathered regularly to attend town meetings where they elected local officials, appointed schoolmasters, and discussed local issues such as repairing fences and building new roads.

8. Puritan women did not play a prominent role in public life. Massachusetts Bay was a patriarchal society in which husbands exercised authority over their wives and children. For example, women did not participate in town meetings and were excluded from decision making in their churches.

9. The Puritans valued education as a means to read and understand the Bible. They promoted public education by requiring each community of 50 families to provide a tax-supported school teacher for reading and writing. The Puritans founded Harvard College in 1636 to ensure an adequate supply of trained ministers.

10. The Puritans emphasized religious conformity. Convinced that they were doing God's work, Puritans did not tolerate outspoken religious dissidents. For example, in 1636 they banished Roger Williams for championing

religious freedom and the separation of church and state. A year later, they banished Anne Hutchinson for challenging the subordinate role of women in Puritan society and the clergy's sole ability to interpret the Bible. Williams promptly founded the Rhode Island colony based upon freedom of religion. Ironically, religious intolerance in Massachusetts Bay fostered a spirit of religious toleration in Rhode Island and other colonies.

TOPIC 4.2
THE FIRST GREAT AWAKENING

1. The First Great Awakening was a period of intense religious revival that began in New England in the mid-1730s and then spread across all of the colonies by the 1740s. This common religious experience became America's first shared national event.

2. As the colonies prospered, more and more people became pre-occupied with earning and spending money. By the 1730s, many ministers worried about a growing sense of religious decline.

3. "Old Light" Puritan ministers continued to deliver long intellectual sermons that emphasized elaborate theological doctrines.

4. Jonathan Edwards provided the initial spark for the Great Awakening by delivering emotional sermons warning congregations in New England to repent and lead pious lives. His most famous sermon, "Sinners in the Hands of an Angry God," painted a terrifying picture of the torments of Hell and the certainty of God's eternal wrath.

5. The Great Awakening reached its peak when George Whitefield, a celebrated English evangelist, set out in 1739 on a two-year speaking tour throughout the colonies. A great open-air orator, Whitefield preached to large and emotional crowds. For example, over 30,000 enthralled listeners crowded into Boston Commons to hear Whitefield's urgent message that they rethink the direction of their lives.

6. As the Great Awakening spread across America it sparked a missionary zeal that led to the conversion of many enslaved Africans.

7. The Great Awakening's impassioned message rekindled religious spirits. The new emotional approach divided American Protestants into "New Light" and "Old Light" denominations. The New Lights favored a spontaneous, impassioned, evangelical style of worship. In contrast, the Old Lights distrusted emotional outbursts and continued to favor traditional sermons.

8. The Great Awakening transformed American higher education. New Light ministers founded Princeton, Dartmouth, Columbia, Brown, and William and Mary to help prepare a new generation of revival-oriented ministers.

9. The Great Awakening led to divisions within the established Anglican, Congregational, and Presbyterian churches. In addition, Baptist and Methodist churches became more popular. These divisions created areligiously pluralistic society that supported toleration since no single denomination could impose its will on the others.

10. The Great Awakening championed individualism by insisting that each person had the right to choose his or her minister. It proved to be a short step from the right of all people to actively participate in their religion to the right of all people to actively participate in their government. Challenging the authority of Old Light ministers prepared a new generation of Americans for challenging the authority of the British Crown.

TOPIC 4.3
THE ENLIGHTENMENT

1. The Enlightenment was an eighteenth century intellectual movement led by a group of English and French thinkers and writers. It spread to the British North American colonies in the 1750s. Enlightenment writers formed a cosmopolitan "republic of letters" that included colonial leaders such as Benjamin Franklin, Thomas Jefferson, Thomas Paine, George Washington, and James Madison.

2. Enlightened leaders opposed intolerance, bigotry, and superstition. Instead,they stressed the use of reason as an informed and rational way to understand the world and an individual's place in it.

3. Enlightened thinkers believed that natural laws regulate the universe and human society. Natural laws can be discovered by human reason. They include the inalienable natural rights of life, liberty, and property.

4. Enlightened leaders believed in social progress. The discovery of laws of economics (such as the operation of supply and demand) and government (such as the separation of powers) would improve society and make progress inevitable.

5. Enlightened writers opposed monarchical forms of government as contrary to the laws of nature. Instead, they favored a social contract in which a government derives its powers from the consent of the people.

6. Enlightened writers lived in societies that placed restrictions on speech, religion, and trade. They wanted to remove these limitations on human

liberty. Enlightened thinkers believed that intellectual freedom was a natural right that would promote progress.

7. Enlightened leaders questioned many religious beliefs and practices, arguing that they perpetuated superstition, intolerance, and bigotry. Led by Thomas Jefferson, they advocated full religious toleration.

8. Much of the educated elite in Western Europe and America embraced deism. Desists thought of God as a cosmic watchmaker who created the universe and then allowed it to run according to immutable natural laws. However, deism's reliance upon reason and its lack of emotion had little appeal for many people. A religious movement known as pietism stressed faith, emotion, and "the religion of the heart."

9. The Enlightenment undermined the political authority of the British Crown and royal officials in the colonies. Enlightened concepts of reason and natural rights reinforced the colonial idea that the colonies could govern themselves.

10. The Enlightenment established the intellectual foundations for ideas that shaped the American revolution and the Declaration of Independence.

CHAPTER 5
CAUSES OF THE AMERICAN REVOLUTION

LOCATION AND STRATEGIC IMPORTANCE

The sequence of events covered in Chapter 5 dominate Period 3 (1754 – 1800). This chapter can stand alone as part of a topical review. Another option would be to use it after Chapter 4 as part of a chronological review of Period 3.

The information in Chapter 5 has generated a significant number of multiple-choice, short-answer, and long-essay questions. Multiple-choice sets have devoted particular attention to the Navigation Acts. Short-answer questions have devoted particular attention to the importance of republican principles in forging a new American identity. There is a strong possibility that the topics presented in this chapter will generate a long-essay question. For example, you should carefully review the influence of mercantilism and the colonial ideas of self-government.

TOPIC 5.1
MERCANTILISM AND SALUTARY NEGLECT

1. Trans-Atlantic trade between Europe, Africa, the West Indies, and the British North American colonies thrived. Great Britain responded by attempting to integrate its North American colonies into a cohesive imperial structure based upon the prevailing economic principles of mercantilism.

2. Mercantilism was intended to enable Great Britain to achieve a favorable balance of trade by exporting more than it imported. Britain expected to achieve this goal by purchasing raw materials such as sugar, tobacco, and furs from its North American colonies and then selling them more expensive manufactured goods such as metal tools, cloth, furniture, dishware, and firearms.

3. Parliament enacted a series of Navigation Acts designed to implement its mercantilist policies. Begun in 1651 and strengthened in 1660 and 1663, the Navigation Acts stipulated that goods could only be shipped in British

and colonial ships, even though Dutch freighters offered lower rates. In addition, certain enumerated articles such as tobacco and sugar had to be transported only to Great Britain, even though markets in Western Europe offered higher prices.

4. The Navigation Acts did not impose an intolerable burden on the colonies. For example, tobacco planters enjoyed a monopoly of the British market. Furthermore, the colonists enjoyed the protection of the British navy without having to pay the cost of maintaining it.

5. Although the Navigation Acts appeared to be strict, Parliament did not rigorously enforce them. Prior to 1763, the British followed a policy of relaxed supervision called "salutary neglect." Crown officials recognized that it cost four times as much to use the Royal navy to collect duties as the value of the duties themselves.

6. Enterprising colonial merchants successfully evaded burdensome mercantilist regulations. For example, New England merchants reaped great profits trading fish and lumber to French sugar islands. As a result, the colonists developed a growing spirit of economic independence.

7. By 1750, one-third of all "British" vessels were actually owned by merchants in New England and the Middle Atlantic colonies. The expansion of colonial shipping hastened urbanization by creating a need for centralized docks, warehouses, and repair shops. The workers, financiers, and merchants who worked in seaport towns later formed the core supporters of the grassroots revolutionary movement.

TOPIC 5.2
THE STAMP ACT AND THE BEGINNING OF COLONIAL RESISTANCE

1. In 1763, the overwhelming majority of American colonists pledged their loyalty to a British king who ruled by divine right. The idea of American independence did not yet exist. However, during the next 13 years a growing dispute over British economic policies strained long-standing political ties binding the colonists to their mother country. A clash over cherished political principles began to forge a new colonial identity.

2. The French and Indian War ended French power in North America. Under the terms of the Treaty of Paris of 1763, the British North American empire now stretched from the Atlantic coast to the Mississippi River and from Canada to the Gulf of Mexico. Colonists celebrated peace by praising their

mother country and optimistically predicting the beginning of a glorious new era of peace and prosperity.

3. The French and Indian War left Britain with a great empire and an enormous national debt that nearly doubled to 130 million pounds. The financial crisis forced Britain's young and untested monarch George III and his first minister George Grenville to reassess their colonial policies. Grenville concluded that the colonies had to begin paying a far share of the "costs of empire." He persuaded Parliament to enact a Stamp Act designed to raise revenue rather than regulate trade.

4. Grenville did not expect opposition to the Stamp Act. He was wrong. Outraged colonial leaders resented the abrupt end of salutary neglect and the sudden threat to their right to set local tax policies. They defended the powers of their provincial assemblies by shouting, "No taxation without representation!"

5. The Virginia House of Burgesses forcefully raised questions about Parliament's right to tax the colonies. In 1765, it passed a series of Resolutions on the Stamp Act. The Resolutions directly challenged Parliament's authority to tax the colonies. While continuing to express loyalty to the king, the Resolutions insisted that local control over taxation represented a "distinguishing characteristic of British freedom." As intended by the House of Burgesses,copies of the Virginia Resolutions quickly spread to other colonial assemblies. The Resolutions thus marked the beginning of a shift in colonial ideas about the need for American independence.

6. The colonists did more than write resolutions and shout slogans. In October 1765, nine colonies sent representatives to a Stamp Act Congress in New York City. The delegates took collective action by drafting a petition to Parliament defending the power of their representative assemblies to enact taxes. In addition, the Stamp Act Congress called for a boycott of imported British goods.

7. Parliament could not ignore the boycott as British exports fell by 15 percent. Pressed by merchants and unemployed workers, Parliament rescinded the Stamp Act while also issuing a little-noticed Declaratory Act reasserting their authority over the colonies.

TOPIC 5.3
THE ROAD TO REVOLUTION

1. No single event caused the American Revolution. Instead, it was precipitated by the cumulative effects of a series British actions and colonial reactions.

2. In 1767, Charles Townshend, the head of the British treasury, persuaded Parliament to enact a new revenue act. The Townshend Act imposed import duties on such everyday items as paint, glass, paper, and tea. Townshend proposed to use the revenue to pay for military expenses and the salaries of royal officials.

3. The Townshend Act reignited the dispute over taxation. The Massachusetts legislature promptly condemned the new taxes and urged other colonial assemblies to join their protest. At the same time, merchants in Boston began a nonimportation movement to boycott British goods.

4. American resistance stiffened Townshend's determination to impose his will on the Bostonians. In late 1768, the first of 4,000 royal troops began to arrive in Boston. City residents deeply resented the presence of these troops. On the night of March 5, 1770, a rowdy crowd of hecklers taunted a squad of British soldiers stationed outside the Boston Customs House. An alarmed soldier fired into the crowd. When the smoke cleared, five townspeople lay on the ground, dead or dying.

5. On the same day the Boston Massacre occurred, Parliament repealed all the Townshend duties except the one on tea. Although harmony seemed to have been restored, the Townshend Act crisis exacerbated feelings of distrust between British officials and a new and increasingly radical generation of American leaders.

6. On December 16, 1773, a group of Boston patriots disguised as Mohawk Indians boarded three British ships and threw 342 chests of tea into the harbor. The so-called Boston Tea Party infuriated British authorities.

7. Parliament promptly passed the Coercive Acts to punish Boston for the wanton destruction of private property. Known in the colonies as the Intolerable Acts, the legislation closed the port of Boston, sharply curtailed town meetings, and authorized the army to quarter troops wherever they were needed. Parliament's punitive action seemed to confirm the colonists' fear that Britain intended to restrict each colony's right to self-government.

TOPIC 5.4
COMMITMENT TO REPUBLICAN VALUES

1. Parliament enacted the Intolerable Acts to tighten its control over the increasingly rebellious colonists. Instead, the acts punitive measures intensified colonial resistance to British rule and their commitment to the republican principle that government should be based on the consent of the governed.

2. Enlightenment ideas about the rights of individuals and self-government circulated throughout the colonies. Colonial newspapers familiarized their readers with John Locke's argument that the people had a right to replace a monarch who did not protect their lives, liberties, and property. They also closely studied Baron de Montesquieu's contention that power should not be concentrated in the hands of a single individual. Montesquieu instead recommended separating power among executive, legislative, and judicial branches of government.

3. Republican ideas played a key role in shaping the American revolutionary movement. They helped overcome regional colonial differences by providing a common ideological set of principles.

4. Tom Paine published *Common Sense* in January 1776. The pamphlet offered the colonists a convincing answer to why they should declare independence from Great Britain. Paine attacked monarchy as an institution insisting that kings were forcibly imposed upon people capable of self-government. He assailed George III as an "oppressive royal brute" who should be scorned and not venerated. Paine argued that independence was inevitable since a prosperous and growing continent could not be permanently tied to a small and distant island. Paine concluded by exhorting the colonists to declare independence and "begin the world over again."

5. *Common Sense* became an instant bestseller, as people throughout the colonies agreed with Paine's compelling arguments why America should pursue its own destiny.

6. The Continental Congress responded to the shift in public sentiment by formally adopting the Declaration of Independence on July 4, 1776. The Declaration created a new American identity by transforming a debate over taxes into a fight for independence.

7. The impact of the Declaration of Independence extended beyond justifying a war for political independence. Jefferson did not base his revolutionary arguments upon the narrow rights of Englishmen. Instead, he drew upon the ideas of the Enlightenment thinkers to base his arguments upon universal principles derived from "the Laws of Nature" and "Nature's God." The Declaration's "self-evident" truths became an enduring expression of America's highest principles and goals.

CHAPTER 6
FEDERALISTS AND ANTI-FEDERALISTS

LOCATION AND STRATEGIC IMPORTANCE

The ratification debate between the Federalists and the Anti-Federalists occurred toward the end of Period 3 (1754–1800). This chapter can stand alone as part of a topical review. Another option would be to use it after Chapter 5 as part of a chronological review of Period 3.

The information in Chapter 6 has generated a significant number of points on multiple-choice and short-answer questions. For example, a recent short-answer question asked students to discuss achievements and weaknesses of the Articles of Confederation.

TOPIC 6.1
THE FEDERALISTS AND THEIR KEY ARGUMENTS

1. The Federalists supported the proposed Constitution. They welcomed a national government that would protect private property from debtors and irresponsible state legislatures.

2. Federalists drew support from large landowners, enterprising seaport merchants, established lawyers, land speculators, and influential preachers and newspaper editors. They typically lived and worked in ports, market towns, and along navigable rivers.

3. Federalists argued that the Articles of Confederation created a badly flawed government that hindered America's future growth and prosperity. For example, the Confederation Congress could not raise revenue or regulate interstate commerce. In addition, the government lacked a chief executive and did not provide for a national court system.

4. Federalists pointed to Shays' Rebellion in Massachusetts as an example of "the excesses of democracy." They argued that the proposed Constitution would strengthen national authority and protect property rights.

5. Federalists argued that the proposed Constitution would create a balance between republican principles and the need to place limits on popular democracy. For example, the House of Representatives would give people a direct voice in their government. However, a Senate chosen by state legislatures for six-year terms and a President selected by an Electoral College would provide necessary protection from demagogues and sudden shifts in popular opinion.

6. Federalists argued that the proposed Constitution would create a federal system in which power would be shared by state and federal governments. They insisted that day-to-day affairs of government such as education and law enforcement would remain under local control.

7. Federalists argued that the creation of three separate branches of government would disperse power, thus making it difficult for any one faction to gain control over the government. In addition, the system of checks and balances would prevent one branch of the government from dominating the other two.

8. The Federalists were skilled and pragmatic political leaders who understood the art of compromise. For example, the ratification debates in state conventions indicated strong public support for a Bill of Rights. Rather than defy public opinion, the Federalists promised to add a Bill of Rights that would enumerate individual rights and explicitly restrict the powers of the central government.

9. The Federalists argued that rejecting the proposed Constitution would lead to disunion, disorder, and inevitable disaster.

10. James Madison, Alexander Hamilton, and John Jay wrote a series of 85 essays now known as the *Federalist Papers* to defend and explain the Constitution. The *Federalist Papers* are now considered a definitive explanation of the theoretical underpinnings of the Constitution. For example, Madison argued in *Federalist No. 10* that political factions are undesirable but inevitable.

TOPIC 6.2
THE ANTI–FEDERALISTS AND THEIR KEY ARGUMENTS

1. The Anti-Federalists opposed the proposed Constitution. They favored strong state governments and a limited national government.

2. Anti-Federalists drew support from state officials, small farmers, debtors, and shopkeepers. They typically lived and worked in less developed, more isolated parts of their states.

3. Anti-Federalists argued that a few well-chosen amendments would correct the flaws in the Articles of Confederation.

4. The Anti-Federalists argued that popular self-government flourishes in small communities, where public officials and their constituents frequently interact. The proposed Constitution violated this principle by creating a House of Representatives with just 65 districts. Anti-Federalists pointed out that the proposed House of Representatives would have fewer members than any of the state legislatures. For example, the Massachusetts assembly had 200 members.

5. Anti-Federalists feared excessive centralized authority. They warned that the proposed Constitution would create a powerful President who could easily become an "elected despot." For example, the proposed Constitution gave the President vast new powers, including the ability to veto legislation passed by the people's representatives. In addition, the President had the power to appoint federal judges for life terms.

6. Anti-Federalists argued that popular self-government is most effective when there are few competing factions. They believed that the continental republic contemplated by the proposed Constitution would create far too many different rival interests. This would encourage "a constant clashing of opinions" that would "retard the operation of government" and pose a threat to the common good.

7. The Anti-Federalists repeatedly stressed that the proposed Constitution failed to include a Bill of Rights to safeguard such essential individual liberties as freedom of speech, the press, and religion.

8. The Anti-Federalists warned that the proposed Constitution would create "one grand, consolidated national government" that would give too much power to a small group of men who controlled a disproportionate amount of wealth and influence.

9. The Anti-Federalists were unable to overcome their well-organized Federalist opponents. They lost close but decisive votes in Virginia and New York.

10. Although they lost, the Anti-Federalists did persuade the Federalists to add a Bill of Rights to the Constitution.

PART II

AFRICAN AMERICAN HISTORY

CHAPTER 7

AFRICAN AMERICAN HISTORY

FROM THE ORIGINS OF SLAVERY TO
THE BEGINNING OF ABOLITIONISM

1607–1831

STRATEGIC IMPORTANCE

African American history generates the most questions and points of any topic on the APUSH exam. We have devoted four of our twelve narrative chapters to help you thoroughly master the key events, trends, and leaders associated with this all-important historic experience. A careful analysis of recent APUSH exams reveals that the period from the founding of Jamestown to the beginning of the abolition movement generated an average of about 15 points per exam. Remember, you only need 75 points to earn a three, 95 points to earn a four, and 110 points to earn a five. This chapter is thus a particularly important part of your coalition of points.

KEY POINTS AND HISTORIC GENERALIZATIONS

- A combination of geographic, economic, and social factors enabled slavery to take root in Southern society.

- Tobacco and sugar played key roles in causing the African slave trade.

- The expansion of liberty coexisted with the simultaneous expansion of slavery.

- The Declaration of Independence did not have an immediate effect on the lives of enslaved Africans living in America. However, Jefferson's stirring statement that "all men are created equal" created a language of liberty that inspired future reformers.

- The Constitution adopted a pragmatic approach to slavery by including the Three-Fifths Compromise and allowing the slave trade to continue to 1808.

- As the South devoted more and more resources to maintaining its "peculiar institution," the region failed to fully participate in the economic changes transforming the American economy.

- William Lloyd Garrison's bold call for the immediate and unconditional end of slavery marked the beginning of the abolitionist movement.

TOPIC 7.1
THE ORIGINS OF AMERICAN SLAVERY

A. VIRGINIA AND TOBACCO

The Virginia Company founded the Jamestown colony in 1607 to make a profit for its investors. At first, Jamestown tottered on the brink of collapse. Within ten years about 80 percent of its colonists perished from disease and malnutrition.

Life in Virginia changed when John Rolfe learned how to raise a sweet form of tobacco that thrived in the colony's rich Tidewater soil. Within a short time, Rolfe and other planters began exporting their new cash crop to Europe. As a result, tobacco production soared from under 5,000 pounds in 1614 to ten million pounds in 1670.

B. INDENTURED SERVANTS

Tobacco provided a valuable cash crop that saved the fledgling Virginia colony. Rapidly rising tobacco profits created a demand for inexpensive labor. At first, Virginia planters relied upon INDENTURED SERVANTS from England. These young men and women received passage across the Atlantic in exchange for working four to seven years without wages. The number of indentured servants exceeded the number of enslaved Africans for most of the seventeenth century. The shift to enslaved Africans began in the years following Bacon's Rebellion in 1676.

C. BACON'S REBELLION

Bacon's Rebellion began with the grievances of former indentured servants. A combination of falling tobacco prices, rising taxes, and dwindling opportunities to purchase fertile land along navigable streams caused mounting levels of frustration and resentment.

Led by Nathaniel Bacon, discontented former indentured servants known as yeoman farmers rebelled against the arbitrary rule of Governor Berkeley and the haughty class of wealthy planters he represented. The rebels even managed to capture and then burn down Jamestown. However, Bacon's sudden death from dysentery enabled Governor Berkeley to regain the upper hand. He promptly crushed the rebellion and hanged over 20 rebels, calling them "a rabble of the basest sort of people."

Bacon's Rebellion exposed tensions between poor former indentured servants and the wealthy tidewater gentry. The rebellion did not overthrow Virginia's wealthy planter elite. But it did much to persuade planters to replace troublesome indentured servants with more easily controlled slaves imported from Africa. The number of enslaved Africans in Virginia rose from 300 in 1650 to 150,000 or 40 percent of the colony's population in 1750.

D. CAUSES OF THE GROWTH OF SLAVERY IN THE SOUTHERN COLONIES

Geography played a crucial role in the growth of slavery in the Southern colonies. Fertile land, a warm climate, abundant rainfall, and a long growing season enabled planters in Virginia and South Carolina to grow tobacco, rice, and indigo as cash crops. Numerous navigable rivers provided convenient routes for transporting goods to ports such as Norfolk, Charleston, and Savannah.

Tobacco and rice required a large supply of inexpensive labor. Enslaved Africans provided a number of economic advantages. Unlike indentured servants, slaves were compelled to work for the duration of their lives. In addition, their dark skin color made it difficult for them to escape and then blend into the surrounding society.

By the mid-1700s, a small but powerful group of wealthy planters dominated Southern society. Although the majority of white families in the South did not own slaves, they did aspire to become slave owners. Impoverished whites felt superior to enslaved Africans, thus providing social support for slavery. Few seventeenth- and early eighteenth-century white colonists questioned human bondage as either morally unacceptable or a contradiction of their belief in liberty.

Taken together, these geographic, economic, and social factors supported the growth of slavery. In 1705, the Virginia General Assembly enacted laws codifying slavery as a system of race-based, inherited, and perpetual bondage. The law further provided for strict punishments designed to enforce rigid racial boundaries. The Virginia statutes served as models for similar laws in other Southern states.

TOPIC 7.2
THE GROWTH OF TRANS-ATLANTIC TRADE

A. THE IMPORTANCE OF SUGAR

Columbus introduced sugar cane to Hispaniola. Within a short time, a "white gold" rush began as sugar plantations spread across the island. By 1700, sugar quickly became the most valuable crop grown in the British Empire. Led by planters in Barbados, the English West Indies produced about 25,000 tons of sugar, worth four times the value of Chesapeake tobacco.

Sugar plantations required large fields, costly equipment, and a huge labor force working under strict supervision. Like the tobacco planters in Virginia, sugar planters in Barbados began with indentured servants and then shifted to importing enslaved Africans. In 1644, only about 800 slaves worked in

Barbados. Just 16 years later the number swelled to 27,000. Between 1701 and 1810, sugar planters imported 252,000 enslaved Africans to Barbados and 662,000 to Jamaica.

B. TRANS–ATLANTIC TRADE

West Indian sugar plantations and Chesapeake tobacco plantations generated immense profits. In addition, rice from South Carolina and coffee from Brazil also emerged as valuable cash crops. Fueled by these crops, highly profitable TRANS-ATLANTIC TRADE routes criss-crossed the Atlantic Ocean.

The Industrial Revolution enabled British merchants to ship textiles, guns, and other manufactured goods to West Africa and to their New World colonies. In exchange, planters exported sugar, tobacco, rice, and coffee to Great Britain and Europe. At the same time, a vast and inhuman ATLANTIC SLAVE TRADE uprooted more than ten million Africans. Less than five percent of the slaves reached Britain's mainland North American colonies. The overwhelming majority worked on plantations in Brazil and the Caribbean.

C. CONSEQUENCES

The exchange of goods and labor between Africa, the Americas, and Europe led to the emergence of a trans-Atlantic economy. The ships did more than transport agricultural products and slaves; they also brought newspapers and books to readers in colonial ports. This led to the growth of a trans-Atlantic print network that featured the spread of ENLIGHTENMENT ideas about the ability of human reason to reshape political and religious institutions.

As trans-Atlantic trade expanded, Parliament began to implement MERCANTILE economic policies designed to regulate commerce and manufacturing for the benefit of Great Britain. During much of the eighteenth century Parliament failed to fully enforce its Navigation Acts. This period of benign neglect allowed colonial merchants to prosper and become more independent. Britain's later attempt to regain control over colonial trade triggered an economic and political dispute that ultimately ignited the Revolutionary War.

TOPIC 7.3
THE LANGUAGE OF LIBERTY AND THE PRESENCE OF SLAVERY

A. A DEEP CONTRADICTION

Colonial America witnessed a dramatic expansion of political liberty. New England town meetings and assemblies such as the Virginia House of Burgesses gave white men an opportunity to participate in public life. At the same time, Enlightened thinkers such as Benjamin Franklin and Thomas Jefferson accepted

John Locke's argument that every person was entitled to enjoy natural rights that included life, liberty, and property.

However, the enjoyment of liberty coexisted with the simultaneous expansion of slavery. Between 1700 and 1775, enslaved Africans comprised just under half of the 585,000 persons who arrived in colonial America. The presence of slavery in a land dedicated to promoting liberty posed a deep contradiction that would not be resolved until the Civil War.

B. THE DECLARATION OF INDEPENDENCE

Jefferson opened the Declaration of Independence with a concise and compelling statement of principles and self-evident truths. Inspired by John Locke's philosophy of natural rights, Jefferson asserted that governments derive "their just powers from the consent of the governed." The governed are entitled to "alter or abolish" their ties to a government that denies them their "unalienable rights" to "life, liberty, and the pursuit of happiness."

The Declaration of Independence created a new American identity by transforming a debate over taxes into a fight for independence. By creating a new national identity, the Declaration decisively answered what John Adams called "the greatest question" of the day. The impact of Jefferson's words accomplished more than justifying a war for political independence—they also proclaimed broad "self-evident" truths that became an enduring expression of America's founding principles and goals.

The Declaration of Independence did not have an immediate impact upon the condition of enslaved Africans. Jefferson's original draft did contain a clause condemning the slave trade. However, representatives from Georgia and South Carolina successfully lobbied to remove it. The harsh reality of slavery thus contradicted Jefferson's eloquent expression of republican ideals. Although not originally fulfilled, Jefferson's stirring statement that "all men are created equal" created a language of freedom that became an inspiring part of the American dream.

C. THE "FIRST EMANCIPATION"

The American Revolution created a new ideal of a society based upon liberty and human rights. This language of liberty did not fall upon deaf ears in the North. Motivated by political and religious opposition to slavery, Mid-Atlantic and New England states initiated a "First Emancipation" by enacting laws eliminating slavery.

The Continental Congress further underscored the growing antislavery sentiment in the North. Passed in 1787, the Northwest Ordinance contained the spread of slavery by prohibiting it in the territories comprising the Old

Northwest. As a result, slavery rapidly became identified as a distinctive Southern institution.

TOPIC 7.4
THE CONSTITUTION AND SLAVERY

A. THE THREE-FIFTHS COMPROMISE

The Constitution did not actually use the words "slave" or "slavery." Afraid of alienating the Southern states, the Framers agreed to the Three-Fifths Compromise, whereby slaves (euphemistically called "other persons") were treated as three-fifths of a person for purposes of both taxation and representation. This gave the Southern states an enlarged vote in the House of Representatives and thus a larger voice in the Electoral College.

B. THE SLAVE TRADE

Many delegates abhorred the slave trade and wanted to immediately abolish it. Gouverneur Morris underscored slavery's moral outrage by declaring that "The inhabitant of Georgia and South Carolina who goes to the Coast of Africa, and in the defiance of the most sacred laws of humanity tears away his fellow creatures from their dearest connections and damns them to the most cruel bondage, shall have more votes in a Government instituted for the protection of the rights of mankind than the citizens of Pennsylvania and New Jersey."

Morris's moral plea failed to persuade the delegates from South Carolina and Georgia. They pointed out that their states needed to continue the slave trade in order to replace the slaves evacuated by the British during the Revolutionary War.

Led by James Madison, pragmatic delegates wanted to avoid a dispute with the South that would fracture the convention. "Great as the evil is," Madison wrote, "a dismemberment of the union would be worse." Determined to distinguish the possible from the impossible, the convention resolved the issue by agreeing to a compromise in which Congress would not abolish the slave trade until 1808.

C. IMPACT ON SLAVERY

The Constitution marked a milestone event in American political history. However, it did not mark the beginning of momentous social changes for enslaved Africans. While new emancipation laws in the North ended human bondage in this region, over 90 percent of slaves lived in the South where conditions did not change.

TOPIC 7.5
SLAVERY AND THE OLD SOUTH

A. "COTTON IS KING"

During the second half of the eighteenth century, a series of inventions revolutionized the textile industry in Great Britain. These advances created a seemingly limitless demand for raw cotton. However, Southern planters could not supply enough cotton because of the difficulty of separating the fluffy cotton fibers from their sticky seeds. It required a full day for a field hand to separate a pound of cotton.

In 1793, Eli Whitney invented a machine to more efficiently perform this tedious chore. His cotton gin enabled slaves to separate 50 times as much fiber as could be done by hand. Improvements in Whitney's invention enabled cotton production to soar to previously undreamed of heights. In 1791, the South only produced 9,000 bales of cotton. The total harvest rose to one million bales in 1831 and then skyrocketed to over four million bales in 1860.

The cotton gin transformed cotton into America's most valuable cash crop. By 1860, a vast cotton belt stretched from South Carolina to the Mississippi River Valley. Known as the Deep South, this region produced three-fourths of the world's supply of cotton. Proud Southern planters confidently boasted, "Cotton is King."

B. THE IMPACT OF THE COTTON ECONOMY

Cotton irrevocably altered the South's attitude toward slavery. Prior to the invention of the cotton gin, thoughtful Southerners regarded slavery as a necessary evil that would gradually be phased out. However, as the South became committed to a cotton economy, it also became committed to slavery.

The presence of unpaid slave labor discouraged European immigrants from settling in the South. In 1860, foreign-born residents comprised just 4.4 percent of the South's population. Meanwhile, between 1844 and 1854 over three million immigrants from Ireland and Germany flooded into the North and Midwest.

As the South devoted more and more resources to slave labor and cotton, the region failed to fully participate in the transportation revolution transforming the rest of America's economy. For example, while the South lagged behind in canal and railroad construction, the Erie Canal and new railroad lines forged strong commercial ties between the North and the Midwest. By contrast, most Southern internal improvements connected plantations with nearby rivers and ports.

The South's commitment to growing cotton also slowed the growth of cities. With the exception of New Orleans and Charleston, the South had few urban areas. Instead, most Southerners lived on widely dispersed farms and plantations.

C. WHITE SOCIETY IN THE OLD SOUTH

Planters commanded great economic resources. In 1860 a "prime field hand" between the ages of 18 and 40 cost approximately $1,800. Just over 40,000 families possessed 20 or more slaves. This small but powerful group of planters owned more than half of the region's slaves. Prior to the Civil War the wealthiest Americans were not Northern industrialists but planters living in South Carolina and Natchez, Mississippi.

The majority of white families in the antebellum South were independent yeoman farmers who owned few, if any, slaves. Although the South's numerical majority, yeoman farmers did not set the region's political and social tone. Instead they deferred to the planters, since many aspired to become prosperous landowners themselves.

A large group of unskilled laborers occupied the bottom of the South's social pyramid. These "poor whites" often lived in the backwoods, where they scratched out a meager living doing odd jobs.

The planters, yeoman farmers, and poor whites all supported the South's biracial social structure. Despite the vast disparities in their standards of living, these groups all shared a belief in white supremacy.

D. THE DOMESTIC SLAVE TRADE

Congress outlawed the African slave trade in 1808. However, as the cotton economy expanded so did the slave population. In the half-century before the Civil War, the number of slaves increased from 1.2 million to about 4 million. Most of this increase was due to the natural population increase of American-born slaves.

The spread of cotton plantations into the Deep South caused a major change in the movement and distribution of slavery. In 1790, planters in Virginia and Maryland owned 56 percent of all American slaves. During the 1800s, Chesapeake planters sold as many as 700,000 slaves to planters in the cotton belt. By 1860, just 15 percent of all slaves lived in Virginia and Maryland, while half lived in the Deep South.

The domestic slave trade uprooted countless families. Despite forced separation and harsh living conditions, slaves maintained strong kinship networks while creating a separate African American culture. Religion played a particularly important role. For example, spiritual songs enabled slaves to express their sorrows, joys, and hopes for a better life.

E. ATTITUDES TOWARDS THE SOUTH'S "PECULIAR INSTITUTION"

Antebellum white Southerners did not view the phrase "peculiar institution" as a dry term that had to be memorized for a test. The word "peculiar" did not mean odd or strange. Instead, it referred to something distinctive or characteristic of the Southern way of life.

During the late 1700s and early 1800s, many Southern leaders referred to slavery as a "necessary evil" inherited from their colonial past. However, during the 1820s and 1830s slaveholders worked out a systematic proslavery argument to justify their "peculiar institution" as a "positive good."

John C. Calhoun and other defenders of slavery as a "positive good" insisted that the slaves benefited from a benign and paternalistic institution. They argued that their well-cared-for slaves actually had lives that were as good as or better than the lives of wage slaves working in Northern factories. The proponents of slavery identified the institution as an integral part of the South's economy and way of life.

F. "LIBERTY! LIBERTY!"

The overwhelming majority of enslaved Africans did not consider slavery a "positive good." The first significant slave rebellion occurred south of Charleston, South Carolina, in September 1739. The Stono Rebellion began when about 20 slaves raided a store, killed two shopkeepers, and seized a supply of guns and ammunition. The rebels quickly gathered new recruits, burned several plantations, and killed over 20 whites. They then marched south, headed for Spanish Florida, where they hoped to gain their freedom. As the exuberant rebels fled south they joyously shouted, "Liberty! Liberty!"

The Stono Rebellion only lasted a day. Alerted by what happened, the local militia pursued and caught the rebels. A brief but bloody battle claimed the lives of at least 34 slaves.

The Stono Rebellion underscored the tension between slaves and their owners. For white Southerners the most terrifying slave revolt occurred in Southampton County, Virginia, in August 1831. In two violent days about 75 enslaved Africans led by Nat Turner killed over 50 whites.

Nat Turner's Rebellion made alarmed slaveholders sensitive to any threat to their "peculiar institution." The fear of slave rebellions led Southern states to place severe restrictions on the ability of enslaved Africans to receive an education and assemble in large groups.

TOPIC 7.6
THE CRUSADE AGAINST SLAVERY

A. THE SECOND GREAT AWAKENING

During the early 1800s a wave of intense religious enthusiasm known as the SECOND GREAT AWAKENING swept across much of America. Thousands of people attended emotionally charged camp meetings featuring fervent appeals to faith. Preachers such as Charles Grandison Finney emphasized that a merciful and loving God granted people free will and therefore the ability to do good. The Second Great Awakening inspired a belief in PERFECTIONISM—faith in the human ability to consciously build a just society.

The Second Great Awakening inspired people to believe in the possibility of improving their own lives and also addressing social problems. It was a short step from the Second Great Awakening's emphasis upon spiritual progress to a belief in social progress. Enthusiastic reformers worked to improve public education, limit the sale of alcoholic beverages, and expand women's rights. But at first, most Americans accepted slavery as an entrenched part of the Southern way of life.

B. THE AMERICAN COLONIZATION SOCIETY

Founded in 1817, the American Colonization Society (ACS) advocated the gradual abolition of slavery combined with the goal of returning freed slaves to Africa. Although Society members opposed slavery, many held openly racist views. Leaders of the ACS did not believe that freed blacks could be integrated into American society. For example, Henry Clay argued that since an "unconquerable prejudice" would prevent free blacks from assimilating into white society, it would be better for them to return to Africa.

The American Colonization Society played an instrumental role in founding the colony of Liberia on the west coast of Africa. However, the Society's gradual approach could never resolve the problem of slavery. By 1860 the ACS helped approximately 12,000 free blacks migrate to Liberia. At that time four million slaves continued to live and work in the South.

C. WILLIAM LLOYD GARRISON: "I WILL BE HEARD!"

William Lloyd Garrison was a young reformer who at first supported the ACS's gradual approach to ending slavery. However, his contact with slavery in Baltimore convinced him that the South's "peculiar institution" was cruel, brutal, and sinful. He therefore rejected the ACS's strategies of gradual emancipation and colonization in Africa. Unlike the overwhelming majority of the American public, Garrison viewed blacks as his fellow citizens and not as aliens who should be returned to Africa.

As Garrison's views became more militant, he resolved to move to Boston and publish his own antislavery newspaper. Even though his views initially lacked public support and even though he faced hostile opposition, Garrison began publishing *The Liberator*, a newspaper devoted to promoting the abolitionist cause. On New Year's Day 1831, the 26-year-old Garrison published an open letter rejecting moderation and compromise. He boldly denounced slave owners as oppressors who defended a sinful institution that contradicted the Declaration of Independence's self-evident truth that all men are created equal. He defiantly concluded by declaring, "I WILL BE HEARD!"

Garrison's uncompromising call for immediate and uncompensated emancipation helped galvanize antislavery sentiment in the Northeast. In 1833, he co-founded the American Anti-Slavery Society. Calling slavery America's "foulest stain," Garrison vowed "to deliver our land from its deadliest curse." Within just five years, the new organization claimed to have 250,000 members and 1,350 local affiliates.

D. FREDERICK DOUGLASS: "I STOLE THIS HEAD"

Born a slave in Maryland, Frederick Douglass escaped from what he later called "the dark night of slavery" in 1838 when he was just 22 years old. He became a gifted orator who captivated antislavery audiences with his authentic stories about the horrors of slavery. For example, he told a spellbound audience in Massachusetts, "I appear before this immense assembly this evening as a thief and a robber. I stole this head, these limbs, this body from my master and ran off with them."

Douglass was also a compelling writer. In 1845 he published his *Narrative of the Life of Frederick Douglass*, describing his brutal fight with a slave driver and dramatic escape to the North. In 1847, he founded the *North Star*, an influential antislavery newspaper.

Douglass's eloquent speeches and writings played an important role in refuting proslavery arguments and persuading a growing number of Northerners that slavery was evil and that its further spread into the western lands must be halted.

CHAPTER 7
PRACTICE QUESTIONS

MULTIPLE-CHOICE QUESTIONS

Questions 1–4 refer to the excerpt below:

Five of our number in the passage dy'd,
Who were cast into the ocean wide,
And, after sailing seven weeks and more,
We, at Virginia all were put ashore.

Into the field I next did go,
Among tobacco plants all day to hoe,
At day break in the morn our work begun,
And lasted till the setting of the sun.

My fellow slaves were five transports more,
With eighteen Negroes which is twenty four,
Besides four transport women in the house,
To wait upon his daughter and his spouse.

We and the Negroes both alike did fare,
Of work and food we had an equal share…
My countrymen, take warning e'er too late,
Lest you shou'd share my unhappy fate.

> James Revel, "A Poor Unhappy Transported Felon's Sorrowful Account of His Fourteen Years' Transportation at Virginia, in America," 1680

1. **The excerpt was most likely intended to do which of the following?**
   A. Address the need to import more African slaves into the Virginia colony
   B. Alleviate concerns about the difficulties faced by indentured servants
   C. Raise questions about the efficacy of becoming an indentured servant
   D. Question the Virginia colony's growing dependence upon cultivating tobacco as a cash crop

2. **The excerpt serves as evidence of which of the following trends during the last quarter of the seventeenth century?**

   A. The increasing reliance on the labor of indentured servants
   B. The continuing conflicts between the Virginia colonists and the Powhatan Confederacy
   C. The flourishing trade between Virginia and the West Indies
   D. The growing use of enslaved Africans on Virginia tobacco plantations

3. **Compared to New England, early English settlements in the Chesapeake colonies were characterized by**

   A. lower life expectancy, a larger population of indentured servants, and a greater tolerance for the property rights of Native Americans
   B. lower life expectancy, increased importation of African slaves, and a more unequal distribution of wealth
   C. higher life expectancy, compact self-governing villages, and a diverse economy
   D. higher life expectancy, greater gender balance, and rapid industrialization

Questions 4–6 refer to the excerpt below:

"Let us trace…the men in authority and favor to whose hands the dispensation of the country's wealth has been committed. Let us observe the sudden rise of their estates…compared with the quality in which they first entered this country. Let us consider their sudden advancement. And let us also consider whether any public work for our safety and defense or for the advancement and propagation of trade, liberal arts or sciences is in any way adequate to our vast charge. Now let us compare these things together and see what sponges have sucked up the public treasure and whether it has not been privately contrived away by favorites and juggling parasites whose tottering fortunes have been repaired and supported at the public charge."

Nathaniel Bacon, "Manifesto," 1676

4. **Which of the following could be used as evidence to support Bacon's argument in the excerpt?**

    A. Port records showing the number of pounds of tobacco shipped to England between 1640 and 1675
    B. Ship records documenting the number of African slaves sold in Virginia between 1640 and 1675
    C. Diaries describing how to run a tobacco planation
    D. Tax records showing the average incomes of tobacco planters between 1640 and 1675

5. **The reference in the excerpt to "any public work for our safety and defense" most directly refers to**

    A. the governor's policy of protecting Indian tribes engaged in the fur trade
    B. the construction of a fleet to protect Virginia from Spanish attacks
    C. the construction of a series of dams to ensure a supply of irrigation water for the tobacco fields
    D. the passage of strict slave codes to restrict the freedom of enslaved Africans

6. **Which of the following historical developments most directly resulted from the tensions that led Bacon to write his Manifesto?**

    A. The British Parliament disbanded the House of Burgesses
    B. The House of Burgesses enacted a Toleration Act, granting all Christians the right to follow their beliefs
    C. King James I revoked the Virginia Company's charter, thus making Virginia a royal colony
    D. Virginia tobacco planters began to replace indentured servants with enslaved Africans

Questions 7–8 refer to the excerpt below:

"But when a long train of abuses and usurpations, pursuing inevitably the same object, evinces a design to reduce them under absolute despotism, it is their right, it is their duty, to throw off such government, and to promote new guards for their future security. Such has been the patient sufferance of these colonies; and such is now the necessity which constrains them to alter their former systems of government. The history of the present King of Great Britain is a history of repeated injuries and usurpation, all having in direct object the establishment of an absolute tyranny over these states. To prove this, let facts be submitted to a candid world."

  Thomas Jefferson, Declaration of Independence, 1776

7. **The ideological content of the Declaration of Independence was most directly influenced by**

  A. the Enlightenment belief that human conditions could be improved through the use of reason
  B. statements about the rights of Englishmen issued by Virginia's House of Burgesses
  C. John Locke's philosophy of natural rights
  D. John Winthrop's "City Upon a Hill" sermon

8. **The "facts" Jefferson submitted to "a candid world" did NOT include criticism of the**

  A. slave trade
  B. Boston Port Act
  C. sending of mercenary troops to the colonies
  D. quartering of British troops in colonial homes

Questions 9–10 refer to the excerpt below:

"The migration or importation of such persons as any of the States now existing shall think proper to admit, shall not be prohibited by the Congress prior to the year one thousand eight hundred and eight, but a tax or duty may be imposed on such importation, not exceeding ten dollars for each person."

  Article I, Section 9, United States Constitution, 1787

9. **The expression "such persons" was used to mean**

  A. loyalists
  B. slaves
  C. indentured servants
  D. Anti-Federalists

10. **Which of the following was a reason northern delegates accepted this provision?**

  A. They wanted to collect badly needed revenue
  B. They wanted to let the Supreme Court resolve the issue
  C. They wanted to establish a limited federal government
  D. They wanted to avoid a dispute that could fracture the convention

Questions 11–12 refer to the excerpt below:

"Representatives and direct taxes should be apportioned among the several states which may be included in this Union according to their respective number, which shall be determined by adding to the whole number of free persons, including those bound to service for a term of years, and excluding Indians not taxed, three-fifths of all other persons."

Article I, Section II, paragraph 3, United States Constitution, 1787

11. This provision overcame a major impasse between

A. agricultural and industrial states
B. small and large states
C. Southern and Northern states
D. Eastern and Western states

12. Which of the following was a direct effect of this provision?

A. It led to a major economic downturn
B. It led to an upsurge in abolitionist sentiment
C. It led to the displacement of American Indians from the Southeast
D. It led to an increase in the political power of the Southern states

Questions 13–15 refer to the excerpt below:

"We have met together for the achievement of an enterprise, without which that of our fathers is incomplete…. We maintain that no compensation should be given to the planters emancipating their slaves…. We regard as delusive, cruel, and dangerous, any scheme or expatriation which pretends to aid, either directly or indirectly, in the emancipation of the slaves, or to be a substitute for the immediate and total abolition of slavery…. We will do all that in us lies consistently with this Declaration of principles, to overthrow the most execrable system of slavery that has ever been witnessed upon earth."

William Lloyd Garrison, "Declaration of Sentiments of the American Anti-Slavery Society," 1833

13. **Which of the following contributed most directly to the sentiments expressed in this excerpt?**

    A. The religious spirit of the Second Great Awakening
    B. The egalitarian spirit of the Seneca Falls "Declaration of Sentiments and Resolutions"
    C. The defiant spirit of Bacon's Manifesto
    D. The conciliatory spirit of the U.S. Constitution

14. **The excerpt most directly rejects**

    A. a scheme by Southern planters to annex Cuba
    B. a proposal to reduce cotton exports to Great Britain
    C. a bill to revive and fund the importation of indentured servants
    D. a plan by the American Colonization Society to return freed slaves to Africa

15. **Garrison and his supporters believed that the principles in this excerpt were consistent with**

    A. the legal requirements of the Three-Fifths Compromise
    B. the ideas expressed in the Declaration of Independence
    C. the provisions of the Missouri Compromise
    D. the provisions of the Fugitive Slave Act

MULTIPLE-CHOICE ANSWERS

1. C	5. A	9. B	13. A
2. D	6. D	10. D	14. D
3. B	7. C	11. C	15. B
4. D	8. A	12. D	

SHORT-ANSWER QUESTIONS

Question 1
Using the chart below, answer A, B, and C.

Number of African Slaves Imported to the Americas by Various Nations

Years	Spain/Uruguay	Portugal/Brazil	Great Britain	USA
1501-1550	31,738	32,387	0	0
1551-1600	88,223	121,804	1,922	0
1601-1650	127,809	469,128	33,695	824
1651-1700	18,461	542,065	394,567	3,327
1701-1750	0	1,011,143	964,639	37,281
1751-1800	10,654	1,201,860	1,580,659	111,395
1801-1825	168,087	1,160,601	283,959	109,545
1826-1866	616,552	1,399,278	0	2,326
TOTAL	**1,061,524**	**5,848,265**	**3,259,440**	**305,326**

Source: Voyages Database, Emory University

A. Briefly explain how ONE major historical factor contributed to the dramatic increase in the number of Africans transported to the New World between 1601 and 1800.

B. Briefly explain ONE specific historical effect that resulted from the increase in enslaved Africans transported to the mainland British North American colonies between 1601 and 1800.

C. Briefly explain ONE specific historical factor that contributed to the decline in the number of enslaved Africans transported to the mainland British North American colonies between 1801 and 1866.

Question 2
Using the excerpts below, answer A, B, and C.

"In all respects the comforts of our slaves are greatly superior to those of the English [factory] operatives, or the Irish and continental peasantry, to say nothing of the millions of paupers crowded together in those loathsome receptacles of starving humanity, the public poorhouses…. From this excess of labor, this actual want, and these distressing cares, our slaves are entirely exempted."

> Governor George McDuffie to the South Carolina legislature, 1835

"I am not included within the pale of this glorious anniversary! Your high independence only reveals the immeasurable distance between us. The blessings in which you, this day, rejoice, are not enjoyed in common. The rich inheritance of justice, liberty, prosperity and independence, bequeathed by your fathers, is shared by you, not by me. The sunlight that brought life and healing to you, has brought stripes and death to me. This Fourth of July is yours, not mine. You may rejoice, I must mourn."

> Frederick Douglass, speech to an antislavery group in Rochester, New York, July 5, 1852

A. Briefly describe ONE major difference between McDuffie's and Douglass's views of the condition of slaves in the United States.

B. Briefly explain how ONE specific historical event or development from the period 1607 to 1844, that is not explicitly mentioned in the excerpts, could be used to qualify McDuffie's argument.

C. Briefly explain how ONE specific historical event or development from the period 1607 to 1844, that is not explicitly mentioned in the excerpts, could be used to qualify Douglass's argument.

SHORT-ANSWER ANSWERS

Question 1

A. The development of lucrative New World plantation economies, based upon the cultivation and export of sugar, tobacco, and coffee, created a rising demand for enslaved Africans.

B. The Southern colonies became committed to a "peculiar institution" based upon a system of race-based, inherited, and perpetual bondage. White supremacy united white Southerners in support of a cruel system that contradicted their belief in liberty.

C. Congress outlawed the African slave trade in 1808. However, the number of slaves continued to rise because of the natural increase of American-born slaves.

Question 2

A. McDuffie reflects the prevailing Southern "positive good" argument that enslaved Africans benefited from a benign and paternalistic institution. In contrast, Douglass reflects the abolitionist argument that slavery was a sinful institution that contradicted America's most cherished founding ideals.

B. Slave rebellions underscored the underlying tension between slaves and their owners. The Stono Rebellion and Nat Turner's Rebellion both forced Southern states to adopt severe restrictions on slaves that contradicted McDuffie's argument.

C. The language of liberty did not fall upon deaf ears in the North. Motivated by political and religious opposition to slavery, Mid-Atlantic and New England states instituted a "First Emancipation" by enacting laws that eliminated slavery.

CHAPTER 8

AFRICAN AMERICAN HISTORY

THE IMPACT OF SLAVERY ON TERRITORIAL
EXPANSION AND THE CIVIL WAR

1820–1865

STRATEGIC IMPORTANCE

African American history generates the most questions and points of any topic on the APUSH exam. We have devoted four of our twelve narrative chapters to help you thoroughly master the key events, trends, and leaders associated with this all-important historic experience. A careful analysis of recent APUSH exams reveals that questions from the Louisiana Purchase to the Emancipation Proclamation generated an average of 15 points per exam. Remember, you only need 75 points to earn a three, 95 points to earn a four, and 110 points to earn a five. This chapter is thus a particularly important part of your coalition of points.

KEY POINTS AND HISTORIC GENERALIZATIONS

- Jefferson approved the Louisiana Purchase in order to fulfill his vision of enabling America to become "an Empire of Liberty."

- The Missouri Compromise temporarily defused the political crisis between free and slave states over the status of slavery in the Louisiana Territory.

- The idea of MANIFEST DESTINY justified America's westward expansion.

- The Wilmot Proviso opened sectional divisions over the status of slavery in the lands acquired in the Mexican Cession.

- The Compromise of 1850 failed to remove slavery from the center stage of American politics.

- The Fugitive Slave Act inflamed antislavery sentiment in the North.

- The Kansas–Nebraska Act created a political upheaval that led to the demise of the Whig Party and the rise of the Republican Party.

- The Supreme Court decision in *Dred Scott v. Sanford* held that black people were not citizens of the United States. The ruling also struck down the Missouri Compromise of 1820.

- The Republican Party platform accepted slavery where it existed but opposed the further expansion of slavery into the Western territories.

- The Emancipation Proclamation transformed the Civil War into a crusade against slavery.

TOPIC 8.1
SLAVERY AND TERRITORIAL EXPANSION, 1803-1850

A. "AN EMPIRE OF LIBERTY"

On July 4, 1803, President Thomas Jefferson proudly informed the American people that his representatives in Paris had signed a treaty to purchase the Louisiana Territory from France. Under the terms of the Louisiana Purchase Treaty, the United States acquired vast new lands doubling the nation's size. The Louisiana Territory included 828,000 square miles of land that would ultimately embrace part or all of 15 future states.

Jefferson believed that these new lands would enable America to become "an Empire of Liberty." Jefferson did not envision a continental empire controlled by a central government in Washington. Instead the new lands would promote a broad distribution of property ownership, supporting an agrarian republic devoted to the principles of liberty and equality he eloquently set forth in the Declaration of Independence.

Jefferson would live to see that organizing and governing the Louisiana Territory proved more difficult than purchasing it. During the next half-century, the contentious issue of slavery repeatedly threatened to disrupt national unity. Bitter disputes over the status of Missouri, California, Kansas, and Nebraska forced American leaders to face a divisive and fateful question: Could slave states coexist with free states in an Empire of Liberty?

B. THE MISSOURI COMPROMISE OF 1820

In early 1819, Missouri petitioned Congress for admission to the Union as a slave state. The request stunned and angered Northern members of Congress. Representative James Tallmadge of New York responded by introducing an amendment providing that no more slaves could be introduced into Missouri and that all children born into slavery in the new state would become free at the age of 25.

The Tallmadge Amendment ignited a passionate debate in both houses of Congress. At that time free-state representatives in the House outnumbered those from slave states. However, the Senate was evenly but precariously balanced between 11 free states and 11 slave states. As a result, the House approved the Tallmadge Amendment while the Senate rejected it.

The votes in Congress reflected the widening divide between the North and the South. With each passing year, the South became committed to a plantation economy relying on slave labor to harvest the region's ever- expanding fields of cotton. At the same time, the North became a region of small independent farmers and growing urban and industrial centers.

The bitter debates in Congress featured heated exchanges between Southern and Northern representatives. Thomas Cobb of Georgia warned Tallmadge, "You have kindled a fire which all the waters of the ocean cannot put out which seas of blood can only extinguish." Tallmadge refused to back down and defiantly proclaimed, "If a dissolution of the Union must take place, let it be so!" These dire threats deeply concerned Secretary of State John Quincy Adams. The future President grimly predicted the debate marked, "a title page to a great tragic volume."

As emotional arguments raged back and forth, Congressional leaders turned to their Speaker, Henry Clay of Kentucky, to find middle ground that would end the crisis. Clay proved equal to the challenge. Known as the Missouri Compromise, his proposal maintained the balance of power in the Senate by admitting Missouri as a slave state and Maine as a free state. The compromise also provided that any other new states from the Louisiana Territory north of parallel 36 degrees, 30 minutes would remain free.

The Missouri Compromise temporarily defused the political crisis over the expansion of slavery into the western territories. However, it did not resolve the issue. The debates hardened the South's defense of slavery as a positive good essential to the region's economy. Jefferson recognized the gravity of the situation when he likened the Missouri crisis to "a fire-bell in the night," which "awakened and filled me with terror." He correctly predicted that the Missouri Compromise represented "a reprieve only, not a final sentence."

C. MANIFEST DESTINY

The Missouri Compromise seemingly settled the status of slavery in the western territories. American leaders carefully avoided policies that would reopen the sectional strife over the future of slavery. Furthermore, Jefferson's vision of an Empire of Liberty did not disappear. As Andrew Jackson left the White House in 1837, he confidently predicted Providence chose Americans to be "the guardians of freedom to preserve it for the benefit of the human race." The American people wholeheartedly agreed with Jackson. Convinced of the superiority of their customs and institutions, the public enthusiastically supported western expansion.

As the United States reached across the continent toward the Pacific Ocean, Americans discussed expansion as though it was a great crusade. In 1845, New York newspaper editor John L. O'Sullivan gave the nation's expansionist spirit a name when he coined the term "MANIFEST DESTINY." According to O'Sullivan, Manifest Destiny represented America's clear and unavoidable mission "to overspread and to possess the whole of the continent which Providence has given us for the development of the grand experiment of liberty and federated self-government."

The phrase Manifest Destiny successfully captured the linkage between territorial expansion and America's self-proclaimed mission to spread the blessings of liberty and progress across the continent. But territorial expansion inevitably placed slavery at the center of American politics. During the 1840s and 1850s, American leaders proved unable to find a satisfactory way to avoid the gathering storm over slavery.

D. POLK, OREGON, AND THE MEXICAN WAR

Manifest Destiny excited the American imagination. Settlers and adventurers eagerly looked to the western frontier for new lands to cultivate and new opportunities to exploit. The Democrat candidate James K. Polk won a narrow victory in the 1844 presidential election by promising voters an aggressive program of territorial expansion.

Polk pledged to annex all of the Oregon Territory. Despite his belligerent campaign slogan, "All of Oregon or none," Polk secretly negotiated an agreement with Great Britain to divide the Oregon Territory at the 49th parallel. The agreement opened fertile new lands in the Pacific Northwest for American settlers.

While Polk avoided conflict with Great Britain, he deliberately provoked a war with Mexico. American forces won a series of victories in New Mexico, California, and Mexico itself. Led by General Winfield Scott, American troops seized Mexico City, and then forced a negotiated settlement to end the war. By the terms of the Treaty of Guadalupe Hidalgo, Mexico gave up all claims to Texas above the Rio Grande and ceded California and New Mexico to the United States for $15 million. Known as the Mexican Cession, these territorial acquisitions fulfilled the goal of Manifest Destiny by transforming the United States into a transcontinental republic stretching from the Atlantic coast to the great Pacific harbors of San Diego, Monterey, and San Francisco.

E. THE WILMOT PROVISO AND THE FUTURE OF SLAVERY

President Polk believed that America's victory in the Mexican War would strengthen "the bonds of Union." He was wrong. Instead, the Mexican Cession reopened the divisive question of the status of slavery in the Western territories.

No other issue had the power to arouse intense sectional emotions in both the North and the South.

On August 8, 1846, David Wilmot, a first-term congressman from Pennsylvania, attached an amendment, or proviso, to a military appropriations bill. The Wilmot Proviso banned slavery from all the territories acquired from Mexico. Wilmot pointed out that the Northwest Ordinance of 1787 and the Missouri Compromise provided precedents for the right of Congress to restrict slavery in the new territories.

Wilmot and his supporters defended the proviso as a necessary measure to insure the "rights of white freemen" to live and work in the new territories without the unfair disadvantage of competing with slave labor. "Free soil" would guarantee liberty, equal competition, social mobility and a worker's "right to rise."

The House of Representatives passed the Wilmot Proviso. However, the South successfully blocked the legislation in the Senate. Although the Wilmot Proviso did not become law, it did become a rally point for an antislavery coalition that formed the Free Soil Party. The new party pledged to support "free soil, free speech, free labor and free men."

F. GOLD, SLAVERY, AND A DEEPENING CRISIS

Unforeseen events begun by previously unknown people have altered the course of American history. On the morning of January 24, 1848, a 37-year-old carpenter named James Marshall supervised the construction of a new sawmill along the south fork of the American River east of San Francisco. Marshall unexpectedly spotted several glittering, golden-colored nuggets. He later recalled that his discovery "made my heart thump. I was certain it was gold."

The lure of easily obtained gold proved to be irresistible. As news of Marshall's discovery spread across the country, a great human wave of fortune hunters rushed to California. During 1849 over 80,000 forty-niners reached the once thinly populated territory. The new Californians promptly drew up a constitution and asked Congress to admit them into the Union as a free state.

California's petition for statehood renewed the still-unresolved debate over the spread of slavery into the territories won in the Mexican War. In 1850 the Union included 15 free states and 15 slave states. The South continued to demand a new slave state to balance every new free state.

The balance of power in the Senate was not the only issue dividing the North and the South. In 1850, Washington, D.C. served as a thriving and profitable center of the domestic slave trade. Groups of chained slaves often passed by the Capitol building and the White House. Although the sight reassured slavery's supporters, it deeply offended abolitionists who denounced the odious practice as a national disgrace.

Reaching an agreement between the North and South had been difficult in 1820. It proved to be even harder in 1850. Southern leaders feared that the North would use its growing strength to threaten slavery and reduce the proud region to the status of a permanent minority. Representative H.W. Hilliard of Alabama reflected the growing crisis when he grimly warned, "The Union of these states is in grave peril."

G. THE COMPROMISE OF 1850

Henry Clay recognized that the growing sectional crisis threatened the Union. The 73-year-old senator from Kentucky hoped to once again play his historic role as the "Great Compromiser." After deliberating with Daniel Webster, Clay formulated a package of resolutions designed to settle the outstanding issues and restore sectional harmony. Clay's proposals included the following five key points:

1. The immediate admission of California as a free state.

2. The abolition of the domestic slave trade, but not slavery itself, in Washington, D.C.

3. The establishment of territorial governments in the rest of the Mexican Cession "without the adoption of any restriction or condition on the subject of slavery." This provision conciliated the South by reaffirming the permanence of slavery and rejecting the Wilmot Proviso.

4. The monetary compensation to Texas for the withdrawal of its claims to portions of New Mexico.

5. The enactment of a strict new Fugitive Slave Act.

The Senate debate over Clay's proposals featured a dramatic speech by Daniel Webster. On March 7, 1850, a full Senate and packed gallery listened intently as Webster implored Northern and Southern senators to find common ground "for the preservation of the Union." His great plea had a calming effect that helped mobilize public support for Clay's compromise. After months of debate, Senator Stephen A. Douglas of Illinois successfully maneuvered each of Clay's proposals through the Senate.

The Compromise of 1850 seemed to defuse the crisis and establish an uneasy sectional peace. Americans now turned to what they hoped would be a bright future, undisturbed by the issue of slavery in the western territories. This hope, however, proved to be fleeting.

TOPIC 8.2
SLAVERY AND THE ROAD TO WAR

A. THE FUGITIVE SLAVE ACT

The Compromise of 1850 did not end the agitation over slavery. Each year about 1,000 slaves successfully escaped to freedom in the Northern states. A significant number of these fugitives began their perilous journeys in the border slave states of Delaware, Maryland, Kentucky, and Missouri. Outraged slave owners viewed the Fugitive Slave Act as a test of the North's good faith in enforcing the Compromise of 1850.

The Fugitive Slave Act pledged the full weight of the federal government to recapture escaped slaves. The law required local officials to aid federal agents. It also permitted federal marshals to require private citizens to assist in the capture and return of suspected runaways. Violators could be imprisoned for up to six months and fined $1,000.

Designed to placate the South, the Fugitive Slave Act had the unintended consequence of inflaming Northern public opinion against slavery. The law compelled previously uncommitted Northerners to confront the harsh reality of slavery by assisting in the arrest of fugitives. Moral indignation filled the columns of northern newspapers. For example, a local paper in Quincy, Illinois, denounced the Fugitive Slave Act as "an outrage to humanity" and declared that anyone obeying the immoral law ought to be "marked and treated as a moral leper."

The Fugitive Slave Act presented abolitionist leaders with a new focus for their crusade against slavery. Many redoubled their support for the Underground Railroad, a name given to the loosely organized group of individuals who helped escaped slaves flee to the North. Dedicated opponents of slavery sheltered runaways in their homes during the day and then guided them at night to another stop along a changing network of back roads and safehouses. Renowned as "The Moses of Her People," Harriet Tubman repeatedly risked her life by leading more than 300 slaves to freedom on a network of trails and safe houses known as the Underground Railroad.

The Fugitive Slave Act exacerbated fears and concerns in both the North and the South. The sight of professional slave hunters roaming across the Northern free states raised fears of a "slave power conspiracy." At the same time, slave owners viewed Northern resistance as yet another sign of antipathy toward the South and its way of life.

B. HARRIET BEECHER STOWE AND *UNCLE TOM'S CABIN*

The Fugitive Slave Act appalled Harriet Beecher Stowe. As the law took effect, she wrote, "that the time is come when even a woman or a child who can speak a word for freedom and humanity is bound to speak." Stowe published *Uncle Tom's Cabin* in March 1852. It became an instantaneous success, selling over 300,000 copies within nine months. The *Boston Morning Post* declared, "everybody has read, is reading, or about to read it."

Uncle Tom's Cabin dramatized the horrors of slavery. Although often contrived and melodramatic, Stowe's narrative successfully denounced slavery's brutal effect on all people associated with it. For example, her poignant description of the desperate runaway slave Eliza bravely crossing the frozen Ohio River, with her baby in her arms, provided a compelling moral argument against slavery.

Uncle Tom's Cabin helped shape public attitudes in both the North and the South. It expanded and solidified antislavery sentiment in the North. However, it aroused deep resentment in the South. Many Southerners wondered how they could remain in a political union with a region whose citizens view their way of life as morally tainted by an evil institution.

C. THE KANSAS-NEBRASKA ACT, 1854

As 1854 began, most Americans accepted the Compromise of 1850 as a permanent settlement for separating free and slave territory in the Louisiana Territory. The Democrats and Whigs formed a seemingly stable two-party system that had dominated American political life since the Jackson Administration. At that moment the Republican Party did not exist, and Abraham Lincoln remained an obscure former Whig congressman from Illinois.

In January 1854, Senator Stephen A. Douglas of Illinois changed the course of American history when he proposed a bill allowing settlers moving into Kansas and Nebraska to use POPULAR SOVEREIGNTY to decide whether or not slavery would be permitted within their borders. If enacted into law, Douglas's bill would repeal the Missouri Compromise by allowing slavery north of the 36-30 line. Congress finally passed the Kansas–Nebraska Act after a bitter and divisive debate that lasted almost four months.

The passage of the Kansas–Nebraska Act had immediate and profound consequences. The act aroused public opinion in both the North and the South. The national uproar mobilized antislavery opinion as abolitionists, Free-Soilers, and former Whigs united to form the new Republican Party. The Republicans pledged to keep slavery out of the western territories. The rise of the Republicans led to the demise of the Whigs and the emergence of political parties representing rival sectional interests.

D. BLEEDING KANSAS

Kansas marked the first important test of popular sovereignty. Within a short time, proslavery and antislavery groups streamed into Kansas to influence the elections. Proslavery forces won a disputed election and promptly enacted legislation legalizing slavery. Free state supporters countered by electing delegates to a convention of their own, which adopted a constitution excluding slaves. A civil war erupted, claiming almost 200 lives. The violence gave the territory the nickname "Bleeding Kansas."

E. THE *DRED SCOTT* DECISION

Dred Scott was a slave whose master took him from the slave state of Missouri to the free state of Illinois. The pair then moved to the Wisconsin Territory, an area where the Missouri Compromise expressly forbade slavery. When his owner died Scott returned to Missouri, where he was placed under the authority of his former master's wife. Helped by abolitionists, Scott sued for his freedom. He contended that living in a free state and a free territory made him a free man.

Led by Chief Justice Roger B. Taney, the Supreme Court ruled that neither slaves nor free blacks were citizens in the political community created by the Constitution. Taney ruled that slaves were "chattel property ... so far inferior that they have no rights which the white man is bound to respect." Since Dred Scott was not a citizen, he was not entitled to sue in a federal court.

The Court also declared that as a constitutionally protected form of property, neither Scott nor any slave became free by living in a free state or a free territory. The *Dred Scott* decision therefore declared the Missouri Compromise unconstitutional. This marked the first time the Supreme Court had struck down an act of Congress since the *Marbury v. Madison* decision in 1803.

The *Dred Scott* decision exacerbated sectional tensions. It reinforced the Southern view that that Constitution safeguarded slavery. At the same time it dealt a blow to the Republican Party's platform pledging to oppose the extension of slavery into the western territories.

F. THE RISE OF LINCOLN

Abraham Lincoln began his political career in Illinois. He served eight years in the Illinois House of Representatives. In 1846, voters elected Lincoln to the U.S. House of Representatives. Like other Whigs, Lincoln opposed the Mexican War and supported the Wilmot Proviso. When his term ended in March 1849, Lincoln returned to Illinois to resume his career as a lawyer.

During the next five years Lincoln concentrated on expanding his law practice and raising his growing family. Although he supported the Compromise of 1850, Lincoln remained largely indifferent to national politics. However, the Kansas–Nebraska Act jolted Lincoln into action. He denounced slavery as a "monstrous injustice" and lambasted the Kansas–Nebraska Act for allowing the South's "peculiar institution" to enter free territories.

Events now propelled Lincoln into the national spotlight. In 1856, he joined the newly formed Illinois Republican Party. As sectional tensions mounted, Lincoln emerged as a leading Republican spokesman. In June 1858 he delivered his famous "House Divided" speech warning, "A House divided against itself cannot stand. I believe this government cannot endure permanently half slave and half free." Later that summer Lincoln engaged Stephen A. Douglas in a series of debates for a U.S. Senate seat. Lincoln challenged Douglas's support for popular sovereignty by declaring that people do not "have a right to do wrong."

At that time state legislatures selected U.S. senators. Although Lincoln enjoyed widespread support, the Democrat-controlled Illinois state legislature selected Douglas. Lincoln accepted his defeat, calling it "a slip and not a fall." Lincoln's analysis proved to be accurate. The Lincoln-Douglas debates transformed him into a figure of national importance.

In 1860 the Democratic Party split into rival factions, as its leaders proved unable to bridge divisions over slavery. Sensing that they had an excellent chance to defeat the divided Democrats, the Republicans nominated Lincoln.

He carried all 18 free states but did not win a single state in the South. Lincoln's electoral victory prompted South Carolina and six other Deep South states to secede from the Union.

In a final desperate effort to save the Union, Senator John Crittenden of Kentucky proposed a binding constitutional amendment to extend the Missouri Compromise line to the West coast. Lincoln rejected the compromise, saying that it violated the Republican platform position opposing the further extension of slavery into the western territories. Shortly after Lincoln took office, Confederate troops fired on Fort Sumter, leading to the secession of additional Southern states and the beginning of the Civil War.

TOPIC 8.3
THE EMANCIPATION PROCLAMATION

A. CONTEXT

The Union's narrow victory at Antietam enabled President Lincoln to turn his attention to the pressing issues of when and how to emancipate the South's four million slaves. By the fall of 1862, Congress had already prohibited slavery in Washington, D.C., and in the western territories. Lincoln feared that Britain and France would recognize the Confederacy unless the Union war aims included abolition as a moral cause. And finally, thousands of escaped slaves were seeking refuge behind the Union lines. The first Confiscation Act provided a stopgap measure by authorizing Union troops to seize all rebel property, including slaves.

B. A "RIGHTEOUS MOMENT"

President Lincoln issued the Emancipation Proclamation on January 1, 1863. The proclamation justified emancipation as a "necessary measure" intended to cripple the Confederacy's use of slaves in their war effort. The Emancipation Proclamation only applied to slaves in states or parts of states then in rebellion. It excluded freeing slaves in border states still within the Union and in other areas where Union forces were in control. Thus, the Emancipation Proclamation did not actually free any slaves. Since the Confederacy did not recognize Lincoln's authority, its slaves remained in bondage until they were freed by advancing Union armies.

Although the Emancipation Proclamation did not immediately free a single slave, it widened the war into a crusade against slavery. Recognizing this paramount fact, the abolitionist leader Frederick Douglass hailed the proclamation as a "righteous moment" that would ultimately doom slavery.

C. IMPACT

Prior to the Emancipation Proclamation, Britain and France considered supporting the Confederacy in order to weaken the United States and expand their influence in the Western Hemisphere. With slavery now doomed, public opinion in Europe swung decisively behind the Union cause. The Emancipation Proclamation thus ended any chance that European powers would actively aid the Confederacy.

The Emancipation Proclamation permitted blacks to join the Union army. Frederick Douglass urged blacks to rally to the Union cause declaring, "The iron gate of our prison stands half open." Approximately 180,000 African Americans served in the Union army and navy. Although these "blacks in blue" fought with great valor, they were paid less than white soldiers of equal rank. More than 38,000 black soldiers lost their lives during the Civil War.

Lincoln considered the Emancipation Proclamation the crowning achievement of his presidency. "If my name ever goes into history," he declared, "it was for this act." History has vindicated Lincoln's prediction. The Emancipation Proclamation became a necessary complement to the soaring rhetoric in the Declaration of Independence that "all men are created equal."

D. THE THIRTEENTH AMENDMENT

The Emancipation Proclamation was not a law passed by Congress. Instead it was an executive order, based upon Lincoln's constitutional authority as commander-in-chief of the armed forces. Although the Emancipation Proclamation was never contested in court, Lincoln realized that its legal standing could be challenged after the war. Determined to prevent the newly freed slaves from being re-enslaved, Lincoln skillfully organized support for passage of the Thirteenth Amendment, abolishing slavery in the United States.

CHAPTER 8
PRACTICE QUESTIONS

MULTIPLE-CHOICE QUESTIONS

Questions 1–3 refer to the excerpt below:

"This momentous question, like a fire bell in the night, awakened and filled me with terror. I considered it at once as the knell of the Union. It is hushed indeed for the moment. But this is a reprieve only, not a final sentence. A geographical line, coinciding with a marked principle, moral and political, once conceived and held up to the angry passions of men, will never be obliterated; and every new irritation will mark it deeper and deeper."

Thomas Jefferson to John Holmes, April 22, 1820

1. **The excerpt most directly responds to which "momentous question"?**
   A. The passage of the Indian Removal Act
   B. The passage of the Missouri Compromise
   C. The decision by the House of Representatives to ban the discussion of antislavery petitions
   D. The debate over William Lloyd Garrison's demand for the uncompensated emancipation of all slaves

2. **The "geographic line" referenced in the excerpt refers to**
   A. the dispute over the southern boundary of Texas
   B. the line closing most of the Louisiana Territory to slavery
   C. the exclusion of slavery from all territories north of the Ohio River and east of the Mississippi River
   D. the exclusion of slavery from all territories ceded to the United States in the Treaty of Guadalupe Hidalgo

3. **Which of the following historical developments provides the best evidence in support of Jefferson's warning about "the angry passions of men"?**

   A. Bleeding Kansas
   B. The Trail of Tears
   C. The Mexican-American War
   D. A continuous series of slave revolts

Questions 4–6 refer to the excerpt below:

"An old age was dying, a new age being born; and such stormy transitions always bear harshly upon party structures. Facing the new issues which the war created, both Whigs and Democrats showed the strain. Being in power, the Democratic Party suffered the more. A few years earlier it has seemed homogeneous and closely knit. Actually, it was composed of disparate interests bound together by very loose ties and ready to quarrel the moment a sufficient motive appeared; and now the war revealed its essential lack of unity. A powerful body of Northern Democrats, their greatest strength lying in New England and upper New York, stood opposed to any expansion of slavery. A still more powerful body of Southern Democrats, counting many Northern supporters, held that slavery had the right to spread through any areas where climate and other conditions favored it."

   Allen Nevins, historian, *Ordeal of the Union*, 1950

4. **Which of the following was one of the "new issues" referenced in the excerpt?**

   A. The industrialization of the South
   B. The nullification crisis caused by Southern resistance to federal policy
   C. The rise of the Whig Party in the South
   D. The expansion of slavery into the Mexican Cession

5. **Most of the Southern Democrats referenced in the excerpt strongly opposed**

   A. the use of popular sovereignty
   B. the concept of Manifest Destiny
   C. the passage of the Wilmot Proviso
   D. the Mexican–American War

6. **Most of the Northern Democrats referenced in the excerpt strongly supported**

   A. the Kansas–Nebraska Act
   B. the Fugitive Slave Act
   C. the Free Soil position on the expansion of slavery
   D. the annexation of overseas territories

Questions 7–9 refer to the except below:

"An immoral law makes it a man's duty to break it, at every hazard...By law of Congress September, 1850, it is a high crime and misdemeanor, punishable with fine and imprisonment, to resist the reenslaving a man on the coast of America...What kind of legislation is this? What kind of Constitution which covers it?...One thing appears certain to me, that, as soon as the Constitution ordains an immoral law, it ordains disunion. The law is suicidal, and cannot be obeyed. The Union is at an end as soon as an immoral law is enacted."

   Ralph Waldo Emerson, "The Fugitive Slave Law: Address to Citizens of Concord, 3 May, 1851"

7. **The excerpt most directly provides evidence for which of the following?**

   A. The outbreak of violence in Kansas
   B. The failure of the Compromise of 1850 to lessen sectional tensions
   C. The growing number of cotton planters urging the South to reevaluate support for their "peculiar institution"
   D. The growing number of armed rebellions by enslaved people in the South

8. **The sentiments in this excerpt would have been most strongly condemned by**

   A. advocates of women's rights
   B. reformers influenced by the Second Great Awakening
   C. planters in coastal South Carolina
   D. members of the American Colonization Society

9. **Based on this excerpt, Emerson would have been most likely to endorse all of the following EXCEPT:**

    A. The view of slavery articulated by Free Soil candidates
    B. The view of slavery articulated by William Lloyd Garrison
    C. The view of slavery articulated by Harriet Beecher Stowe
    D. The view of slavery articulated by Stephen A. Douglas

Questions 10–11 refer to the excerpt below:

"The conspiracy is nearly complete. The Legislation of the Republic is in the hands of Slaveholders…The body which gives the supreme law of the land, has just acceded to their demands, and dared to declare that under the charter of the Nation, men of African descent are not citizens of the United States and cannot be…that human Slavery is not a local thing, but pursues its victims to free soil, clings to them wherever they go, and returns with them—that the American Congress has no power to prevent the enslavement of men in the National Territories—that the inhabitants themselves of the Territories have no power to exclude human bondage from their midst—and that men of color cannot be suitors for justice in the Courts of the United States!"

The *Evening Journal* of Albany, New York, March 1857

10. **The ideas expressed in this excerpt most directly challenged**

    A. the Supreme Court's decision in *Dred Scott v. Sanford*
    B. the Senate's rejection of the Wilmot Proviso
    C. the Senate's passage of the Kansas–Nebraska Act
    D. The Supreme Court's decision in *McCulloch v. Maryland*

11. **The "supreme law of the land" referenced in this excerpt effectively repealed the**

    A. Missouri Compromise
    B. Fugitive Slave Act
    C. Wilmot Proviso
    D. Three-Fifths Compromise

Questions 12–15 refer to the excerpt below:

"I now come back to the question, why cannot this Union exist forever, divided into Free and Slave States, as our fathers made it? It can thus exist if each State will carry out the principles upon which our institutions were founded; to wit, the right of each State to do as it pleases, without meddling with its neighbors. Just act upon that great principle, and this Union will not only live forever, but it will extend and expand until it covers the whole continent, and makes this confederacy one grand, ocean-bound Republic."

Stephen A. Douglas, Lincoln–Douglas Debates, 1858

12. Which of the following ideas supported Douglas's vision of an "ocean-bound Republic"?

A. Abolitionism
B. Manifest Destiny
C. Perfectionism
D. Republicanism

13. The Kansas–Nebraska Act heightened the sectional crisis because it

A. repealed the Fugitive Slave Act
B. repealed the Missouri Compromise
C. made Kansas and Nebraska free states
D. signaled acceptance of the position advanced by the Wilmot Proviso

14. The sentiments expressed in this excerpt would have been most strongly supported by

A. Western Free Soilers
B. New England abolitionists
C. Northern Republicans
D. Southern Democrats

15. Both Lincoln and the Republican Party took which of the following stands on Douglas's position on the expansion of slavery into the Western territories?

A. Slavery could remain where it existed but should not be allowed to enter the new Western territories
B. Residents of the new Western territories could decide on the basis of popular sovereignty whether to have slavery
C. The federal government should purchase slaves from their masters and then relocate them to the west coast of Africa
D. The federal government should abolish slavery

MULTIPLE-CHOICE ANSWERS

1. B	5. C	9. D	13. B
2. B	6. C	10. A	14. D
3. A	7. B	11. A	15. A
4. D	8. C	12. B	

SHORT-ANSWER QUESTIONS

Question 1
Answer A, B, and C.

A. Briefly describe ONE specific historical similarity between how the Missouri Compromise and the Compromise of 1850 attempted to reduce sectional tensions.

B. Briefly describe ONE specific historical difference between how the Missouri Compromise and the Compromise of 1850 attempted to reduce sectional tensions.

C. Briefly explain ONE specific historical impact of either the Missouri Compromise or the Compromise of 1850.

Question 2
Using the excerpts below, answer A, B, and C.

"As sectional tension mounted in late 1860 and early 1861, five states in the lower South—Mississippi, Alabama, South Carolina, Georgia, and Louisiana—appointed commissioners to other slave states and instructed them to spread the secessionist message across the entire region…They were not talking about constitutional differences or political arguments. They were talking about the dawning of an abominable new world in the South, a world created by the Republican destruction of the institution of slavery…By illuminating so clearly the racial content of secession persuasion, the commissioners would seem to have laid to rest, once and for all, any notion that slavery had nothing to do with the coming of the Civil War. To put it quite simply, slavery and race were absolutely critical elements in the coming of the war."

Charles B. Dew, historian, *Apostles of Disunion: Southern Secession Commissioners and the Causes of the Civil War*, 2001

"In the eyes of many white Southerners, Lincoln's victory placed their future at the mercy of a party avowedly hostile to their region's values and interests. Those advocating secession did not believe Lincoln's administration would take immediate steps against slavery in the states. But if, as seemed quite possible, the election of 1860 marked a fundamental shift in power, the beginning of a long period of Republican rule, who could say what the North's antislavery sentiment would demand in five years, or ten? Slaveowners, moreover, feared Republican efforts to extend their party into the South by appealing to non-slave holders. Rather than accepting permanent minority status to a nation governed by their opponents, Deep South political leaders boldly struck for their region's independence. At stake, they believed, was not a single election, but an entire way of life."

Eric Foner, historian, *Give Me Liberty!*, 2014

A. Briefly describe ONE major difference between Dew's and Foner's historical interpretations of the causes of the Civil War.

B. Briefly explain how ONE specific historical event or development from the period 1820 to 1860 that is not explicitly mentioned in the excerpts could be used to support Dew's argument.

C. Briefly explain how ONE specific historical event or development from the period 1820 to 1860 that is not explicitly mentioned in the excerpts could be used to support Foner's argument.

SHORT-ANSWER ANSWERS

Question 1
A. Both compromises attempted to reduce sectional tensions. The Missouri Compromise reduced tensions by maintaining the sectional balance of power in the Senate. The Compromise of 1850 reduced tensions by reaffirming the permanence of slavery and rejecting the Wilmot Proviso.

B. The Missouri Compromise maintained the sectional balance of power in the Senate. In contrast, the Compromise of 1850 allowed California to enter the Union as a free state, thus giving the North 16 free states while leaving the South with 15 slave states.

C. The Missouri Compromise defused the political crisis over the expansion of slavery into the western territories. The 36°30' compromise line held for 34 years, until the passage of the Kansas-Nebraska Act inflamed sectional tensions.

Question 2

A. Dew argued that the Republican victory in the 1860 presidential election would result in the "destruction of the institution of slavery." He concluded that slavery and race were critical causes of the Civil War. In contrast, Foner believes that the election of 1860 would usher in a "long period of Republican rule" that would relegate the South to a "permanent minority status."

B. The failure of the North to enforce the Fugitive Slave Act provides evidence of the South's fear that the North intended to destroy slavery.

C. The Compromise of 1850 left the South with a weakened position in the Senate. The election of 1860 further intensified Southern fears that a long period of Republican rule had begun.

CHAPTER 9

AFRICAN AMERICAN HISTORY

FROM SEGREGATION TO THE FIRST
STIRRINGS OF BLACK PRIDE

1866–1939

STRATEGIC IMPORTANCE

African American history generates the most questions and points of any topic on the APUSH exam. We have devoted four of our twelve narrative chapters to help you thoroughly master the key events, trends, and leaders associated with this all-important historic experience. A careful analysis of recent APUSH exams reveals that the period from Reconstruction to the New Deal generated an average of about seven points per exam. Remember, you only need 75 points to earn a three, 95 points to earn a four, and 110 points to earn a five. This chapter is thus an important part of your coalition of points.

KEY POINTS AND HISTORIC GENERALIZATIONS

- The Fourteenth Amendment overturned the BLACK CODES, Three-Fifths Compromise, and the *Dred Scott* decision. It also established a principle of equality before the law that played a key role in the landmark *Brown v. Board of Education* decision.

- SHARECROPPING trapped African American farmers in an endless cycle of debt and poverty.

- REDEEMER governments reestablished white supremacy throughout the South. They used poll taxes and literacy tests to disenfranchise black voters.

- The *Plessy v. Ferguson* decision provided legal support for "separate but equal" Jim Crow laws.

- Booker T. Washington urged African Americans to follow a policy of accommodation by accepting segregation, avoiding political agitation, and concentrating on economic advancement.

- W.E.B. Du Bois urged African Americans to follow a policy of "ceaseless agitation" to challenge Jim Crow segregation and demand full economic, social, and political equality.

- Both the Progressive Era reformers and presidents neglected the plight of African Americans living in the South.

- The NAACP used lawsuits in federal courts as its primary weapons against segregation.

- The push of discrimination and the pull of a booming Northern job market combined to cause a GREAT MIGRATION of African Americans from the rural South to the urban North.

- The HARLEM RENAISSANCE marked an outpouring of literary and artistic works that expressed the assertive spirit of the "New Negro."

- Marcus Garvey preached a message of black pride and black self-help.

- African American voters became an important part of the NEW DEAL political coalition.

TOPIC 9.1
BLACK CODES AND CONSTITUTIONAL AMENDMENTS

A. A PERIOD OF UNCERTAINTY

The aftermath of the Civil War ushered in a period of great uncertainty. The defeated Southern states faced difficult questions about the future place of over four million freedmen. In a speech given to the House of Representatives, Thaddeus Stevens recognized that "the infernal laws of slavery" left African Americans impoverished and illiterate. He warned his colleagues that they faced a difficult road and a "great duty."

B. BLACK CODES

Slavery's long legacy of prejudice and discrimination would not be easy to overcome. Prior to the Civil War, slave codes rigorously regulated the South's African American population. In the months following the Civil War, Southern states enacted BLACK CODES designed to limit the labor, mobility, and rights of African Americans. For example, a law in Mississippi required every freedman to annually sign a one-year labor contract. The law made it a crime to give food, clothing, or shelter to any African American worker who left his or her employer while still under contract. Other laws forbade blacks from owning guns, marrying whites, or assembling in groups.

Frederick Douglass recognized that the Black Codes had the common goal of returning the freedmen to a system resembling slavery. He denounced the laws for making the promise of the Emancipation Proclamation "a mockery and delusion." Douglass grimly warned that the Black Codes "defeat the beneficent intention of the Government, if it has beneficent intention, in regards to the freedom of our people."

C. THE FOURTEENTH AMENDMENT, 1868

The intentions of the federal government quickly became a hotly disputed issue. President Johnson did not object to the Black Codes. His lenient view of Reconstruction placed the president on a collision course with a Congress dominated by Radical Republicans who wanted to transform the South by extending civil and political rights to African Americans.

The Fourteenth Amendment countered Johnson's lenient program and overturned the Black Codes. The first section granted citizenship to "all persons born or naturalized in the United States." This famous definition overturned both the *Dred Scott* decision and the Three-Fifths Compromise.

The Fourteenth Amendment also prohibited the states from depriving "any person of life, liberty, or property, without due process of law; nor deny to any person within its jurisdiction equal protection of the laws." The phrase "equal protection of the laws" is the only reference to the idea of equality in the Constitution. The full force of these words would not be felt until the 1954 Supreme Court decision in *Brown v. Board of Education*. In this landmark ruling, the high court used the equal protection clause of the Fourteenth Amendment to strike down segregation in the public schools. (See Chapter 5 for a full discussion).

D. THE FIFTEENTH AMENDMENT, 1870

Frederick Douglass recognized the importance of the Fourteenth Amendment. At the same time, he also pressed for the "immediate, unconditional, and universal enfranchisement of the black man, in every State in the Union." Douglass forcefully argued for a Constitutional amendment granting African American men "this all-important right of suffrage."

After extensive debates, Congress ratified the Fifteenth Amendment on February 3, 1870. The amendment marked the last of the three Reconstruction Amendments. It forbade either the federal government or the states from denying citizens the right to vote on the basis of "race, color, or previous condition of servitude."

As Douglass hoped, the Fifteenth Amendment enabled African Americans to exercise political influence for the first time. Freedmen provided about 80 percent of the Republican votes in the South. Over 600 blacks served in reconstructed state legislatures. In addition, voters elected 14 blacks to the House of Representatives and two to the Senate. Black voters supported the Republican Party by casting ballots that helped elect Grant in 1868 and 1872.

TOPIC 9.2
FROM SLAVE TO SHARECROPPER

A. SHARECROPPING

The Reconstruction amendments brought African Americans freedom and political rights. However, the new laws did not bring economic prosperity. Many former slaves stayed on their old plantations because they could not afford to leave.

During the late 1860s, cotton planters and black freedmen entered a new labor system called SHARECROPPING. Under this system, black families exchanged their labor for the use of land, tools, and seed. The sharecropper typically gave the landowner half of the crops as payment for the use of his property.

B. AN ENDLESS CYCLE OF DEBT AND POVERTY

Sharecropping did not lead to economic independence. Unscrupulous landowners and shopkeepers charged sharecroppers exorbitant prices and unfair interest rates. An Arkansas sharecropper recalled, "We couldn't make nothing, just overalls and something to eat." He warned, "A man that didn't know how to count would always lose…. They didn't give no itemized statement. No, you just had to take their word." This system of economic exploitation trapped African Americans in a seemingly endless cycle of debt and poverty.

TOPIC 9.3
THE RESTORATION OF WHITE SUPREMACY

A. THE KU KLUX KLAN

White Southerners believed that vindictive Republicans sought to punish them by repealing Black Codes and enfranchising African Americans. The years following the Civil War witnessed the proliferation of white supremacist organizations. The Ku Klux Klan began in Tennessee in 1866 and then quickly spread across the South.

Anonymous Klansmen dressed in white robes and pointed cowls. They believed that this ghostlike appearance would intimidate and frighten superstitious blacks. The Klansmen used whippings, house-burnings, kidnappings, and lynchings to keep blacks "in their place." For example, an African American woman from South Carolina testified that Klansmen beat her and then burned her house for the "crime" of "bragging and boasting that I would have land."

The Klan's reign of terror worked. As black voting declined, Democrats regained power. By 1876, Democrats replaced Republicans in eight of the eleven former

Confederate states. Only South Carolina, Louisiana, and Florida remained under Republican control.

B. THE COMPROMISE OF 1877

Republicans grew weary of pressing their agenda to reconstruct Southern society. Sympathy for the freedmen began to wane as radical leaders such as Thaddeus Stevens and Charles Sumner died or left office. A new generation of "politicos" began to focus their attention on Western expansion, Indian wars, tariffs, and the construction of transcontinental railroads.

The disputed 1876 presidential election provided an opportunity for the North to end Reconstruction. After tense negotiations, Democratic leaders agreed to support the Republican candidate Rutherford Hays. In return, Hays agreed to adopt a "Let 'Em Alone Policy" that included the withdrawal of all federal troops from the South. The remaining Republican governments quickly collapsed as Southern Democrats proclaimed a return to "home rule" and white supremacy. After reviewing these events, historian Jill Lapore concluded, "The Confederacy had lost the war, but it had won the peace."

C. THE DISENFRANCHISEMENT OF BLACK VOTERS

The end of Reconstruction left political control in the South in the hands of Democratic Party leaders known collectively as REDEEMERS because they claimed to redeem or save the South from Republican rule. The Redeemers were committed to white supremacy. Poor whites did not see impoverished blacks as fellow victims of economic forces they could not control. Instead, they supported the Redeemers' policy of disenfranchising African American voters.

The Redeemers employed a number of tactics to circumvent the Fifteenth Amendment. For example, poll taxes forced poor sharecroppers to pay a tax for the right to vote. In addition, many states enacted literacy tests requiring voters to read and then answer difficult questions about their state constitutions. Not surprisingly, registrars declared far more blacks ineligible than whites.

These tactics achieved their purpose of excluding African Americans from voting. In 1887 no African Americans served in the 50th Congress. In Louisiana the number of blacks registered to vote plunged from 130,000 in 1894 to just 1,342 a decade later.

D. "SEPARATE BUT EQUAL"

During the 1890s more and more white Southerners rejected the idea of racial equality. The crash of 1893 and the ensuing economic depression further sharpened racial tensions. The African American reformer Ida B. Wells protested that the Redeemer governments "did everything in their power to render our freedom a curse rather than a blessing."

The curse of racial injustice soon turned into the demeaning reality of JIM CROW laws mandating segregated facilities. For example, a Separate Car Act in Louisiana required railroad companies to maintain "colored cars" for African American passengers. Supported by a New Orleans Citizens Committee, a light-skinned African American named Homer Plessy challenged the law by refusing to give up his first-class seat on a white-only car. A detective promptly arrested Plessy.

Plessy and his supporters challenged the Separate Car Act as a violation of the Fourteenth Amendment's guarantee of equal protection before the law. When New Orleans Judge John H. Ferguson ruled against Plessy, his lawyer appealed the case to the U.S. Supreme Court. The justices ignored Plessy's argument that "Citizenship is neutral and knows no color." Instead, they ruled that segregated facilities do not discriminate as long as they are "separate but equal."

The "SEPARATE BUT EQUAL" DOCTRINE allowed Jim Crow segregation laws to spread across the South. Soon there were segregated schools, restaurants, hotels, and even cemeteries. Segregation affected every detail of daily life. Courthouses provided black and white witnesses with separate Bibles, while playgrounds provided black and white children with separate swings. Ubiquitous signs declaring "White Only" or "Colored" appeared on restroom doors, above water fountains, and inside stores.

TOPIC 9.4
RESPONSES TO "THE COLOR LINE"

A. "THE COLOR LINE"
By 1900 Jim Crow segregation, political disenfranchisement, and Klan-inspired violence defined race relations in the South. The editor of the *Richmond Times* expressed a widespread Southern attitude when he wrote, "God Almighty drew the color line and it cannot be obliterated. The Negro must stay on his side, and the sooner both races recognize this fact and accept it, the better it will be for both."

The harsh realities of racism and Jim Crow segregation laws forced African American leaders to speak out. Booker T. Washington and W.E.B. Du Bois offered very different approaches for how blacks should respond to the color line imposed across the South.

B. BOOKER T. WASHINGTON AND ACCOMMODATION
Booker T. Washington was born in 1856 as a slave on a Virginia plantation. After the Civil War his family moved to West Virginia. Washington worked from 4 a.m.

to 9 a.m. in a coal mine before going to school. He later recalled, "Few were too young, and none too old, to make the attempt to learn." Determined to get an education, Washington studied for three years at Virginia's Hampton Institute, a black vocational school. He graduated in 1875 as a brick mason.

In 1881 the founder of Hampton Institute selected Washington to establish an industrial and professional school for blacks in Tuskegee, Alabama. Washington faced a daunting challenge. When he arrived in Tuskegee the facility included just two small buildings, no equipment, and very little money. Washington worked the next 34 years teaching his students the values of self-sufficiency and industry while promoting Tuskegee in speeches around the country. At his death in 1915, Tuskegee was a thriving institution with more than 100 buildings, over 1,500 students, a faculty of 200 instructors, and an endowment of $2 million.

In 1895, organizers for the Cotton States and International Exposition in Atlanta took the then-unprecedented step of inviting Washington to be one of the featured speakers for the event's opening ceremonies. Washington did not disappoint his hosts. He delivered a conciliatory message that blacks and whites could lead separate social lives while working together for economic progress. Washington encouraged blacks to follow a policy of accommodation by accepting segregation, avoiding politics, and concentrating on economic advancement. In a memorable moment he thrust out his hand, declaring, "In all things purely social we can be as separate as the fingers, yet one as the hand in all things essential to mutual progress."

Washington's white audience praised his message of accommodation and self-help. In a short time his "Atlanta Compromise Speech" catapulted him into the national limelight as America's leading spokesperson for African Americans.

C. W.E.B. DU BOIS AND "CEASELESS AGITATION"

Washington's conciliatory message did not inspire W.E.B. Du Bois. Born in 1868 in Great Barrington, Massachusetts, Du Bois grew up in a relatively tolerant community where he attended school with white students. He earned a bachelor's degree at Fisk University, a historically black institution in Nashville, Tennessee. Du Bois pursued his education at Harvard University, where he became the first African American to earn a Ph.D.

Du Bois represented a younger generation of African Americans who criticized Washington's commitment to gradual progress. In his groundbreaking book *The Souls of Black Folk*, Du Bois charged that Washington's strategy of accommodation would only serve to perpetuate segregation and racial injustice. He advanced an alternative program of "ceaseless agitation" to challenge Jim Crow segregation and demand full economic, social, and political equality.

Du Bois understood that overcoming centuries of discrimination and racism would not be easy. He urged a "talented tenth" of educated blacks to spearhead the fight for equal rights. In 1909, Du Bois and a number of prominent black and white reformers founded the National Association for the Advancement of Colored People. The NAACP adopted a strategy of using lawsuits in federal courts to fight Jim Crow segregation.

Du Bois lived to see the NAACP lawyers argue and win the historic *Brown v. Board of Education* decision striking down the "separate but equal" doctrine. He died on August 27, 1963, one day before Dr. King delivered his famous "I Have a Dream" speech calling for the integrated society Du Bois had dedicated his life to achieving.

TOPIC 9.5
AFRICAN AMERICANS AND PROGRESSIVE REFORM

A. PRESIDENTIAL PREJUDICE

Progressive reformers addressed a wide range of issues including child labor laws, antitrust legislation, urban corruption, and women's rights. However, they conspicuously neglected the plight of African Americans in the South. President Taft reflected the depth of white prejudice when he applauded Jim Crow laws as necessary to "prevent entirely the possibility of domination by… an ignorant electorate."

President Wilson shared Taft's racist views. In 1915, Hollywood director D.W. Griffith released *The Birth of a Nation*, an explicitly racist film glorifying the Ku Klux Klan. Wilson allowed the film to be the first movie screened inside the White House. He enthusiastically endorsed Griffith's racist message by saying, "It is like writing history with lightning, and my only regret is that it is so terribly true."

B. THE NATIONAL ASSOCIATION FOR THE ADVANCEMENT OF COLORED PEOPLE

In 1908 a bloody riot in Springfield, Illinois, claimed the lives of at least 16 black and white residents. The riot in Lincoln's hometown shocked concerned citizens. The following year, W.E.B. Du Bois and a number of white and black reformers founded the National Association for the Advancement of Colored People (NAACP). The founding of the NAACP marked the first major attempt since Reconstruction to make civil rights the focus of national reform.

The NAACP used lawsuits in federal courts as its primary weapons against segregation. The organization achieved a noteworthy success in 1915 when the Supreme Court struck down a grandfather clause in an Oklahoma law. The statute had denied the vote to any citizen whose ancestors had not been enfranchised in 1860.

C. IDA B. WELLS

Ida B. Wells could not ignore racial injustice. The daughter of former slaves in Mississippi, Wells worked as a teacher in a segregated school in Memphis. She experienced the humiliation of Jim Crow segregation while riding on a train from Nashville to Memphis. Although Wells purchased a first-class ticket, the train conductor ordered her to move to a crowded smoking car reserved for blacks. When Wells refused, the conductor and two men forcibly removed her from the train. Wells sued the train company, and won a $500.00 settlement. However, the Tennessee Supreme Court later overturned the payment. This injustice led Wells to found a newspaper and become a vocal critic of segregation.

Wells experienced a second major personal turning point in 1892. That year three black friends opened a People's Grocery in Memphis. Their new business drew customers away from a nearby white-owned store. Tensions quickly escalated as supporters of the white owners clashed with the black proprietors. One night the black owners shot three white vandals who threatened their store. The police arrested and jailed the black men. But they didn't have a chance to defend themselves in court. A lynch mob stormed the prison and lynched the three men.

The brutal murders incensed Wells. Putting her life at risk, she wrote scathing articles condemning the deaths of her friends. A mob retaliated by burning her newspaper office and destroying all her equipment. Undaunted, Wells published her first investigative book, *Southern Horrors: Lynch Law in All Its Phases*.

Wells's book documented how white supremacists used lynchings to intimidate blacks and enforce Jim Crow laws. She indignantly pointed out, "Nowhere in the civilized world save the United States of America do men, possessing all civil and political power, go out in bands of 50 and 5,000 to hunt down, shoot, hang or burn to death a single individual, unarmed and absolutely powerless." While white progressives largely ignored these acts of terror, Wells emerged as an effective leader of an anti-lynching crusade. She also worked tirelessly for the women's suffrage movement and helped found the NAACP.

TOPIC 9.6
THE GREAT MIGRATION, 1910-1930

A. LEAVING THE LAND OF COTTON

In 1900, nine out of every ten black Americans lived in the South, and three out of four lived on farms. The humiliation of Jim Crow segregation crushed the brief spirit of optimism following Emancipation. Grinding poverty, along with the Ku Klux Klan's relentless campaign of intimidation and violence, provided compelling reasons for Southern blacks to leave their homes.

A sudden labor shortage in the North provided the essential economic opportunity for a better life. The outbreak of World War I created a tremendous demand for wartime supplies. At that same time, the war cut the flow of European immigrants to America. Northern assembly lines, steel mills, and meatpacking companies turned to Southern blacks to fill the shortage of jobs.

The push of discrimination and the pull of a booming Northern job market convinced about 1.5 million African Americans to leave the South in the years between 1910 and 1930. This mass movement from the rural South to the cities in the North and Midwest is known as the GREAT MIGRATION.

B. LIVING IN THE "COLD, COLD MINDED NORTH"

The North offered migrants a complex mix of fulfilled promises and thwarted expectations. Migrants often earned salaries two to three times higher than those they had earned in the South. They attended better schools, visited free public libraries, and enjoyed watching films in the new movie palaces. At the same time, however, African Americans were barred from joining many unions and confined to living in dilapidated, overpriced housing. In a popular song called the "Cotton Belt Blues," a woman living in the "cold, cold minded North" laments that she is "broke and disgusted." Despite the sometimes harsh realities of life in Northern cities, the overwhelming majority of black migrants did not return to the South.

TOPIC 9.7
THE HARLEM RENAISSANCE AND THE "NEW NEGRO"

A. "THE GREATEST NEGRO CITY IN THE WORLD"

The Great Migration fostered the growth of a new urban black culture. During the 1920s a creative generation of black writers and artists transformed Manhattan's Harlem district into what they proudly called "the greatest Negro city in the world." Langston Hughes, Jean Toomer, Claude McKay, and

Zora Neale Hurston formed a core group of writers who contributed to an outpouring of black literary, artistic, and political expression known as the HARLEM RENAISSANCE.

Alain Leroy Locke described the new black pride and assertive spirit in his essay "The New Negro." Locke explained that in the past, black Americans shared the common conditions of slavery and segregation. In contrast, blacks living in Harlem formed the vanguard of a new common consciousness rooted in their collective racial identity. Harlem thus became the nerve center of black America's thrust toward "group expression and self-determination."

B. MARCUS GARVEY

For millions of black Americans, Marcus Garvey embodied the spirit of the New Negro. An unknown 30-year-old black Jamaican publisher and labor organizer, Garvey arrived in Harlem in 1917. A flamboyant and charismatic speaker, Garvey projected a compelling vision. He rejected integration and instead preached a message of black pride and self-help. Garvey exhorted his followers to embrace their African heritage and rejoice in the beauty of their black skin. "We have a beautiful history," Garvey told enthralled listeners, "and we shall create another one in the future."

Garvey's vision of black pride and black nationalism fueled the rapid growth of the Universal Negro Improvement Association. Within a short time, the UNIA became the first mass movement in African American history. By the mid-1920s, Garvey's organization had 700 branches in 38 states and the West Indies. The UNIA also published a newspaper with as many as 200,000 subscribers. By 1923, Garvey was one of the most famous black spokesmen in the world.

Garvey's fame proved to be short-lived. In the mid-1920s he was charged with mail fraud, jailed, and then deported to Jamaica. Nonetheless, the man whose followers called him the "Black Moses" left behind a rich legacy. Dr. King captured the essence of Garvey's message of racial pride when he told an audience in Jamaica that Garvey "was the first man of color to lead and develop a mass movement. He was the first man on a mass scale and level to give millions of Negroes a sense of dignity and destiny. And make the Negro feel he was somebody."

TOPIC 9.8
THE GREAT DEPRESSION, NEW DEAL, AND AFRICAN AMERICANS

A. "LAST HIRED, FIRST FIRED"

During the 1920s soaring stock prices reinforced optimism about America's booming economy. However, Wall Street's speculative bubble burst on Black Thursday, October 24, 1929, beginning a devastating economic collapse known as the Great Depression. Within three years stocks lost 89 percent of their value, thousands of banks closed, and millions of workers lost their jobs.

The burden of hard times fell most heavily on African Americans. As the "last hired and first fired," black families did not have far to fall. The African American unemployment rate soared to approximately 50 percent, twice the rate of white workers. Harlem did not escape the Great Depression's ever-tightening grip. As the Roaring Twenties came to an abrupt end, the creative spirit inspiring the Harlem Renaissance also came to an end.

B. A LIMITED NEW DEAL

President Roosevelt pledged to use the power of the federal government to address the nation's economic crisis. Known as the NEW DEAL, his program of relief, recovery, and reform included about 15 pieces of landmark legislation.

The New Deal did not directly confront racial injustice. For example, the Civilian Conservation Corps allowed racially segregated camps, while the Federal Housing Administration refused to insure mortgages for African Americans trying to buy homes in white neighborhoods. Because he needed the support of Southern Democrats, FDR did not challenge the poll tax or support passage of a federal anti-lynching law.

Although New Deal programs did not challenge segregation, they did help African Americans survive the Great Depression. For example, blacks living in northern cities benefited from WPA work relief programs. In addition, FDR appointed the first African American federal judge and tripled the number of blacks working in the federal government.

C. THE NEW DEAL COALITION

Following Reconstruction, white-led Redeemer governments took power across the South. They shared an antipathy toward both Republicans and blacks. African American voters in the North responded by forming a reliable Republican voting bloc. In the 1932 presidential election, 75 percent of African American voters supported Herbert Hoover as the candidate of the party of Lincoln.

The New Deal caused a dramatic shift in how African Americans viewed the Republican and Democratic parties. Unlike the Hoover administration, FDR's programs did provide modest but welcome relief. In the 1936 presidential election, over three-fourths of black voters switched their allegiance to FDR and the Democratic Party. African Americans thus became a key component in a Democratic coalition of voters that included union members, urban Catholics, Jews, liberal Progressives, and white Southerners.

D. MORE THAN A CONCERT

FDR was a pragmatic politician who carefully considered what he could and could not do. In contrast, First Lady Eleanor Roosevelt's actions often reflected her deep personal convictions. In 1939 the all-white Daughters of the American Revolution (DAR) barred Marion Anderson, the world-renowned African American singer, from performing in Constitution Hall in Washington, D.C. Outraged by this blatant act of discrimination, the First Lady resigned from the DAR. She then arranged for Anderson to give a free outdoor concert from the steps of the Lincoln Memorial. An integrated audience of 75,000 people attended Anderson's Easter Sunday performance.

The event had a significance beyond that of a mere concert. The unprecedented gathering of a white and black audience removed a barrier in American society. When Marion Anderson opened the concert by singing "My Country, Tis of Thee," the power and beauty of her voice struck at the foundations of racism. Many in the audience openly wept as she sang the words "Sweet land of liberty...Let freedom ring." Marian Anderson's groundbreaking performance marked a milestone in American history by setting the stage for the Civil Rights era that was about to begin.

CHAPTER 9
PRACTICE QUESTIONS

MULTIPLE-CHOICE QUESTIONS

Questions 1–2 refer to the excerpt below.

Sec. 1 *Be it ordained by the police jury of the parish of St. Landry, That no negro shall be allowed to pass within the limits of said parish without special permit in writing from his employer....*

Sec. 4 ... Every negro is required to be in the regular service of some white person, or former owner, who shall be held responsible for the conduct of said negro....

Sec. 5 ... No public meeting or congregations of negroes shall be allowed within said parish after sunset....

Sec. 7 ... No negro who is not in the military service shall be allowed to carry firearms or any kind of weapons, within the parish....

   Louisiana Black Code, 1865

1. **Section 4 most directly contributed to the**
    A. migration of African Americans to cities in the West and North
    B. election of African Americans to Congress between 1869 and 1877
    C. emergence of sharecropping during Reconstruction
    D. creation of a federal jobs program to help African American farmers

2. **Which of the following late nineteenth-century developments best represents a continuation of the ideas expressed in this excerpt?**
    A. A movement focused on women's voting rights.
    B. Support for outlawing the production and sale of alcohol.
    C. The industrialization of some segments of the Southern economy.
    D. The South's determined resistance and the North's waning resolve.

Questions 3–4 refer to the excerpt below.

"All persons born or naturalized in the United States, and subject to the jurisdiction thereof, are citizens of the United States and of the States wherein they reside. No state shall make or enforce any law which shall abridge the privileges or immunities of citizens of the United States; nor shall any State deprive any person of life, liberty, or property,without due process of law; nor deny to any person within its jurisdiction the equal protection of the laws."

Fourteenth Amendment, 1868

3. Which of the following was a direct consequence of the ratification of the Fourteenth Amendment?

A. The promotion of suffrage for all women
B. The election of former slaves to Congress
C. The protection of the rights guaranteed by the First Amendment
D. The invalidation of the *Dred Scott v. Sanford* decision

4. One direct long-term effect of the Fourteenth Amendment was that it

A. refined the meaning of the "necessary and proper" clause
B. altered the meaning of the Preamble to the Constitution
C. served as the basis for successful civil rights court suits in the 1950s and 1960s
D. Repudiated the Thirteenth Amendment

Questions 5–6 refer to the 1867 cartoon below, "First Vote" by Alfred R. Waud (Library of Congress).

5. **The cartoonist most likely supported the**

    A. enactment of Black Codes
    B. ratification of the Fifteenth Amendment
    C. growth of corporate economic power
    D. development of political machines

6. **Which of the following groups most strongly opposed the event depicted in this cartoon?**

    A. Redeemers in the South
    B. Radical Republicans in Congress
    C. Founders of the NAACP
    D. Supporters of the cult of domesticity

Questions 7–8 refer to the excerpt below.

"To everyone applying to rent land upon shares, the following
conditions must be read and agreed to...
The sale of every cropper's part of the cotton to be made by me
when and where I choose to sell, and after deducting all they owe
me and all sums that I may be responsible for on their accounts, to
pay them this half of the net proceeds."

　　　A contract in North Carolina, 1882

"De White man he got ha'f de crop
　Boll-Weevil took de res'
　Ain't got no home,
　Ain't got no home.

　　　A Southern African American folk saying, 1910s

7. **The problem described in both examples illustrates
    which of the following developments in the decades
    after the Civil War?**
    A. The emergence of a New South economy based upon a balanced mix
       of agriculture and industry
    B. The emergence of sharecropping as the dominant labor system in the
       South
    C. The mass migration of African Americans to cities in the North and
       West
    D. The emergence of a lucrative cotton economy that promoted
       widespread economic prosperity

8. **Which of the following was a direct effect of the
    problem illustrated in the two excerpts?**
    A. The formation of the Ku Klux Klan
    B. The passage of Black Codes
    C. The major redistribution of land ownership in the South
    D. The entrapment of tenant farmers in a cycle of debt and poverty

Questions 9–10 refer to the excerpt below.

"In all things that are purely social we can be as separate as the fingers, yet
one as the hand in all things essential to mutual progress...The wisest among
my race understand that the agitation of questions of social equality is the

extremest folly, and that progress in the enjoyment of all the privileges that will come to us must be the result of severe and constant struggle rather than artificial forcing…The opportunity to earn a dollar in a factory job just now is worth infinitely more than the opportunity to spend a dollar in an opera-house."

Booker T. Washington, Atlanta Compromise Speech, 1895

9. **The excerpt most directly advocates which of the following strategies for African Americans living in the South?**
   A. An aggressive campaign of nonviolent demonstrations
   B. Political activism to promote Black Power
   C. Legal action to challenge Jim Crow segregation laws
   D. Widespread participation in vocational education programs

10. **Which of the following groups would have been most likely to oppose the perspective of Booker T. Washington in the excerpt?**
    A. Proponents of the New South economic program
    B. Owners of new textile mills in the South
    C. Leaders of Du Bois's "talented tenth"
    D. Organizers of the Cotton States and International Exposition in Atlanta

Questions 11–12 refer to the excerpt below.

"While much is said about moneymaking, not enough is said about efficient, self-sacrificing toil of head and hand. Are not all these things worth striving for? The Niagara Movement proposes to gain these ends…. If we expect to gain our rights by nerveless acquiescence in wrong, then we expect to do what no other nation ever did. What must we do then? We must complain. Yes, plain, blunt complain, ceaseless agitation, unfailing exposure of dishonesty and wrong— this is the ancient, unerring way to liberty, and we must follow it."

W.E.B. Du Bois, "The Niagara Movement," 1905

11. **The beliefs expressed in the excerpt most directly challenged the prevailing idea in early twentieth-century America that**

   A. African Americans should migrate from the South to cities in the North and West
   B. separate but equal public facilities for African Americans were appropriate
   C. sharecropping was the best route to economic advancement
   D. African American voters should shift their allegiance to the Democratic Party

12. **The excerpt was a direct response to**

   A. Booker T. Washington's policy of accommodation
   B. Ida B. Wells's campaign against lynching
   C. Theodore Roosevelt's Square Deal programs
   D. Susan B. Anthony's campaign for women's suffrage

Questions 13–15 refer to the excerpt below.

"The road for the serious black artist, then, who would produce a racial art is most certainly rocky and the mountain is high. Until recently he received almost no encouragement for his work from either white or colored people… to my mind it is the duty of the younger Negro artist…to change through the force of his art that old whispering 'I want to be white,' hidden in the aspirations of his people, to 'Why should I want to be white? I am Negro—and beautiful.'"

   Langston Hughes, "The Negro Artist and the Racial Mountain," 1926

13. **The message advocated in this excerpt was an integral part of which of the following developments in the 1920s?**

   A. The New South movement
   B. Cubism and Modern Art
   C. The Harlem Renaissance
   D. The Niagara movement

14. **The ideas about racial pride expressed by Hughes were most consistent with the views of**

    A. Marcus Garvey
    B. Booker T. Washington
    C. D.W. Griffith
    D. Franklin D. Roosevelt

15. **Which of the following groups would have been most likely to support the views expressed in this excerpt?**

    A. The Daughters of the American Revolution
    B. The Progressive era presidents
    C. The Universal Negro Improvement Association
    D. The Ku Klux Klan

MULTIPLE-CHOICE ANSWERS

1. C	5. B	9. D	13. C
2. D	6. A	10. C	14. A
3. D	7. B	11. B	15. C
4. C	8. D	12. A	

SHORT-ANSWER QUESTIONS

Question 1
Answer A, B, and C.

A. Briefly describe ONE specific example of how New Deal programs helped African Americans.

B. Briefly describe ONE specific example of how New Deal programs failed to help African Americans.

C. Briefly describe a specific political effect that resulted from the reaction of African Americans to FDR and the New Deal.

Question 2
Using the excerpts above, answer A, B, and C.

"Four centuries had passed since continents, separated by oceans, had met again. A century had passed since Jefferson had declared all men equal. Three decades had passed since the Fourteenth Amendment had declared all persons born or naturalized in the United States to be citizens. And now the Supreme Court ruled that those who would set aside equality in favor of separation had not violated the nation's founding truths. In one of the most wrenching tragedies in American history—a chronicle not lacking for tragedy— the Confederacy had lost the war, but it had won the peace."

Jill Lapore, historian, *These Truths, A History of the United States*, 2018

"We stirred in our shackles, and our unrest awakened justice in the hearts of a courageous few, and we re-created in America the desire for true democracy, freedom for all, the brotherhood of man, principles on which the country had been founded. We were freed and as before, we fought America's wars, provided the labor, gave the music, kept alive her flickering conscience, prodded her on toward the yet unachieved goal, democracy, until we became more than a part of America! We—this kicking, yelling, touchy, sensitive, scrupulously demanding minority—are the personification of the ideal begun by the Pilgrims about 350 years ago… We are more than a few isolated instances of courage, valor, achievement. We're the injection, the shot in the arm, that has kept America and its gotten principle alive in the fat and corrupt years intervening between our divine conception and our near-tragic present."

Edward Kennedy "Duke" Ellington, composer and musician, speech given on February 12, 1941

A. Briefly describe ONE significant difference between Lapore's understanding and Ellington's understanding of the African American experience during the Jim Crow era.

B. Briefly explain how ONE specific historical event or development from the period 1896–1941 could be used to support Lapore's interpretation.

C. Briefly explain how ONE specific historical event or development from the period 1896 to 1941 could be used to support Ellington's interpretation.

SHORT-ANSWER ANSWERS

Question 1

A. Blacks living in northern cities benefited from WPA relief programs. In addition, FDR tripled the number of blacks working in the federal government.

B. The New Deal did not directly confront racial injustice. For example, FDR did not challenge the poll tax or support passage of a federal anti-lynching law.

C. Black voters overwhelmingly switched their allegiance to FDR and the Democratic Party. They became a key component of the New Deal coalition of Democratic voters.

Question 2

A. Lapore argues that Reconstruction was a tragic experience of African Americans because America betrayed its founding principles. In contrast, Ellington argues that African Americans continued to make major contributions to American culture. He believes that African Americans kept American principles alive.

B. The Supreme Court ruling in *Plessy v. Ferguson* illustrates Lapore's view that the Confederacy "won the peace." The "separate but equal" doctrine nullified the Fourteenth Amendment and relegated African Americans to second-class citizenship.

C. The Harlem Renaissance illustrates Ellington's view that African Americans continued to make vital contributions to American culture. It provided a "shot in the arm" that asserted a new black pride and assertive spirit.

CHAPTER 10

AFRICAN AMERICAN HISTORY

FROM WORLD WAR II TO THE MODERN
CIVIL RIGHTS MOVEMENT

1940–1970

STRATEGIC IMPORTANCE

African American history generates the most questions and points of any topic on the APUSH exam. We have devoted four of our twelve narrative chapters to help you thoroughly master the key events, trends, and leaders associated with this all-important historic experience. A careful analysis of recent APUSH exams reveals that questions from World War II to the Black Power movement generated an average of five points per exam. Remember, you only need 75 points to earn a three, 95 points to earn a four, and 110 points to earn a five. This chapter is thus an important part of your coalition of points.

KEY POINTS AND HISTORIC GENERALIZATIONS

- FDR's Executive Order 8802 marked the first time since Reconstruction that the federal government committed itself to opposing racial discrimination.

- The Double V campaign called for African Americans to fight against fascism in Europe and racism in America. It marked the beginning of a new assertive attitude toward fighting against segregation.

- The Supreme Court decision in *Brown v. Board of Education of Topeka* reversed the legal principle of "separate but equal" established in *Plessy v. Ferguson*. The Court ruled that racial segregation in public schools was a denial of the equal protection of the laws guaranteed by the Fourteenth Amendment. The decision reflected the growing belief after World War II that the power of the federal government should be used to promote greater racial justice.

- The Dixiecrats were dissident Southern Democrats who opposed President Truman's proposals for civil rights legislation. The Dixiecrat Party marked the first break in the previously Solid South.

- Southern segregationists called for "massive resistance" to the *Brown* decision. The Little Rock school crisis marked a major test of the federal government's willingness to enforce the *Brown* decision.

- Dr. King galvanized the black community with his message of nonviolent civil disobedience. Dr. King worked to achieve equal rights and racial integration.

- The March on Washington was a massive demonstration to build a "coalition of conscience" to support President Kennedy's civil rights bill. Passed in 1964, the Civil Rights Act banned segregation in housing, jobs, education, and public facilities.

- The Voting Rights Act of 1965 outlawed poll taxes, literacy tests, and other practices used to prevent African Americans from exercising their constitutional right to vote.

- Malcolm X advocated black separatism, black pride, and the expansion of links with the newly independent nations in Africa.

- Stokely Carmichael and other advocates of BLACK POWER argued that African Americans should build economic and political power by forming black-owned businesses and voting for black candidates for political offices.

TOPIC 10.1
WORLD WAR II AND A NEW ASSERTIVE SPIRIT

A. THE POOREST OF THE POOR

When the 1940s opened, a vast gap still existed between the American Creed of democracy and equality and the reality of racial injustice. Despite the Great Migration, three-fourths of African Americans continued to live in the South, where they remained the poorest inhabitants of the nation's poorest region. The average black worker earned just 37 percent as much as the average white worker. A staggering nine out of ten black families survived on an income at or near the poverty level.

B. EXECUTIVE ORDER 8802

The outbreak of World War II in 1939 ignited the American economy. As orders for defense materials poured in, America's economy roared to life. However, frustrated and angry black leaders watched helplessly as defense plants turned away black job applicants. For example, in 1940 black workers held just 300 of the 100,000 well-paying aircraft jobs.

The exclusion of black workers from defense industries outraged A. Philip Randolph, the president of the all-black Brotherhood of Sleeping Car Porters. When a meeting with President Roosevelt failed to produce any concrete results, Randolph threatened to call for a mass protest march in Washington, D.C.

Randolph's strategy worked. Anxious to avoid a divisive and politically embarrassing protest, FDR issued Executive Order 8802, banning discrimination in defense jobs. His order also established a Fair Employment Practices Commission to investigate complaints. Hailed by the black press as a new Emancipation Proclamation, the presidential order promoted an increase in the black workforce in defense industries from three percent in 1942 to nine percent in 1945. Executive Order 8802 marked the first time since Reconstruction that the federal government committed itself to opposing racial discrimination.

The lure of jobs sparked a second phase in the Great Migration. During the 1940s, a massive wave of about one million Southern blacks boarded "liberty trains" heading for urban areas in the Northeast, Midwest, and Pacific coast. In 1943 alone over 100,000 African Americans abandoned their homes in Texas and Louisiana and moved to southern California.

The Second Great Migration far exceeded the movement of 1.5 million African Americans between 1910 and 1930. In the quarter-century following World War II, more than five million blacks left the South in search of better jobs, higher wages, and greater social equality. By 1970, about 80 percent of African Americans lived in cities.

C. THE DOUBLE V CAMPAIGN

More than one million black soldiers served in America's armed forces during World War II. Black Americans were keenly aware of the contradiction between fighting for democracy abroad while facing discrimination at home. The famous black poet and social activist Langston Hughes demanded to know, "How long I got to fight both Hitler and Jim Crow?"

In February 1942, the *Pittsburgh Courier* responded to Hughes' question by calling for blacks to support a Double V campaign to win victory over fascism in Europe and victory over racism in America. This new assertive attitude signaled both rising expectations and a determination to fight racial injustice.

TOPIC 10.2
THE TRUMAN YEARS: PROGRESS AND RESISTANCE, 1945–1952

A. "TO SECURE THESE RIGHTS"

In the months before the 1946 congressional election, black leaders attempted to start a voter registration drive in the South. Ku Klux Klan members and their supporters responded by threatening, assaulting, and even killing African Americans who tried to exercise their constitutional rights. When Truman learned about a particularly brutal assault on a black soldier in South Carolina he vowed, "We've got to do something."

The violence outraged the black community. President Truman responded to their angry complaints by appointing a presidential commission to study mob violence and civil rights. Issued in the Fall of 1947, the committee's report, "To Secure These Rights," called for 35 reforms including a federal anti-lynching law, a civil rights division within the Justice Department, a permanent Fair Employment Practices Committee, and a law abolishing poll taxes. Although Truman seemed ready to lead, Southern opposition blocked any congressional actions.

The battle over civil rights continued at the 1948 Democratic Convention. Minneapolis mayor Hubert H. Humphrey called upon the delegates to support a civil rights plank in the party platform. He passionately declared, "The time has arrived for the Democratic Party to get out of the shadow of states' rights and walk forthrightly into the bright sunshine of human rights."

B. THE "DIXIECRATS"

Humphrey's impassioned plea failed to inspire delegates from Alabama and Mississippi who marched out of the convention hall waving Confederate battle flags. Two weeks later, Deep South delegates met in Birmingham, Alabama, and nominated South Carolina governor Strom Thurmond to head a new States' Rights or "Dixiecrat" Party. Although Truman eventually won the 1948 presidential election, the Dixiecrats carried Alabama, Mississippi, Louisiana, and South Carolina.

The Dixiecrat Party marked the beginning of a significant change in the Democratic Party coalition. In the presidential elections following Reconstruction, Southern states formed a politically unified block known as the Solid South. With black voters effectively disenfranchised, Southern states gave their electoral votes to Democratic candidates. The Dixiecrat success in the 1948 presidential election marked the first crack in the Solid South. The election demonstrated that life-long Southern Democrats would abandon their party over the issues of civil rights and desegregation.

C. THE END OF MILITARY SEGREGATION, 1948

Southern resistance continued to block civil rights legislation in Congress. Determined to take a meaningful action, Truman signed Executive Order 9981, abolishing discrimination "on the basis of race, color, religion, or national origin" in the United States Armed Forces. This historic action marked a major victory in the emerging Civil Rights Movement.

D. JACKIE ROBINSON

On April 14, 1947, major league baseball mirrored American society. The rosters of all 16 major league teams contained only white players. But everything changed the next day, when Jackie Robinson took the field for the Brooklyn Dodgers. The grandson of slaves, Robinson became the first black major league baseball player in the twentieth century.

Crossing baseball's color line proved to be a daunting challenge. Branch Rickey, the president of the Dodgers, warned Robinson to expect a torrent of abuse. Rickey's dire prediction proved to be all too accurate. Opposing pitchers threw at Robinson, base runners tried to spike him, and fans taunted him. But Robinson persevered and excelled. He proved that talent and character are more important than skin color.

Robinson's success illustrated the shift in attitudes taking place across America. While Robinson changed minds in crowded baseball stadiums, the fight for justice and equal rights reached the dignified chamber of the United States Supreme Court.

TOPIC 10.3
BROWN V. BOARD OF EDUCATION OF TOPEKA

A. SEPARATE BUT NOT EQUAL

Ratified in 1868, the Fourteenth Amendment forbade states from denying their residents "the equal protection of the laws." However, in 1896 the Supreme Court narrowed the equal protection clause by ruling in *Plessy v. Ferguson* that racially "separate but equal" public facilities are constitutional. In his dissent, Justice John Marshall Harlan warned "the thin disguise" of equality "will not mislead anyone." Harlan's admonishment proved to be prophetic. Once legally sanctioned, Jim Crow segregation became a pervasive part of life in the South.

The "separate but equal" doctrine created separation but it did not create equality. When the 1953–54 school year opened, 2.5 million African American children attended all-black schools in the nation's capital and in 17 Southern and border states. The NAACP's Legal Defense Fund discovered appalling disparities between the white and black school systems. For example, in Clarendon County, South Carolina, the local school board spent $179.00 to educate each white child and just $43.00 for each black child. Black students in Clarendon County attended classes in buildings lacking running water or indoor toilets.

B. THURGOOD MARSHALL AND OLIVER BROWN

Thurgood Marshall understood the humiliation caused by legal segregation. In 1933, the University of Maryland Law School denied Marshall admission because he was black. Undeterred by this rejection, he attended law school at the historically black Howard University. Charles Houston, the program's dynamic new dean, taught Marshall to apply the tenets of the Constitution to all Americans. After graduating first in his class, Marshall eventually became the Chief Counsel for the NAACP's Legal Defense Fund. He soon compiled an impressive record of court challenges to state-sponsored discrimination.

Oliver Brown also understood the humiliation caused by legal segregation. A welder and part-time pastor, Brown and his family lived in an integrated neighborhood in Topeka, Kansas. In September 1950, Brown and his seven-year-old daughter Linda walked four blocks to an all-white neighborhood elementary school. The principal refused to enroll Linda because she was black. This degrading rejection forced Linda to walk across dangerous railroad tracks to reach an all-black elementary school two miles from her home.

Linda Brown's father and Thurgood Marshall together changed the course of American history. In February 1951, Oliver Brown filed a federal lawsuit against the Topeka, Kansas Board of Education. His suit soon became one of five test cases chosen by Marshall and the NAACP legal team to challenge state laws mandating segregation in the public schools. Oliver Brown's famous case became the first name on the list.

C. "WE CONCLUDE..."

Thurgood Marshall and his team argued that segregated schools placed a stigma or badge of second-class citizenship on black children by implying that they were not fit to be educated with white children. He forcefully insisted that this denied black children the "equal protection of the laws" guaranteed by the Fourteenth Amendment.

On May 17, 1954, a hushed audience of reporters closely watched as all nine Supreme Court justices solemnly entered the Court's ornate chamber. Americans and indeed people all over the world anxiously waited to hear the Court's decision in *Brown v. Board of Education of Topeka*. The wait soon ended. Chief Justice Earl Warren firmly announced the Court's unanimous decision: "We hold that in the field of public education the doctrine of 'separate but equal' has no place. Separate educational facilities are inherently unequal."

The decision marked a momentous turning point in American history. The ruling overturned the "separate but equal" doctrine established in *Plessy v. Ferguson*. It thus opened a new era in the African American struggle for equal rights. The unanimous *Brown* decision placed the Supreme Court on the side of racial justice. Galvanized by the Court's ruling, America's 15 million black citizens began to demand "Freedom Now!"

TOPIC 10.4
MASSIVE RESISTANCE

A. THE SOUTHERN MANIFESTO

Outraged Southern leaders did not applaud the Court for becoming an active agent of social change by opening a new era in the African American struggle for equal rights. Instead they responded by calling for "massive resistance" to the *Brown* decision. In Congress, 82 representatives and 19 senators signed a Southern Manifesto accusing the Supreme Court of "a clear abuse of judicial power."

The Southern Manifesto inspired widespread resistance to integration. Deep South states successfully evaded or defied plans to integrate their schools. Three years after the *Brown* decision, none of the 1.4 million African American children in Alabama, Mississippi, Louisiana, Georgia, and South Carolina attended integrated schools.

B. CRISIS AT CENTRAL HIGH SCHOOL IN LITTLE ROCK

Little Rock's Central High School first opened its doors in 1927. State officials hailed the new building as America's most expensive, most beautiful, and most spacious public high school. Nearly 2,000 white students expected to attend Central when it opened for the new school year on September 3, 1957. According to a desegregation plan adopted by the Little Rock school board, nine carefully selected black students would join them.

Arkansas Governor Orval Faubus had other plans. The defiant governor denounced the school board's desegregation plan and warned, "blood will run in the streets." In order to deter violence he dispatched over 250 Arkansas National Guardsmen to surround Central High School and prevent the nine black students from entering the building.

Massive resistance became painfully visible on September 3, 1957. A howling mob of over 1,000 white segregationists threatened the black students. Televised images of black students confronted by armed soldiers and their white tormentors stunned America. After three weeks of mob rule, Little Rock's mayor sent President Eisenhower an urgent wire declaring, "Situation is out of control and police cannot disperse the mob…Immediate need for federal troops is urgent."

C. PRESIDENT EISENHOWER ACTS

The mayor's emergency plea and the mob's direct challenge to the federal government forced President Eisenhower to intervene. Acting as America's commander in chief, Ike ordered 1,200 paratroopers from the famous 101st Airborne Division to Little Rock to protect the black students and enforce the desegregation order. He explained his action in a stern, nationally televised address: "The very basis of our individual rights and freedoms rests upon the certainty that the President and the Executive Branch of Government will support and insure the carrying out of the decisions of the federal courts, even, when necessary, with all the measures at the President's command."

The Screaming Eagles of the 101st Airborne Division arrived in Little Rock within eight hours of the president's order. Their deployment marked the first time since Reconstruction federal troops were sent into the South to protect the rights of African Americans. Shocking images of armed soldiers escorting the Little Rock Nine into Little Rock's Central High School became symbols of America's struggle for racial equality. The events in Little Rock began to build public support for desegregation. However, they did not end determined and often violent Southern resistance to integration.

TOPIC 10.5
THE BEGINNING OF NONVIOLENT PROTESTS, 1954-1960

A. ROSA PARKS

Rosa Parks grew up on a small farm outside Montgomery, Alabama. Like other blacks, she faced the daily struggle of living with humiliating Jim Crow segregation laws. Knowing her place meant drinking from colored-only water fountains, eating in colored-only restaurants, and sitting in colored-only seats on public buses.

On December 1, 1955, Parks finished a long day's work in a Montgomery department store and boarded a bus to ride home. When she sat down, Parks was an unknown and very tired 42-year-old seamstress. A few minutes later a white bus driver ordered her to give up her seat to a white passenger. As the bus driver impatiently waited for an answer, Rosa Parks did the unexpected. In a calm and unwavering voice she refused the driver's order by saying just one fateful word—"No." The driver promptly called the police, who arrested Parks and fined her $10.00.

B. DR. MARTIN LUTHER KING, JR.

Parks's act of defiance shifted attention to her 26-year-old minister, Dr. Martin Luther King, Jr. The son of a well-respected Atlanta pastor, King showed great academic promise as a student at Morehouse College. After choosing to become a minister, he attended Crozer Theological Seminary in Chester, Pennsylvania. King distinguished himself as both a scholar and a student leader. The mostly-white student body voted him president of their class. He left Crozer to earn a Ph.D. at Boston University.

Dr. King's force of personality and strong moral convictions made him a charismatic leader. He mobilized Montgomery's black community by organizing a boycott of the city buses. During the 381-day boycott, blacks walked, carpooled, and bicycled to their destinations. Extremists retaliated by bombing Dr. King's home.

Dr. King did not apologize for his "crime" of violating unjust segregation laws. Influenced by the writings of Henry David Thoreau and the actions of Mahatma Gandhi, he inspired boycotters by urging them to meet hate with love and violence with nonviolent civil disobedience. Dr. King convinced his followers that "noncooperation with evil is a moral duty." He refused to retreat or compromise. "If I am stopped," he told his fellow boycotters, "this movement will not stop, because God is with this movement." The Montgomery Bus Boycott finally prevailed when the Supreme Court declared the Montgomery and Alabama laws segregating buses unconstitutional.

Dr. King's leadership in the Montgomery Bus Boycott transformed him from an unknown local minister into America's foremost civil rights leader. Within a short time he founded the Southern Christian Leadership Conference (SCLC) to apply the principles of nonviolent civil disobedience to test cases across the South.

C. THE SIT-IN MOVEMENT

The victories in Montgomery and Little Rock did not end segregation's iron grip on Southern life. While moderates urged patience, Joe McNeil and three black college students disagreed. Calling segregation "evil pure and simple," the four students sat down at a Woolworth's lunch counter in Greensboro, North Carolina, and ordered cups of coffee and slices of apple pie. The Greensboro Four did not leave when their waitress refused to serve them. Even though segregationists shouted obscenities, threatened violence, and poured ketchup and mustard on their heads, the students remained resolute. During the next days, more and more students joined the sit-in. Faced with mounting losses, the Greensboro Woolworth desegregated its lunch counter.

The Greensboro Four pioneered a successful tactic of student-led sit-ins. Encouraged by the civil rights organizer Ella Baker, black and white students formed the Student Nonviolent Coordinating Committee (SNCC). Soon a wave of student protesters held "read-ins" at libraries, "watch-ins" at movie theaters, and "wade-ins" at pools and beaches.

TOPIC 10.6
"WE SHALL OVERCOME"

A. THE FREEDOM RIDERS

Young black and white activists continued to press for a faster pace of desegregation. In May 1961, the Congress of Racial Equality (CORE) sent an integrated group of 13 "freedom riders" on a bus trip scheduled to begin in Washington, D.C., and end in New Orleans. They hoped to find out if a 1960 Supreme Court decision outlawing segregation in bus stations was being obeyed. They quickly learned that it wasn't. A mob of angry whites attacked the freedom riders in Anniston, Montgomery, and Birmingham, Alabama.

Violence did not stop the freedom riders. By the end of 1961, Attorney General Robert Kennedy convinced the Interstate Commerce Commission to issue an order banning segregation in interstate bus terminals. The freedom riders thus proved that direct action would work. Across the country, more and more black and white demonstrators marched against segregation as they sang the civil rights anthem, "We Shall Overcome."

B. BIRMINGHAM, "A VISUAL DEMONSTRATION OF SIN"

In April 1963, Dr. King led a campaign of demonstrations designed to topple segregation in Birmingham, Alabama. "If we could break through the barriers in Birmingham," Dr. King predicted, "all the South would go the same way." However, segregationists led by Eugene "Bull" Conner, the city's Commissioner of Public Safety, offered forceful resistance. Connor's police officers promptly arrested over 3,000 demonstrators, including Dr. King.

While in jail, Dr. King composed an eloquent plea for racial justice, the "Letter from Birmingham Jail." Dr. King defended civil disobedience as a justified response to unjust laws. He called upon white clergymen to join him in being

"extremists for the cause of justice." He reminded them that "segregation distorts the soul and damages the personality. It gives the segregator a false sense of superiority and the segregated a false sense of inferiority."

Bull Connor responded by being an extremist for the cause of segregation. He unleashed snarling police attack dogs and high-pressure fire hoses to disperse peaceful protestors. Widespread television coverage exposed the American public to what one journalist called a "visual demonstration of sin, vivid enough to rouse the conscience of the entire nation."

C. PRESIDENT KENNEDY, "WE ARE CONFRONTED WITH A MORAL ISSUE"

Public outrage forced President Kennedy to act. In a televised address on June 11, 1963, he argued for racial justice: "We are confronted primarily with a moral issue…The heart of the question is whether all Americans are to be afforded equal rights and equal opportunities, whether we are going to treat our fellow Americans as we want to be treated." Eight days later, the President called upon Congress to pass a sweeping civil rights bill prohibiting segregation in public places.

D. THE MARCH ON WASHINGTON, "I HAVE A DREAM"

Dr. King and other civil rights leaders called for a massive March on Washington to build a "coalition of conscience" to support Kennedy's civil rights bill. The climax of the day came when Dr. King addressed a crowd of over 200,000 black and white supporters. His famous "I Have a Dream" speech featured an eloquent call for a society based on racial harmony. Stating that his dream was "deeply rooted in the American dream," Dr. King yearned for a day when his children would "live in a nation where they will not be judged by the color of their skin but by the content of their character."

E. THE CIVIL RIGHTS ACT OF 1964

President Johnson plunged into his duties in the dark days following the assassination of President Kennedy. Johnson used his legendary legislative skills to overcome strong Southern opposition and win passage of the landmark Civil Rights Act of 1964. The new law was the most comprehensive civil rights legislation ever enacted by Congress. It banned segregation in housing, jobs, education, and public facilities such as hotels, restaurants, and theatres. The law also authorized the attorney general to bring suits to speed school desegregation.

The landmark act played an unexpected role in promoting women's rights. Title VII outlawed discrimination in employment on the basis of race, religion, national origins, or sex. Women's groups used this provision to secure government support for greater equality in education and employment.

F. THE VOTING RIGHTS ACT OF 1965

Following this victory, civil rights activists shifted their attention to black voter registration. A major campaign in Mississippi failed to overcome fierce resistance from segregationists who intimidated blacks and murdered three civil rights workers. Dr. King then launched a voting rights campaign in Selma, Alabama, a city that allowed just 355 of its 15,000 blacks residents to vote. Dr.

King hoped to use Selma as a test case for voting rights, in the same way he had used Birmingham as a test case for civil rights.

On Sunday March 7, 1965, about 600 activists began a peaceful march from Selma to the state capitol in Montgomery. However, a large contingent of deputies and state troopers attacked and brutally beat the marchers with nightsticks, tear gas, and electric cattle prods. Known as "Bloody Sunday," the shocking event provided yet another graphic demonstration of violent resistance.

Bloody Sunday galvanized civil rights activists who poured into Selma to complete the march. President Johnson delivered a nationwide address endorsing a strong voting rights bill, vowing "We Shall Overcome." Five months later Congress passed the Voting Rights Act of 1965, outlawing poll taxes, literacy tests, and other practices that had been used to block blacks from voting. The new law thus made the Fifteenth Amendment an effective part of the Constitution.

TOPIC 10.7
A NEW MILITANCY

A. MALCOLM X

The Civil Rights Act of 1964 and the Voting Rights Act of 1965 represent historic achievements that struck down Jim Crow segregation. However, these victories did not satisfy a new generation of militant black leaders living in urban ghettos. They pointed to decaying cities, soaring crime rates, and depression-level unemployment rates as evidence of problems that could not be solved by sit-ins and freedom marches.

Malcolm X emerged as a charismatic black leader who demanded radical change. He first came to public attention as a militant minister for the Nation of Islam, a religious group known as the Black Muslims. Malcolm X rejected Dr. King's strategy of nonviolence and vision of a racially integrated society. Instead, he advocated black separatism, black pride, and the expansion of links with the newly independent black nations in Africa. He chose the surname "X" as a tribute to the memory of his unknown African ancestors.

Malcolm X expressed the growing anger and frustration of urban African Americans. He condemned white racism and the failure of liberal whites and moderate blacks to address the pressing economic needs of the African American community. Malcolm X underscored his differences with Dr. King when he declared, "I don't see any American dream. I see an American nightmare."

Within a short time, Malcolm X became America's most effective militant voice. However, his growing national notoriety sparked rivalry and jealousy with leaders in the Nation of Islam. On February 21, 1965, Malcolm X gave a scheduled speech before a crowd of several hundred followers in Harlem's Audubon Ballroom. Black Muslim assassins suddenly unleashed a barrage of bullets, silencing the most articulate spokesmen for black militants since Marcus Garvey.

B. STOKELY CARMICHAEL AND BLACK POWER

Stokely Carmichael began his activist career as a supporter of Dr. King's philosophy of nonviolent civil disobedience. While still a student at Howard University, Carmichael participated in the first Freedom Ride. After graduating from Howard, he joined the Student Nonviolent Coordinating Committee (SNCC) and within a short time became the organization's national chairman.

Carmichael soon replaced Malcolm X as America's most militant black leader. He promptly turned SNCC in a sharply radical direction by making it clear that white members were no longer welcome. Carmichael expressed his generation's more militant mood when he defiantly proclaimed, "Our grandfathers had to run, run, run. My generation is out of breath. We ain't running no more." In a speech in Mississippi he electrified a crowd of 600 supporters by boldly shouting, "We want Black Power!" When he asked his listeners "What do you want?" the crowd roared, "BLACK POWER!"

Black Power became the rallying cry of a younger, more radical generation of black activists. As explained by Carmichael, Black Power represented a decisive break with the traditional civil rights goals of racial integration and "Freedom Now." Instead, it marked "a call for black people in this country to unite, to recognize our heritage and build a sense of community." Building their own community meant developing black-owned businesses and electing black public officials.

C. THE LONG HOT SUMMERS

The Civil Rights movement raised high hopes that could not be quickly fulfilled. At the same time, the Black Power movement inflamed long-simmering tensions in inner cities across America. The frustration and anger caused by this combustible mix exploded in urban riots that began in 1965 in the Watts section of Los Angeles.

The riot in Watts claimed 34 lives and destroyed millions of dollars of property. It proved to be a harbinger of worse to come. During the long hot summers of 1966 and 1967, racial riots struck over 150 cities and towns. The most serious violence occurred in Detroit, where the worst riot in American history left 43 dead and 5,000 homeless.

As violence exploded in the nation's inner cities, the Black Power movement became angrier and more militant. Stokely Carmichael moved to Oakland, California, where he joined Huey Newton and Bobby Seale's newly formed Black Panther Party. The Black Panthers' menacing appearance and violent rhetoric captured the imagination of inner city black youths while alarming the general public.

D. DR. KING—ASSASSINATION AND LEGACY

The Black Power movement forced Dr. King to expand his focus from civil rights to the deep-rooted problems caused by inner-city poverty. At the same time, he became an outspoken critic of the Vietnam War. Dr. King questioned the war's growing cost and asked why America was sending young black men "eight thousand miles away to guarantee liberties in Southeast Asia which they had not found in southwest Georgia and East Harlem."

Determined to promote economic justice, Dr. King traveled to Memphis to support a strike by the city's underpaid sanitation workers. On the evening of April 4, 1968, a white assassin, later identified as James Earl Ray, fired a high-powered bullet that struck and killed Dr. King as he stood on the balcony of his motel. The tragic news sparked a wave of rioting that impacted over 130 cities.

Dr. King left an enduring legacy that transformed American society. In just over a decade he led a campaign of nonviolent protests dismantling a system of segregation that had stood essentially unaltered since Reconstruction. His famous dream of a just society continues to inspire Americans to work for a future without racial prejudice and discrimination.

CHAPTER 10
PRACTICE QUESTIONS

MULTIPLE-CHOICE QUESTIONS

Questions 1–4 refer to the excerpt below.

"Does segregation of children in public schools solely on the basis of race, even though the physical facilities and other tangible factors may be equal, deprive children of the minority group of equal educational opportunities? We believe that it does…We conclude that in the field of public education, the doctrine of separate but equal has no place. Separate educational facilities are inherently unequal."

> Chief Justice Earl Warren, writing the unanimous opinion of the United States Supreme Court in *Brown v. Board of Education of Topeka*, 1954

1. **The *Brown* decision most directly overturned the legal principle established by**
   A. *Dred Scott v. Sandford*
   B. *Plessy v. Ferguson*
   C. *Roe v. Wade*
   D. *University of California v. Bakke*

2. **The *Brown* decision ruled that racial segregation in public schools**
   A. contradicted the natural rights enumerated in the Declaration of Independence
   B. violated the First Amendment's guarantee of the right to peaceably assemble
   C. denied the equal protection clause of the Fourteenth Amendment
   D. undermined the constitutional goal of forming "a more perfect union"

3. **The *Brown* decision most directly provoked the**
   A. Southern Manifesto
   B. Montgomery Bus boycott
   C. Selma March
   D. Black Power movement

4. **Which of the following civil rights breakthroughs occurred in the decade before the *Brown* decision?**

   A. The racial integration of interstate buses
   B. The racial integration of the Supreme Court
   C. The racial integration of the armed forces
   D. The racial integration of lunch counters and restaurants

Questions 5–8 refer to the excerpt below.

"Just the other day, just last Thursday to be exact, one of the finest citizens in Montgomery...was taken from a bus and carried to jail and arrested because she refused to get up to give her seat to a white person....There comes a time when people get tired of being trampled over by the iron feet of oppression.... If we are wrong the Supreme Court of this nation is wrong. If we are wrong, the Constitution of the United States is wrong. If we are wrong, God almighty is wrong....And we are determined here in Montgomery to work and fight until justice runs down like water and righteousness like a mighty stream."

   Dr. Martin Luther King, Jr,. "Meeting at Holt Street Church," December 5, 1955

5. **Dr. King's main purpose in the excerpt was to**

   A. encourage a voter registration drive
   B. propose a sit-in demonstration
   C. advocate a renewed series of freedom rides
   D. arouse support for a bus boycott

6. **The excerpt best serves as evidence for which of the following trends during the 1950s?**

   A. The beginning of demonstrations to oppose the Vietnam War
   B. The beginning of direct action protests to achieve civil liberties
   C. The beginning of militant organizations to achieve Black Power
   D. The beginning of petitions to lobby states to pass the Equal Rights Amendment

7. **Which of the following best characterizes Dr. King's long-range goal?**

   A. The formation of alliances with newly independent nations in Africa
   B. The use of constant, and if necessary, violent political and social action to achieve long-sought standards of justiceThe removal of legal barriers to social and political equality
   C. The removal of legal barriers to social and political equality
   D. The creation of a national program of job training for unemployed African American youth

8. **Dr. King's theory of nonviolent civil disobedience was most directly influenced by the writings of**

   A. Henry David Thoreau
   B. Woodrow Wilson
   C. Booker T. Washington
   D. Marcus Garvey

Questions 9–11 refer to the excerpt below.

"We are confronted primarily with a moral issue. It is as old as the scriptures and is as clear as the American Constitution. The heart of the question is whether all Americans are to be afforded equal rights and equal opportunities, whether we are going to treat our fellow Americans as we want to be treated…It is time to act in the Congress, in your state and local legislative body and, above all, in all of our daily lives…Next week I shall ask the Congress of the United States to act, to make a commitment it has not fully made in this century to the proposition that race has no place in American life or law."

> President John F. Kennedy, radio and television report to the American people, June 11, 1963

9. **President Kennedy's speech was most directly a response to which of the following events?**

   A. The refusal to serve African American students at a lunch counter in Greensboro, North Carolina
   B. The use of police dogs and fire hoses on civil rights demonstrators in Birmingham, Alabama
   C. The Bloody Sunday attack on civil rights marchers outside Selma, Alabama
   D. The attack on Freedom Riders at the bus station in Montgomery, Alabama

10. **People who agreed with President Kennedy's moral argument would have most likely responded by**

   A. demonstrating against the Tonkin Gulf Resolution
   B. voicing support for the Black Power movement
   C. urging Congress to pass a Civil Rights bill
   D. backing War on Poverty programs

11. **African American leaders responded to President Kennedy's speech by announcing plans for**

   A. a massive nonviolent march in Washington, D.C.
   B. a voting rights march in Selma, Alabama
   C. a summer campaign against racial discrimination in Mississippi
   D. a sustained effort to encourage more liberal Americans to join the National Association for the Advancement of Colored People

Questions 12–15 refer to the excerpt below.

"This is the 27th time I have been arrested, and I ain't going to jail no more! We want Black Power! That's right. That's what we want, Black Power. We don't have to be ashamed of it. We have stayed here. We have begged the President. We've begged the federal government—that's all we've been doing, begging and begging. It's time we stand up and take over."

Stokely Carmichael, Speech in Greenwood, Mississippi, 1966

12. **Which of the following contributed to Carmichael's view that "Black Power" was necessary?**

   A. The success of the Southern Manifesto in blocking school integration
   B. The success of the Civil Rights movement in achieving legal and legislative victories
   C. The failure of nonviolent marches to address the economic plight of many African Americans
   D. The failure of racial desegregation in the United States military

13. The excerpt best reflects which of the following?

A. The growing realization that the Civil Rights movement was part of a global process of social change
B. The successful impact of the Civil Rights Act of 1964
C. The increasing influences of moderate leaders in the Civil Rights movement
D. The growing disillusionment with Dr. King's strategy of peaceful marches

14. The slogan "Black Power" most directly contributed to

A. a greater focus on antiwar demonstrations
B. a greater use of nonviolent demonstrations
C. increasing divisions among activists over strategies and goals
D. growing cooperation with countercultural groups

15. Statistics on which of the following could best be used to support the argument made in the excerpt?

A. The growing percentage of African Americans living in America's largest cities
B. The number of African Americans elected to political offices
C. The percentage of African Americans in labor unions
D. The percentage of female heads of African American familes

MULTIPLE-CHOICE ANSWERS

1.	B	5.	D	9.	B	13.	D
2.	C	6.	B	10.	C	14.	C
3.	A	7.	C	11.	A	15.	B
4.	C	8.	A	12.	C		

SHORT-ANSWER QUESTIONS

Question 1
Answer A, B, and C, confining your response to the period 1954–1968.

A.   Briefly describe ONE specific historical difference between the strategies Thurgood Marshall and Dr. King used to fight racial segregation.

B. Briefly describe ONE specific historical similarity between the strategies Thurgood Marshall and Dr. King used to fight racial segregation.

C. Briefly explain ONE specific historical effect of either of the strategies Thurgood Marshall or Dr. King used to fight racial segregation.

Question 2
Use the chart below to answer A, B, and C.

Black Urban Population
Percentage of Total Population in 10 Largest Cities

	1950	1960	1970
New York	10	14	21
Chicago	14	23	33
Los Angeles	9	14	18
Philadelphia	18	26	34
Detroit	16	29	44
Houston	21	23	26
Baltimore	24	35	46
Dallas	13	19	25
Washington, D.C.	35	54	71
Cleveland	16	29	38

A. Describe ONE specific historic cause of the trend depicted in the chart.

B. Describe a SECOND specific cause of the trend depicted in the chart.

C. Describe a historic effect of the trend depicted in the chart.

SHORT-ANSWER ANSWERS

Question 1

A. Thurgood Marshall used lawsuits to legally challenge Jim Crow segregation laws. In contrast, Dr. King used boycotts, freedom marches, and other forms of nonviolent civil disobedience to challenge Jim Crow segregation laws.

B. Both Thurgood Marshall and Dr. King fought to overturn the doctrine of "separate but equal." They both worked to remove legal barriers to social and political equality.

C. Thurgood Marshall successfully argued for the NAACP in the *Brown v. Board of Education* case. He persuaded the Supreme Court to unanimously overturn the doctrine of "separate but equal" established in *Plessy v. Ferguson*. The *Brown* decision marked a momentous turning point in African American history by placing the Supreme Court on the side of racial justice.

Question 2

A. The push of Jim Crow segregation, poverty, and racial violence all prompted more than five million blacks to leave the South.

B. The lure of jobs in defense plants, along with the relative freedom in the North, prompted more than five million blacks to migrate to urban areas in the Northeast and Midwest.

C. By 1970, African Americans established large communities in Northern cities. These communities became centers of urban unrest as the Black Power Movement began to attract a new generation of African Americans.

PART III

WOMEN'S HISTORY

CHAPTER 11
WOMEN'S HISTORY
FROM ANNE HUTCHINSON TO THE
SENECA FALLS CONVENTION
1637–1848

STRATEGIC IMPORTANCE

Women's history generates a significant and growing number of questions and points on the APUSH exam. We have devoted two of our narrative chapters to help you thoroughly master the key events, trends, and leaders in this important historic experience. A careful analysis of recent APUSH exams reveals that questions from the Colonial period to the Seneca Falls Convention generated an average of five points per exam. Remember, you only need 75 points to earn a three, 95 points to earn a four, and 110 points to earn a five. This chapter is thus an important part of your coalition of points.

KEY POINTS AND HISTORIC GENERALIZATIONS

- Women in both the Chesapeake and New England colonies occupied subordinate positions in male-dominated societies. However, the New England women migrated in families and enjoyed significantly longer lifespans.

- Anne Hutchinson unsuccessfully challenged orthodox Puritan beliefs and the subordinate position of women in New England society.

- Abigail Adams's famous plea to "Remember the Ladies" demonstrated that at least some colonial women were aware of the discrepancy between their subordinate legal status and the republican ideals of equality and independence.

- REPUBLICAN MOTHERHOOD was the belief that women had the responsibility to raise their children to become virtuous and responsible citizens. The concept of republican motherhood placed a new emphasis upon increasing educational opportunities for women.

- The CULT OF DOMESTICITY idealized women in their domestic roles as wives and mothers. As a nurturing mother and faithful spouse, the wife created a home that was a "haven in a heartless world."

- The Lowell mill girls were America's first female factory labor force. They also organized strikes and the first union of working women.

- Women played an important role in antebellum movements to reform American society.

- Many Northern women felt a deep conviction that slavery contradicted Christian morality and corrupted America's democratic mission.

- The Seneca Falls Convention marked the beginning of the women's rights movement in the United States. The resolutions passed at Seneca Falls formed the agenda for what historians call first-wave feminism.

TOPIC 11.1
WOMEN IN COLONIAL AMERICA

A. THE CHESAPEAKE COLONIES

The first women who settled in the Chesapeake colonies faced harsh conditions. Diseases, wars with the Indians, and the hazards of childbirth reduced their average life expectancy to just 39 years, nearly a decade less than the male colonists. Only one couple in three could expect to live in a marriage lasting more than ten years.

Like their counterparts in England, the Chesapeake women were legally subordinate to their husbands. Under common law a woman's legal identity was absorbed into that of her husband. For example, a married woman took her husband's family name. Lacking a legal identity, married women exercised no control over either their property or their children.

During most of the seventeenth century, as many as three-quarters of the Chesapeake women worked as indentured servants. Their lives slowly improved as tobacco plantations grew and prospered. A privileged class of genteel ladies enjoyed lifestyles that included playing music, writing letters, and purchasing luxury goods from England.

B. THE NEW ENGLAND COLONIES

The lives of New England women offered both contrasts and similarities with their counterparts in the Chesapeake colonies. Unlike the Chesapeake indentured servants, New England Puritans migrated in family groups. The cold northern temperatures retarded diseases and enabled Puritan colonists to enjoy lifespans approaching 70 years. But like Chesapeake women, Puritan women occupied subordinate positions in male-dominated families.

C. ANNE HUTCHINSON

Anne Hutchinson's confrontation with the Puritan authorities illustrates the limitations women faced in the New England colonies. An early dissenter, Hutchinson disputed orthodox Puritan beliefs. Even worse, she asserted her right to publicly speak out, thus challenging the subordinate position of women in Puritan society. Outraged Puritan magistrates denounced Hutchinson as a "delusional" woman who had "rather been a Husband than a wife, a preacher than a Hearer, and a Magistrate than a Subject." Given these egregious offenses, the Puritan authorities banished Hutchinson to Rhode Island, a nearby haven for religious dissenters.

TOPIC 11.2
THE EARLY REPUBLIC

A. ABIGAIL ADAMS, "REMEMBER THE LADIES"

Abigail Adams managed her family's farm in Braintree, Massachusetts, while her famous husband attended the Second Continental Congress in Philadelphia. Although Abigail had no formal education, she read widely and displayed a sophisticated understanding of human nature. On March 31, 1776, she wrote a celebrated letter to her husband expressing her concern about how the rights of women would be treated in the new American republic. Abigail urged John to "Remember the Ladies and be more generous and favorable to them than your ancestors."

Adams's famous request underscored the fact that colonial authorities had treated women as second-class citizens. Her letter demonstrated that colonial women were keenly aware of the discrepancy between their subordinate legal status and the republican ideal of equality. However, traditional expectations about women's legal rights and customary roles were deeply entrenched. Given this mindset, it is not surprising that John Adams scornfully dismissed his wife's plea by replying, "As to your extraordinary code of laws, I cannot but laugh....We know better than to repeal our Masculine systems."

B. REPUBLICAN MOTHERHOOD

As John Adams confidently predicted, America's new Constitution did not lead to an expansion of women's legal rights. American women still could not form contracts, buy or sell property, serve on juries, or vote. Given these restrictions, what should be the role of women in the new republic?

Although women's subordinate legal position remained unchanged, the new republic still required well-informed citizens. This need helped give rise to a new ideal for American wives that historians now call REPUBLICAN MOTHERHOOD.

According to its advocates, republican mothers had the responsibility to become exemplary parents who raised their children to become virtuous citizens. Women would thus play a vital role in shaping America's moral character. Catherine Beecher confidently predicted, "Let the women of a country be virtuous and intelligent, and the men will certainly be the same."

Republican motherhood both reinforced and expanded women's traditional role. The concept gave motherhood a new dignity and importance. At the same time, it also placed a new emphasis upon increasing educational opportunities for the nation's republican mothers. During the early 1800s, communities in the Northeast and Mid-Atlantic states opened a number of academic schools for young women. This commitment led to the emergence of educated Northern women who would later play key roles in the reform movements of the 1830s and 1840s.

C. CULT OF DOMESTICITY

Prior to the Industrial Revolution, men and women worked together as an economic team on small family farms. However, as the market revolution gained momentum, it encouraged a division of labor between two separate spheres— work and home. "True Men" were expected to earn success in the ruthlessly competitive world of business and politics. In contrast, "True Women" were expected to devote their energies to creating a stable and peaceful home.

The earlier ideal of republican motherhood gradually evolved into a new cultural model known as the CULT OF DOMESTICITY. This set of beliefs idealized women in their roles of wives and mothers. As a nurturing mother and a faithful spouse, the wife created a home that was a "haven in a heartless world." The home thus became a refuge, and the wife became what one popular women's magazine called "the light of the house."

The cult of domesticity embodied a cultural ideal that best applied to upper- and middle-class families, who could afford to maintain separate spheres for their work and home lives. However, a wide gap separated these privileged groups from the mill women working in factories, the frontier women working on isolated farms, and the enslaved African women working on cotton plantations. The African American abolitionist and women's rights advocate Sojourner Truth pointedly noted, "Nobody ever helped me into carriages, or over mud puddles, or gave me any best places! And ain't I a woman?"

TOPIC 10.3
WOMEN AND THE LOWELL EXPERIMENT

A. THE "CITY OF SPINDLES"

In 1813, Francis Cabot Lowell and a group of investors known as the Boston Associates constructed a textile factory in Waltham, Massachusetts. Their mill used both modern spinning machines and power looms to produce cheap cloth. Inspired by the success of his investment, Lowell built a factory in a nearby town later named for him. His venture proved to be a huge success. Within a short time 32 mills and factories transformed Lowell into the "City of Spindles."

B. THE LOWELL MILL GIRLS

The "City of Spindles" did more than produce cloth; it also marked the beginning of a new chapter in women's history. Lowell recognized that New England farm girls could provide an ideal source of inexpensive labor. In order to attract single girls, he first had to persuade their parents that his town would provide a healthy, well-supervised workplace, unlike the notorious "dark satanic mills" in Great Britain.

Lowell accomplished his goal by building a widely praised factory town. Within a short time his clean red brick dormitories helped attract America's first female labor force. The Lowell "mill girls" lived together under the watchful eyes of older women, who enforced church attendance and strict curfew hours.

The mill girls followed a demanding work schedule that began at 5:00 a.m. and did not end until 7:00 p.m. Despite a tedious six-day workweek, the girls found time to attend public lectures, publish a newspaper, and share a great sense of camaraderie. One mill girl later recalled, "I regard it as one of the privileges of my youth that I was permitted to grow up among these active, interesting girls."

C. THE END OF THE LOWELL EXPERIMENT

The Lowell experiment enjoyed initial success. During the 1830s over 8,000 mill girls comprised three-fourths of Lowell's labor force. However, factory owners soon became more interested in profits than in the welfare of their workers. A sudden drop in the price of cotton cloth forced management to cut wages without reducing working hours.

The outraged women responded by organizing a spontaneous "turn-out," or strike. They also formed America's first union of working women, the Lowell Female Labor Reform Association. The union unsuccessfully petitioned the Massachusetts state legislature to pass a law limiting the workday to ten hours.

A second strike convinced the owners that female workers were too troublesome. They soon began replacing their contentious female workers with more compliant Irish immigrants. By 1860, Irish workers comprised well over half the Lowell labor force. The once-ambitious Lowell experiment ended, and the town became a bleak industrial city.

TOPIC 10.4
WOMEN AND ANTEBELLUM REFORM MOVEMENTS

A. THE CAMPAIGN AGAINST "DEMON RUM"

The Second Great Awakening sparked a spirit of moral and social activism. Women played a notable role in antebellum movements to reform American society.

The crusade against alcoholism attracted widespread support from American women. Long-suffering wives decried the relationship between excessive drinking and poverty. Their campaign focused special attention on the suffering inflicted on innocent children. On pamphlet denounced "Demon Rum" as "the source of nearly all the ills that afflict the human family."

Women contributed time, energy, and moral support to the American Society for the Promotion of Temperance. The organization sponsored 5,000 state and local temperance groups. Its determined campaign to dethrone "King Alcohol" worked. Between 1830 and 1850, the annual per capita (for each man, woman, and child) consumption of alcohol dropped from five gallons to two gallons.

B. THE CAMPAIGN TO HELP THE MENTALLY ILL

The spirit of reform had a profound influence on a Massachusetts school teacher named Dorothea Dix. Her crusade began when she agreed to teach Sunday School to prisoners outside Boston. To her surprise, Dix found that the mentally ill shared jail rooms with hardened criminals. Outraged by the deplorable conditions, Dix launched a crusade to address the problem. An indefatigable champion of reform, Dix travelled more than 10,000 miles as she visited almost every state in the Union. Dix and other like-minded reformers created the first generation of American mental asylums.

C. THE CAMPAIGN AGAINST SLAVERY, "WE CANNOT REMAIN INACTIVE"

The work by women reformers on behalf of the temperance movement was compatible with their accepted role as defenders of the "domestic sphere." However, at the same time, many Northern women felt a deep conviction that slavery contradicted Christian morality and corrupted American's democratic mission. This sense of a compelling moral purpose led many women to join William Lloyd Garrison's American Anti-Slavery Society.

At first, women accepted non-leadership roles in the abolition movement. For example, they circulated petitions and attended mass meetings. But this secondary role changed when women formed the Boston Anti-Slavery Society and the Philadelphia Anti-Slavery Society. In 1836, women activists held the first of three anti-slavery conventions. At their second convention in Philadelphia, Sara T. Smith voiced a more assertive attitude when she questioned why men accused women of "stepping out of your sphere" when they publicly spoke out against slavery. She boldly insisted that slavery was more than "merely a political question, it is likewise a question of justice, of humanity, of morality, of religion." Given the issue's "immense importance," Smith vowed " We cannot remain inactive."

TOPIC 10.5
THE SENECA FALLS CONVENTION

A. "A NEW WORLD OF THOUGHT"

The Seneca Falls Convention had its origins in 1840, when Elizabeth Cady Stanton and Lucretia Mott met in London, England, during the World Anti-Slavery Convention. The all-male organizers confined female delegates behind an opaque curtain and barred them from speaking to the group. The pain of exclusion united Stanton and Mott as they discussed their common experiences as women working in the abolitionist movement. They soon concluded that women and slaves both shared a history of injustice. Stanton later wrote that her conversations with Mott "opened to me a new world of thought."

B. "ALL MEN AND WOMEN ARE CREATED EQUAL"

Stanton and Mott agreed that, upon their return to the United States, they would call a convention to consider the status of women. After a delay of eight years, they finally turned their London decision into a reality. On July 14, 1848, they published a notice in the Seneca Country Courier, asking interested reformers to attend a convention in Seneca Falls, New York, "to discuss the social, civil, and religious condition of and rights of women." Five days later, approximately 300 delegates, including Frederick Douglass, met in the Wesleyan Chapel to conduct America's first convention devoted to women's rights.

After meeting for two days, the convention issued a "Declaration of Sentiments and Resolutions." Written primarily by Stanton, the Declaration opened by asserting, "We hold these truths to be self-evident that all men and women are created equal."

The convention unanimously passed resolutions denouncing the entire structure of inequality confronting American women. For example, the declaration demanded greater access to education, the right to retain property after marriage, and a change in divorce and child custody rights. However, a contentious debate erupted over a controversial resolution calling for the extension of suffrage to women. Douglass made a persuasive speech emphasizing that the right to participate in government is a fundamental principle of equality, from which all other rights would follow. His renowned eloquence swayed the delegates, and the call for women's suffrage narrowly passed.

C. THE FIRST WAVE OF FEMINISM BEGINS

The Seneca Falls Convention marked the beginning of the women's rights movement in the United States. The resolutions passed at Seneca Falls formed the agenda for what historians call first-wave feminism. The women who attended the Seneca Falls Convention faced a long and at times frustrating struggle. Of the 100 delegates who signed the Declaration of Sentiments, just two lived to see passage of the Nineteenth Amendment 72 years later.

CHAPTER 11
PRACTICE QUESTIONS

MULTIPLE-CHOICE QUESTIONS

Questions 1–4 refer to the excerpt below.

"I long to hear that you have declared an independence—and by the way in the new Code of Laws which I suppose it will be necessary for you to make I desire you would Remember the Ladies, and be more generous and favorable to them than your ancestors. Do not put such unlimited power into the hands of the Husbands. Remember, all Men would be tyrants if they could. If particular care and attention is not paid to the Ladies, we are determined to foment a rebellion, and will not hold ourselves bound by any laws in which we have no voice or representation."

Letter from Abigail Adams to John Adams, March 1776

1. Adams's letter most directly indicated that

   A. the new "Code of Laws" would include universal suffrage for all American citizens
   B. some colonial women sought to benefit from republican ideals of equality and individual rights
   C. colonial women would strongly support a compromise with Great Britain
   D. most colonial women would prefer to use their influence over the domestic sphere as a basis for promoting social reform

2. The ideas expressed by Adams in the excerpt were most similar to those later advocated by

   A. supporters of Andrew Jackson
   B. opponents of the Mexican-American War
   C. signers of the Seneca Falls Declaration of Sentiments
   D. advocates of nullification

3. **Opponents of Adams's ideas expressed in the excerpt would most likely have argued that**

    A. women were already guaranteed basic legal rights
    B. women were best suited to be wives and mothers
    C. Adams was far too conservative in her vision of social change
    D. ideas expressed in the Declaration of Independence made Adams's views obsolete

4. **Which of the following provides the best evidence in support of the argument in Adams's letter?**

    A. The legal identity of women under English common law
    B. The growing colonial support to declare independence from Great Britain
    C. The creation of covenants permitting women to serve as Protestant ministers
    D. The widespread colonial opposition to the Intolerable Acts

Questions 5–6 refer to the excerpt below.

"The mother writes the character of the future man; the sister bends the fibres that hereafter are the forest tree; the wife sways the heart, whose energies may turn for good or evil the destinies of a nation. Let the women of a country be virtuous and intelligent, and the men will certainly be the same."

Catherine Beecher, 1837

5. **Catherine Beecher's ideas about the role of women were most directly influenced by**

    A. the Puritan belief in predestination
    B. the concept of republican motherhood
    C. the Enlightenment principle of self-government
    D. the idea of manifest destiny

6. **A person who agreed with Catherine Beecher would most likely have supported encouraging women to**

    A. take an active role in political parties
    B. enter professional occupations such as medicine and law
    C. seek employment in the new industrial factories
    D. nurture their special talent for teaching moral and spiritual values

Questions 7–9 refer to the excerpt below.

"At one time they tell us that our 'free institutions' are based upon the virtue and intelligence of the American people and the influence of the mother, form and mould the man—and the next breath, that the way to make the mothers of the next generation virtuous is to enclose them within brick walls of a cotton mill from twelve and a half to thirteen and a half hours per day."

Sarah Bagley, "The Ten Hour System and Its Advocates," 1846

7. **The trend toward employing young women in textile mills first began in**

A. a cotton plantation located near Charleston, South Carolina
B. a model factory town in Lowell, Massachusetts
C. a tenement building located in Boston, Massachusetts
D. a factory built by Moses Brown in Pawtucket, Rhode Island

8. **According to Bagley the practice of employing young women in cotton mills most directly undermined the prevailing belief in**

A. Jeffersonian democracy
B. federalism
C. the cult of domesticity
D. the Social Gospel

9. **Which of the following evidence would best support Bagley's argument in the excerpt?**

A. Letters describing living and working conditions in a model New England factory town
B. Employment data for women wage earners in New England between 1820 and 1840
C. Tables documenting cotton production in South Carolina between 1820 and 1840
D. Reports documenting profits and losses in New England textile mills

Questions 10–12 refer to the excerpt below.

"But we are assembled to protest against a form of government, existing without the consent of the governed—to declare our right to be free as man is free, to be represented in the government which we are taxed to support, to have such disgraceful laws as give man the power to chastise and imprison his wife….And, strange as it may seem to many, we now demand our right to vote according to the declaration of the government under which we live."

Elizabeth Cady Stanton, Seneca Falls Declaration, August 2, 1848

10. The ideas expressed in the excerpt most directly challenged the prevailing early nineteenth-century commitment to

A. limited government
B. rugged individualism
C. perfectionism
D. the cult of domesticity

11. The goals expressed in this excerpt were most directly influenced by

A. ideas expressed in the Declaration of Independence
B. rights enumerated in the First Amendment
C. commitment to reason expressed by late eighteenth-century Deists
D. commitment to equality in the Constitution of the Brook Farm Associates

12. Which of the following Progressive Era amendments represents the fulfillment of the goals expressed in this excerpt?

A. The Sixteenth Amendment
B. The Seventeenth Amendment
C. The Eighteenth Amendment
D. The Nineteenth Amendment

Questions 13–15 refer to the excerpt below.

"I was disappointed when I came to seek a profession worthy an immortal being—every employment was closed to me, except those of the teacher, the seamstress, and the housekeeper. In education, in marriage, in religion, in everything, disappointment is the lot of woman. It shall be the business of my life to deepen this disappointment in every woman's heart until she bows down to it no longer."

Lucy Stone, Speech at National Women's Rights Convention, 1855

13. Which of the following most directly contributed to the problems described by Lucy Stone in this excerpt?

A. the rise of the sexual revolution in America
B. the prevailing belief that women should be subordinate to men
C. the decline in the number of women in the workforce
D. the failure of the Second Great Awakening to achieve meaningful reforms

14. The excerpt most directly reflects which of the following goals supported by women's rights activists?

A. Strict adherence to the principles of republican motherhood
B. Increased participation of women in factory work
C. Expansion of the settlement house movement
D. Fulfillment of the goals enumerated in the Seneca Falls Declaration of Sentiments

15. One direct long-term effect of the work of Lucy Stone and other women's rights activists was the

A. passage of Progressive Era antitrust laws
B. popularity of Flappers during the 1920s
C. ratification of the Nineteenth Amendment
D. support for the Rosie the Riveter campaign during World War II

MULTIPLE-CHOICE ANSWERS

1. B	5. B	9. A	13. B
2. C	6. D	10. D	14. D
3. B	7. B	11. A	15. C
4. A	8. C	12. D	

SHORT–ANSWER QUESTIONS

Question 1
Using the excerpts below, answer A, B, and C.

"Too much is said of women being better educated, that they may become better companions and mothers for men. They should be fit for such companionship… Earth knows no fairer, holier relation than that of a mother…But a being of infinite scope must not be treated with an exclusive view to any one relation. Give the soul free course, let the organization, both of body and mind, be freely developed, and the being will be fit for any and every relation to which it may be called."

Margaret Fuller, *Woman in the Nineteenth Century*, 1845

"Woman is by nature inferior to man. She is his inferior in passion, his inferior in intellect, and his inferior in physical strength. In ascribing to woman a natural inferiority to man, we by no means seek to depress her in the scale of being, but on the contrary to exalt her. It is this natural inequality of the sexes besides, which constitutes the true ground of their union, and enables woman to be the fountain of unmixed blessing she is to man."

"Woman, and the 'Woman's Movement.'" *Putnam's monthly magazine of American literature, science, and art*, March 1853

A. Briefly describe ONE major difference between Fuller's and *Putnam's* explanation of how a woman's potential should affect her role in society.

B. Briefly explain how ONE specific historical person, event, or development from the period 1776 to 1848 that is not explicitly mentioned in the excerpts could be used to support Fuller's argument.

C. Briefly explain how ONE specific historical person, event, or development from the period 1776 to 1848 that is not explicitly mentioned in the excerpts could be used to support *Putnam's* argument.

Question 2
Answer A, B, and C, confining your response to the period 1776 to 1848.

A. Briefly describe ONE specific historical difference between the roles played by Abigail Adams and Elizabeth Cady Stanton in the women's rights movement.

B. Briefly describe ONE specific historical similarity between the roles played by Abigail Adams and Elizabeth Cady Stanton in the women's rights movement.

C. Briefly explain ONE specific historical effect of the impact of either Abigail Adams or Elizabeth Cady Stanton on the women's rights movement.

SHORT–ANSWER ANSWERS

Question 1

A. Fuller argues that women have unlimited potential that should not be restricted by social relationships. In contrast, *Putnam's* argues that women are inferior to men and that this "natural inequality" restricts women to a domestic sphere centered around helping their husbands and raising their children.

B. The Seneca Falls Convention supports Fuller's argument. The convention demonstrated the ability of women to organize a historic meeting, write a "Declaration of Sentiments and Resolutions," and launch a major reform movement for women's rights.

C. The public response to the market revolution supports *Putnam's* argument. The market revolution encouraged a division of labor between men and women into two separate spheres—work and home. The widespread public acceptance of this division evolved into a socially supported role for women known as the cult of domesticity.

Question 2

A. Abigail Adams confined her thoughts to a private letter to her influential husband. In contrast, Elizabeth Cady Stanton authored a public declaration that contained a number of specific resolutions, including a demand for the extension of suffrage to women.

B. Both Abigail Adams and Elizabeth Cady Stanton sought to use republican ideals of equality and individual rights to improve the legal position of women in American society and challenge prevailing gender norms.

C. Elizabeth Cady Stanton played a major role in organizing the Seneca Falls Convention and authoring its "Declaration of Sentiments and Resolutions." These bold actions provided the agenda for the first wave of American feminism.

CHAPTER 12
WOMEN'S HISTORY
FROM THE PROGRESSIVE MOVEMENT
TO MODERN FEMINISM
1880–1980

STRATEGIC IMPORTANCE

Women's history generates a significant and growing number of questions and points on the APUSH exam. We have devoted two of our narrative chapters to help you thoroughly master the key events, trends, and leaders in this important historic experience. A careful analysis of recent APUSH exams reveals that questions from the Progressive Era to the defeat of the ERA generated an average of 15 points per exam. Remember, you only need 75 points to earn a three, 95 points to earn a four, and 110 points to earn a five. This chapter is thus a very important part of your coalition of points.

KEY POINTS AND HISTORIC GENERALIZATIONS

- During the Progressive Era, women activists took the lead in campaigns to win the suffrage and prohibit the sale of alcoholic beverages.

- Inspired by Jane Addams, the settlement house movement gave a new generation of women organizational and leadership skills that transcended their traditional roles as mothers and wives.

- The women's suffrage movement achieved its first successes in states west of the Mississippi River. Women's valuable service in World War I won additional public support for the Nineteenth Amendment.

- During the 1920s, FLAPPERS ignored the feminist political agenda, choosing instead to focus on a carefree and flamboyant lifestyle.

- During World War II about five million new female workers joined the labor force. These women welcomed their new responsibilities and independence.

- During the 1950s, young families populated suburbs that became havens for a revived CULT OF DOMESTICITY.

- Written by Betty Friedan, *The Feminine Mystique* challenged the cult of domesticity and helped launch a second wave of feminine activism.

- Led by Betty Friedan, The National Organization for Women (NOW) focused on working within the political system to achieve equal opportunity in education and employment, accessible and affordable childcare, and the right to safe and legal abortions.

- RADICAL FEMINISTS focused on personal issues such as reproductive rights, domestic violence, and the objectification of women as sexual objects.

- The second wave of feminism achieved a number of notable successes in education, the workplace, and the Supreme Court decision legalizing abortion.

- The defeat of the ERA signaled the end of the second wave of feminism.

TOPIC 12.1
WOMEN AND THE PROGRESSIVE ERA

A. THE PROGRESSIVE SPIRIT

The term PROGRESSIVE embraced a widespread, multifaceted effort to build a more democratic and just society. Like other Progressives, women worked to reform child labor laws, expose the cutthroat practices in the oil business, and improve sanitation in immigrant neighborhoods. In addition, women took the lead in campaigns to win the suffrage and prohibit the sale of alcoholic beverages.

B. THE "NEW WOMAN"

When the Progressive Era began, most Americans still believed that a woman's proper sphere remained in her home. But the status of women was rapidly changing. By 1900, as many as 700,000 young women left their homes to work as teachers, sales clerks, or office assistants. In addition, a generation of college-educated "New Women" extended their roles from guardians of the home to include activities ranging from driving cars to playing tennis to running a business.

C. THE SETTLEMENT HOUSE MOVEMENT

The nationwide settlement house movement began when Jane Addams founded Hull House in 1889. Addams transformed a decaying mansion, located in the heart of one of Chicago's poorest immigrant neighborhoods, into a thriving community center. The facility rapidly expanded and ultimately provided day care nurseries, English lessons, and a number of practical courses on cooking, dressmaking, and personal hygiene.

Under Addams's leadership, Hull House became an important center of Progressive reform. It served as a model for middle-class women, who founded over 400 similar facilities in cities across America. Settlement house staffs pressured municipal authorities to improve local schools, sewer systems, and garbage pickups. The settlement house experience thus gave a new generation of women organizational and leadership skills that transcended their traditional roles as mothers and wives.

D. THE TEMPERANCE MOVEMENT

Women played a leading role in the temperance movement to outlaw the sale of alcoholic beverages. Organized in 1874, the Women's Christian Temperance Union (WCTU) soon boasted 150,000 dues-paying members, making it the largest women's organization in America. Under the dynamic leadership of Francis Willard, the WCTU organized rallies, revival meetings, and marches in a national campaign to force county after county to pass ordinances closing liquor stores. These activities helped teach women about the importance of having a voice in public affairs.

By the turn of the century, the temperance crusade gathered momentum. Pressured by public opinion, a growing number of the nation's 200,000 liquor dealers closed their doors. In 1918 Congress passed the Eighteenth Amendment, outlawing the manufacture, sale, and transportation of intoxicating liquors.

E. THE SUFFRAGE MOVEMENT

The 1848 Seneca Falls Convention launched the beginning of the women's suffrage movement. The struggle encountered an unexpected setback when the Fifteenth Amendment gave the vote to black men but not to women. When the Progressive Era began, the law denied criminals, lunatics, and women the right to vote.

The Progressive movement sharpened the nation's social conscience and motivated a new generation of suffragists. Led by Carrie Chapman Catt and Alice Paul, women organized rallies, signed petitions, and demonstrated in public marches. With every act of protest, the suffragist army grew larger and more vocal. In 1915, for example, 40,000 women marched down New York City's Fifth Avenue as they were cheered on by over 500,000 supporters.

The momentum for female suffrage proved to be irreversible. By 1910, most states west of the Mississippi River had granted full suffrage rights to women. Women's valuable service during World War I won additional public support for their cause. On June 4, 1919, Congress passed the Nineteenth Amendment, stating that no citizen could be denied the right to vote "on account of sex." The amendment received final state approval 14 months later. The editor of the *Kansas City Star* underscored the historic importance of the Nineteenth Amendment when he proudly declared, "This is not a victory for women alone, it is a victory for democracy and the principle of equality upon which the nation was founded."

TOPIC 12.2
WOMEN AND THE ROARING TWENTIES

A. A NEW MOOD

Feminist leaders hoped that winning the suffrage would enable them to promote an agenda that included child and women's labor laws, health and safety legislation, and municipal reform. However, they were unable to sustain the prewar enthusiasm for Progressive reforms. World War I dealt a shattering blow to the confident Progressive belief that progress was inevitable. Instead of reform, American voters elected Republican presidents who promised a return to "normalcy." At the same time, America's popular culture enthusiastically embraced consumer products and a new carefree lifestyle that became known as the "Roaring Twenties."

B. A NEW GENERATION OF FLAPPERS

A new generation of young women called FLAPPERS provided the most publicized and controversial model of the new American woman. The name derived from the way fashionable young women allowed their galoshes to "flap" about their ankles. Flappers ignored the feminist political agenda, choosing instead to focus on a lighthearted and flamboyant lifestyle. They unceremoniously discarded the ankles-to-neck layers of clothing worn by the older generation in favor of hemlines rising to their knees. The flapper look also included close-cut bobbed hair and heavy makeup. They further jolted their conservative elders by dancing the Charleston, joyriding in their boyfriends' roadsters, smoking once-forbidden cigarettes, and drinking illegal liquor.

The flappers marked the appearance of America's first distinctive youth culture. Magazine advertisements glamorized the flapper's willingness to experience new freedoms. At the same time, the growing movie industry also publicized high-spirited flappers such as Clara Bow, Hollywood's first "It" girl. As critics predicted, the flapper phenomenon proved to be fleeting. However, their spirit of youthful independence inspired future generations of more rebellious youth.

TOPIC 12.3
WOMEN AND WORLD WAR II

A. "DO THE JOB HE LEFT BEHIND"

At the beginning of World War II, President Roosevelt called upon American workers to crush the Axis powers with an overwhelming supply of weapons.

American women did not disappoint FDR. When the war began, about 12 million women held jobs. Encouraged by slogans such as "Do the Job He Left Behind," about five million new female workers joined the labor force.

The popular "Rosie the Riveter" poster celebrated the significant role women played in the nation's armament plants. They worked round-the-clock shifts on assembly lines manufacturing Liberty ships, Sherman tanks, and Flying Fortress bombers. Women welcomed their new responsibilities and independence. A woman who made 155-millimeter howitzers later recalled, "There was an energy in the air and in the people. We were wanted and needed and important to the war effort."

B. WOMEN IN UNIFORM

Women's contribution to the war effort was not limited to the home front. About 350,000 women joined the various branches of the U.S. military. The women workers replaced men in various jobs including airplane mechanics, code clerks, and truck drivers. A specially trained group of female pilots ferried planes to Europe.

TOPIC 12.4
WOMEN AND THE 1950S

A. UNPRECEDENTED PROSPERITY

The Japanese surrender ended World War II and ushered in a new era in American history. With the painful years of economic depression and wartime sacrifice behind them, Americans began to enjoy a period of unprecedented prosperity. The country's gross national product soared from $200 billion in 1945 to $500 billion in 1960. With just six percent of the world's population, Americans drove 75 percent of the world's automobiles, consumed half of its energy, and produced almost half of its manufactured goods.

B. MARRIAGE BOOM AND BABY BOOM

Economic prosperity did not encourage a renewal of women's rights activism. Instead, magazines, movies, and television programs glamorized romantic love and celebrated marriage. Encouraged by the mass media, men and women married at an early age. During the 1950s the average age of marriage for American women dropped to just 20.3. By 1960, almost 75 percent of all women between the ages of 20 and 24 were married.

The marriage boom triggered a postwar baby boom. The 1950s witnessed a tidal wave of 40 million births. These children formed the nucleus of a huge baby boom generation that totaled 76 million births from 1946 through 1964.

C. A REVIVED CULT OF DOMESTICITY

The young families populated suburbs that quickly became havens for a revived cult of domesticity. The mass media reinforced and idealized the traditional gender roles, in which men commuted to work while women stayed home and raised their children. For example, in the popular TV program *Leave It to Beaver*, June Cleaver is a middle-class housewife devoted to her family. When her two boys arrive home from school, June greets them with milk and cookies while she prepares a family dinner in her spotless kitchen. A special issue of *Life* magazine featured "happy homemakers," dedicated to their husbands and children.

TOPIC 12.5
SECOND WAVE FEMINISM, 1963–1980

A. BETTY FRIEDAN, "IS THIS ALL?"

The "happy homemakers" featured in *Life* magazine did not include Betty Friedan. A middle-class mother of three, Friedan discovered that many of her college-educated peers felt unfulfilled by the endless routines of housework and raising children. Although they lived in comfortable suburbs, these women felt bored and dissatisfied with their lives.

Friedan expressed this sense of frustration in her book *The Feminine Mystique*. Published in 1963, *The Feminine Mystique* challenged the culture of domesticity that had prevailed since the end of World War II. It exposed the previously unspoken sense of dissatisfaction felt by suburban housewives who spent their days buying groceries, cooking meals, and chauffeuring their children. Friedan opened her book by describing these routines and then asking a "silent question" that women had been afraid to ask—"Is this all?"

The Feminine Mystique became an instant best seller. It inspired many readers to reevaluate the belief that women should derive fulfillment exclusively through domesticity. Historians credit *The Feminine Mystique* with launching a second wave of feminine activism.

B. THE NATIONAL ORGANIZATION FOR WOMEN (NOW)

Betty Friedan understood "that it was not enough to write a book...there had to be organization and there had to be a movement." In 1966, Friedan and other women activists formed the National Organization for Women (NOW) "to bring women into full participation in the mainstream of American society now." NOW injected new energy into the long-dormant women's movement.

Led by Friedan, NOW focused on working within the political system to achieve equal opportunity in education and employment, accessible and affordable childcare, and the right to safe and legal abortions.

C. RADICAL FEMINISTS—"SISTERHOOD IS POWERFUL"

During the 1960s, many women volunteered to help the Student Nonviolent Coordinating Committee (SNCC) fight racial discrimination in the South. The women soon complained that SNCC and other civil rights organizations practiced discrimination against women by relegating them to such stereotypical jobs as typing speeches, preparing coffee, and cleaning the office. In an influential position paper, Casey Hayden and Mary Kay pointed out that "assumptions of male supremacy are as…crippling to women as assumptions of white supremacy are to the Negro."

Hayden's and Kay's protest struck a responsive chord among a younger, more radical group of feminists. Known as RADICAL FEMINISTS, they challenged NOW's traditional goals and practices by arguing that women faced more obstacles than just economic and legal discrimination. Angry activists demanded a more militant approach to confronting an entrenched patriarchal society based upon male supremacy. Radical feminists focused on personal issues such as reproductive rights, domestic violence, and the objectification of women as sexual objects.

Radicals vowed to end sexism by promoting "women's liberation." While NOW favored lobbying politicians in Washington, militant groups such as New York Radical Women fostered group solidarity by organizing highly visible public protests. For example, the group invited sympathetic women to join a demonstration held on September 7, 1968, at the Miss America pageant in Atlantic City, New Jersey. About 200 radical feminists garnered national publicity by throwing "objects of female torture" such as high-heeled shoes, false eyelashes, hair curlers, and bras into a "Freedom Trash Can." The event underscored a radical motto that "Sisterhood is powerful."

D. FEMINIST SUCCESSES

The second wave of feminist activism recorded a number of notable successes. Women achieved particularly impressive gains in education. Title IX of the Education Amendments of 1972 prohibited sexual discrimination in schools receiving federal funding. The legislation affected over 16,500 local school districts and 7,000 post-secondary institutions. The groundbreaking law led to the end of all-male colleges while also providing equal opportunities to women in athletic programs. For example, the number of girls playing high school sports swelled from fewer than 300,000 in 1974 to more than 3.1 million today.

Both NOW and radical feminist organizations also supported two controversial Supreme Court decisions. In *Griswold v. Connecticut* the Court ruled that a Connecticut law criminalizing the use of contraceptives violated the right to marital privacy. The Court further argued that the Bill of Rights implied a right to privacy. In *Roe v. Wade*, the Supreme Court ruled that abortion is protected by the right to privacy implied by the Bill of Rights.

And finally, women broke through a number of employment barriers. For example, the American labor force welcomed its first female construction workers, railroad engineers, airline pilots, and firefighters. In politics, 39 women entered the House and the Senate between 1955 and 1976. These elected officials provide the foundation for a wave of 218 women elected between 1977 and 2016. The current House of Representatives now includes a record 102 women representatives.

E. THE EQUAL RIGHTS AMENDMENT

Women activists first presented an Equal Rights Amendment (ERA) to Congress in 1921. Fifty years later, NOW revived the struggle to adopt an ERA amendment. In 1972, Congress overwhelmingly passed the ERA and then sent it on to the states for ratification. The amendment stated that "Equality of rights under the law shall not be denied or abridged by the United States or by any State on account of sex." Supporters argued that it would elevate women's legal status while symbolically underscoring gender equality.

Passage of the ERA seemed inevitable when 35 of the 38 needed states ratified the amendment. However, opponents led by Phyllis Schlafly mounted a vigorous Stop ERA movement to defeat the amendment. They argued that it would eliminate legislation designed to protect women. Examples of this type of legislation included laws regulating women's working hours, restricting child labor, and safeguarding the health of mothers and their children. Schlafly marshaled growing support when she asked, "Why should women abandon these good laws?"

The Stop ERA campaign proved to be successful. The time limit for ratifying the amendment expired in 1982. Since no additional state legislatures ratified the ERA, the amendment went down to defeat. The failure to ratify the ERA marked the end of the second-wave feminist era.

CHAPTER 12
PRACTICE QUESTIONS

MULTIPLE-CHOICE QUESTIONS

Questions 1–3 refer to the excerpt below.

"We early learned to know the children of hard-driven mothers who went out to work all day, sometimes leaving the little things in the casual care of a neighbor, but often locking them into their tenement rooms. The first three crippled children we encountered in the neighborhood had all been injured while their mothers were at work: one had fallen out of a third-story window, another had been burned, and the third had a curved spine due to the fact that for three years he had been tied all day long to the leg of the kitchen table, only to be released at noon by his older brother who had hastily ran in from a neighboring factory to share his lunch with him…Hull House was thus committed to a day nursery which we sustained for sixteen years first in a little cottage on a side street and then in a building designed for its use called the Children's House."

Jane Addams, *Twenty Years at Hull House*, 1910

1. **Jane Addams created the Hull House day nursery to address the needs of**

   A. American Indians
   B. Southern sharecroppers
   C. European immigrants
   D. Dust Bowl migrants

2. **The excerpt most directly reflects which of the following trends in the years between 1890 and 1920?**

   A. The ideal that women should promote republican values
   B. The emergence of monopolies that dominated entire businesses
   C. The continued impact of Populist Party reforms
   D. The activities of Progressive reformers

3. **The activity described in this excerpt has the most in common with work performed by**

   A. colonial women during the American Revolution
   B. women reformers during the Second Great Awakening
   C. members of NOW during the 1960s
   D. radical feminists during the 1970s

Questions 4–5 refer to the excerpt below.

"The suffrage for women already established in the United States makes woman suffrage for the nation inevitable....It is too obvious to require demonstration that woman suffrage, now covering half of our territory, will eventually be ordained in all the nation. No one will deny it. The only question left is when and how it will be completely established....The leadership of the United States in world democracy compels the enfranchisement of its own women. The maxims of the Declaration were once called 'fundamental principles of government.' They are now called 'American principles' or even 'Americanisms'.... The time for woman suffrage has come. The woman's hour has struck. If parties prefer to postpone action longer and thus do battle with this idea, they challenge the inevitable."

Carrie Chapman Catt, Address to Congress on Women's Suffrage (1917)

4. **The excerpt's reference to "The suffrage for women already established in the United States" best supports which of the following statements about the status of women's suffrage in 1917?**

   A. No state granted women's suffrage before 1917
   B. Southern states adopted women's suffrage following the ratification of the Fifteenth Amendment
   C. The only states with complete women's suffrage before 1917 were west of the Mississippi River
   D. The six New England states granted women's suffrage after the Spanish-American War

5. **The excerpt most directly reflects the**

   A. wartime mobilization of American society
   B. increased number of women in the paid workforce
   C. revival of the cult of domesticity
   D. growing strength of the women's suffrage movement

6. **The principles referenced in the excerpt were most directly inspired by the**

    A. Mayflower Compact
    B. Articles of Confederation
    C. Declaration of Independence
    D. United States Constitution

7. **The excerpt most directly reflects which of the following developments in the United States during the first two decades of the twentieth century?**

    A. The Progressive Era spirit of reform
    B. Westward expansion
    C. Government actions to combat racial discrimination
    D. Government recognition of labor unions and collective bargaining

Questions 8–10 refer to the excerpt below.

"And here's where you come in: to restore valid, meaningful purpose to life in your home....You may be hitched to one of those creatures we call 'Western man' and I think part of your job is to keep him Western, to keep him truly purposeful, to keep him whole....

"This assignment for you, as wives and mothers, has great advantages. In the first place, it is homework, you can do it in the living room with a baby in your lap or in the kitchen with a can opener in your hand. If you're really clever, maybe you can even practice your saving arts on that unsuspecting man while he's watching television!...Women, especially educated women, have a unique opportunity to influence us, man and boy, and to play a direct part in the unfolding drama of our free society....What you have learned and can learn will, fit you for the primary task of making homes and whole human beings in whom the rational values of freedom, tolerance, charity, and free inquiry can take root."

> Governor Adlai Stevenson, "A Purpose for Modern Woman," Commencement Address, Smith College, 1955

8. **The view of an educated woman's role presented in this excerpt had the most in common with which of the following?**

    A. The concept of republican motherhood in the 1820s
    B. The belief in "the white man's burden" in the 1890s
    C. The image of the flapper in the 1920s
    D. The image of Rosie the Riveter in the 1940s

9. **This excerpt most clearly provides evidence for which of the following?**

    A. The widespread rejection of consumerism and conformity during the 1950s
    B. The widespread rejection of beat poetry and abstract expressionist art during the 1950s
    C. The widespread acceptance of Cold War containment theory during the 1950s
    D. The widespread acceptance of the cult of domesticity during the 1950s

10. **Which of the following most directly undermines Stevenson's argument in the excerpt?**

    A. The role of women as portrayed in such popular television programs as *Father Knows Best* and *Leave it to Beaver*
    B. The emergence of Marilyn Monroe as the most popular female movie star during the 1950s
    C. In 1960, the percentage of married women working outside the home had reached 32 percent, representing 54 percent of all working women
    D. In 1960, women comprised 85 percent of all librarians, 97 percent of all nurses, and 57 percent of all social workers

Questions 11–13 refer to the excerpt below.

"The problem lay buried, unspoken for many years in the minds of American women… The suburban wife struggled with it alone. As she made the beds, shopped for groceries, matched slipcover material, ate peanut butter sandwiches with her children, chauffeured Cub Scouts and Brownies, lay beside her husband at night—she was afraid to ask even of herself the silent question—'Is this all?'"

Betty Friedan, *The Feminine Mystique*, 1963

11. **The ideas expressed by Friedan in the excerpt from *The Feminine Mystique* most directly challenged**

    A. the funding of Head Start programs to promote early education
    B. the discrepancy between the image and reality of suburban life
    C. the growth of bureaucratic corporations
    D. the construction of a national system of interstate highways

12. **The excerpt was most likely intended to do which of the following?**

    A. Dispel concerns about the rapid growth of suburbia
    B. Demand increased educational opportunities for women
    C. Raise questions about the role of women in American society
    D. Decry the shift from a manufacturing to a service economy

13. **Which of the following pieces of evidence could best be used to support the argument in the excerpt?**

    A. Personal diaries written by suburban housewives
    B. Voting records for women in the 1960 presidential election
    C. Statistics showing the changes in average family size during the 1950s
    D. Statistics showing the decline in average age of marriage during the 1950s

Questions 14–15 refer to the excerpt below.

"Women of every political persuasion—all are invited to join us in a day-long boardwalk-theater event…We will protest the image of Miss America, an image that oppresses women in every area in which it purports to represent us. There will be: Picket Lines; Guerrilla Theater; Leafleting; Lobbying Visits to the contestants urging our sisters to reject the Pageant Farce."

Robin Morgan and the New York Radical Women, press release, "No More Miss America!," 1968

14. **The ideas and tactics expressed in this excerpt are most closely aligned with the point of view of**

    A. Progressive-era feminists
    B. New Women during the 1920s
    C. Suburban housewives during the 1950s
    D. Radical feminists

15. Which of the following contributed most directly to the protest movement described in this excerpt?

A. The publication of *The Feminine Mystique*
B. The passage of the Civil Rights Act of 1964
C. The Stonewall riots
D. The widespread publication of cultural images that objectified women

MULTIPLE-CHOICE ANSWERS

1. C	5. D	9. D	13. A
2. D	6. C	10. C	14. D
3. B	7. A	11. B	15. D
4. C	8. A	12. C	

SHORT-ANSWER QUESTIONS

Question 1
Using the excerpts below, answer A, B, and C.

"*Resolved*, That woman is man's equal….

"*Resolved*, That woman has too long rested satisfied in the circumscribed limits which corrupt customs…have marked out for her, and that it is time she should move in the enlarged sphere…assigned her.

"*Resolved*,….That, being invested by the Creator with the same capabilities, and the same consciousness of responsibility for their exercise, it is demonstrably the right and duty of women, equally with man, to promote every righteous cause, by every righteous means."

Declaration of Sentiments and Resolutions, Seneca Falls Convention, 1848

"We, men and women who hereby constitute ourselves as the National Organization for Women, believe that the time has come for a new movement toward true equality for all women in America, and toward a fully equal partnership of the sexes, as part of the world-wide revolution of human rights now taking place within and beyond our national borders…

"We reject the current assumptions that a man must carry the sole burden of supporting himself, his wife, and family, and that a woman is automatically entitled to lifelong support by a man upon her marriage, or that marriage, home and family are primarily woman's world and responsibility—hers to dominate—his to support. We believe that a true partnership between the sexes demands a different concept of marriage, an equitable sharing of the responsibilities of home and children and of the economic burden of their support..."

> Statement of Purpose and Bill of Rights of the National Organization for Women (NOW), 1966

A. Briefly describe ONE major similarity between the Seneca Falls Declaration and the NOW Statement of Purpose.

B. Briefly explain how ONE specific historical person, event, or development from the period 1776 to 1848 that is not explicitly mentioned in the excerpts could be used to support the Seneca Falls Declaration of Sentiments.

C. Briefly explain how ONE specific historical person, event, or historical development from the period 1920 to 1966 that is not explicitly mentioned in the excerpt could be used to support NOW's Statement of Purpose.

Question 2
Answer A, B, and C.

A. Briefly describe ONE specific historical difference between flappers during the 1920s and radical feminists during the late 1960s.

B. Briefly describe ONE specific historical similarity between flappers during the 1920s and radical feminists during the late 1960s.

C. Briefly explain ONE specific historical impact of either the flappers or the radical feminists.

SHORT–ANSWER ANSWERS

Question 1

A. Both documents assume that women have capacities that are equal to those of men. Based upon this assumption, they both directly challenge prevailing gender roles based upon separate spheres and the cult of domesticity.

B. The authors of the Seneca Falls Declaration formally recognized that American women were denied the suffrage. The Seneca Falls Declaration marked the beginning of the women's suffrage movement in the United States.

C. NOW's statement of purpose aimed to advance the women's rights movement into a new agenda. For example, at the time of the NOW Statement of Purpose, women did not have a constitutional right to a safe and legal abortion.

Question 2

A. The flappers ignored the feminist political agenda, choosing instead to focus on a lighthearted and flamboyant lifestyle. In contrast, radical feminists employed a militant approach to confronting an entrenched patriarchal society based upon male supremacy. Radical feminists focused on personal issues such as reproductive rights, domestic violence, and the objectification of women as sexual objects.

B. Both the flappers and the radical feminists refused to accept prevailing gender roles. Both pursued more liberated lifestyles.

C. The flappers successfully challenged prevailing social conventions that dictated how women should dress and behave. Their spirit of youthful independence served as a model for future generations of more rebellious women.

PART IV

KEY TOPICS, MOVEMENTS, AND EVENTS

CHAPTER 13
NATIVE AMERICAN HISTORY
FROM THE COLUMBIAN EXCHANGE TO
THE RED POWER MOVEMENT
1607–1980

STRATEGIC IMPORTANCE

Native American history generates a predictable number of questions and points on the APUSH exam. A careful analysis of recent APUSH exams revealed that questions on Native American history from the Colonial period to 1980 totaled an average of about seven points per exam. Remember, you only need 75 points to earn a three, 95 points to earn a four, and 110 points to earn a five. This chapter is thus an important part of your coalition of points.

KEY POINTS AND HISTORIC GENERALIZATIONS

- The COLUMBIAN EXCHANGE refers to the exchange of plants, animals, and germs between the New World and Europe following the discovery of America in 1492.

- Demographers believe that epidemics of smallpox, influenza, and measles may have caused the deaths of as many as three-quarters of the people living in what is now the continental United States.

- The fur trade shaped French interactions with Native American tribes. Unlike the English, they did not build plantations or family farms on lands occupied by Native Americans.

- The cultivation of tobacco provided the Virginia colony with a prized cash crop. Tobacco planters now valued land far more than Indian friendship.

- Native Americans had no concept of private property. In contrast, the English believed that land could be bought, sold, and transferred in a treaty.

- King Philip's War left the New England tribes a broken and defeated people.

- Great Britain's victory in the French and Indian War posed a dire threat to Native Americans living in the Ohio River Valley and Great Lakes region.

- The Proclamation of 1763 proved to be a fateful failure. Settlers easily evaded the British troops and poured into Tennessee and Kentucky, thus provoking Pontiac's Rebellion.

- The Indian Removal Act voided half a century of treaties and enabled President Jackson to force thousands of Indians to leave their ancestral lands.

- The Supreme Court's ruling in *Worcester v. Georgia* upheld the Cherokee Nation's legal right to their land. But President Jackson refused to enforce the Court's decision.

- As many as 4,000 Native Americans died on the Trail of Tears, a forced relocation from their ancestral lands in the Southeastern United States to areas in the West designated as Indian Territory.

- The construction of the transcontinental railroads, the slaughter of the buffalo, and the spread of epidemic diseases brought irrevocable changes to the Plains Indians' way life.

- The Dawes Act aimed to "civilize" the Plains Indians by turning them into individual homeowners.

- The Ghost Dance aroused erroneous fears that Indians intended to go on the warpath. The army's overreaction led to the tragic loss of life at the Battle of Wounded Knee.

- Indian boarding schools attempted to implement the Bureau of Indian Affairs' policy of using FORCED ASSIMILATION to "Americanize" Native American children.

- Often called the Indian New Deal, the Indian Reorganization Act of 1934 reversed the Dawes Act by ending the policy of dividing tribal lands into small plots for individual families.

- The Red Power movement used militant tactics to publicize Native American grievances. The movement fostered a growing sense of pan-Indian identity.

TOPIC 13.1
NATIVE AMERICANS AND THE EARLY COLONIAL ERA, 1607-1700

A. THE COLUMBIAN EXCHANGE

Columbus's historic voyages shattered the isolation between Europe and the indigenous peoples living in North and South America. The Spanish conquest set in motion a movement of people, plants, animals, and diseases known as the COLUMBIAN EXCHANGE. This interaction continued when the French and English began to explore and colonize North America.

Contagious diseases had a particularly devastating impact on Native Americans living in North America. Demographers believe that epidemics of smallpox, influenza, and measles may have caused the deaths of as many as three-quarters of the people living in what is now the continental United States. This unprecedented demographic catastrophe devastated Native American societies and reduced their ability to resist the European invaders.

B. NATIVE AMERICANS AND THE FRENCH

The first French explorers tried and failed to find a new passage to Asia. However, French trappers did discover an abundant supply of fur-bearing animals. Driven by the lucrative fur trade, the French claimed a vast arc of land stretching from the Saint Lawrence Valley through the Great Lakes and down the Ohio and Mississippi river valleys.

The fur trade shaped French interactions with Native American tribes. Unlike the English, they did not build plantations or family farms on lands occupied by Native Americans. Instead, the French built widely dispersed trading posts at strategic locations. For example, Montreal, Detroit, and St. Louis all began as trading posts. In the best years, Native American trappers captured over 100,000 beaver pelts. In 1693, a fleet of 400 Indian canoes brought furs to Montreal.

The fur trade promoted generally peaceful commercial relations between the French and the Native American tribes. The trade enabled Indians to acquire highly prized guns, metal pots, knives, mirrors, scissors, wool blankets, decorative glass beads, and alcohol. Over time, a gradual process of cultural interaction occurred as French traders intermarried with indigenous women and French priests converted some Native Americans to Catholicism.

C. NATIVE AMERICANS AND THE VIRGINIANS

In 1607 the Powhatan Confederacy numbered about 30,000 Native Americans, living in 30 tribes dispersed along Virginia's coastal plain. Warriors looked to a chief the English later called Powhatan as their paramount leader. The unexpected arrival of English settlers at Jamestown presented Powhatan with a fateful decision. Powhatan viewed the English as a source of valuable manufactured goods and as possible allies. Given these assumptions, he provided Jamestown with desperately needed supplies that enabled the struggling colonists to survive the first harsh winters.

Powhatan overestimated his own strength while misjudging both the power and intentions of the English colonists. The cultivation of tobacco provided the Virginia colony with a prized cash crop. Tobacco planters now valued land far more than Indian friendship.

Powhatan's younger brother, Opechancanough, recognized that Virginia's relentless pressure on tribal lands confronted his people with the greatest threat in their history. In 1622, he led a surprise series of raids designed to destroy the Jamestown colony. Although Opechancanough's warriors killed about one-fourth of the Virginia colonists, they failed to defeat them. Two decades later, a second desperate attack once again failed to dislodge the Virginians. The victorious English forced the defeated Native Americans to cede land and recognize English authority. By 1675, warfare and disease had reduced the once-powerful Powhatan Confederacy to just 3,500 people.

D. NATIVE AMERICANS AND THE PURITANS

The Puritans arrived in Massachusetts in 1629 and founded Boston the following year. Unlike the profit-driven male settlers in Virginia, the Puritans migrated in family groups with a spiritual mission to build an ideal Christian commonwealth. While they differed in many fundamental ways, the Puritans and the Virginia colonists shared a similar pattern of interaction with Native Americans.

Demographers estimate that by 1600 as many as 120,000 Native Americans inhabited New England. In the beginning the Indians welcomed the newcomers by providing them with food and teaching them how to hunt and fish in a new environment. But as in Virginia, tensions quickly developed over differing attitudes toward land. Native Americans had no concept of private property. Tribes viewed land as a collective tribal resource, much like air and water. In contrast, the English believed that land could be bought, sold, and transferred in a treaty.

As the Puritans grew in number and strength, they began to view the native peoples as savages "who are cruel, barbarous, and naturally treacherous." Tensions mounted as Indians complained that the Puritans pushed them off their tribal lands, killed their game, and cheated them in trade. In 1636, the era of amicable relations ended when the New Englanders destroyed a Pequot village, slaughtering about 400 people.

Surviving Indian leaders realized that the Puritans intended to "deprive us of the privileges of our land and drive us to utter ruin." In 1675, Indians led by Chief Metacom (also known as King Philip) attacked and burned settlements across New England. Known as King Philip's War, the series of brutal raids claimed the lives of about 1,000 settlers, or one-tenth of the Massachusetts colony's male population. But the war cost at least 4,000 Indian deaths. As in Virginia, the clash of cultures left the Native Americans a broken and defeated people.

TOPIC 13.2
THE IMPACT OF THE FRENCH AND INDIAN WAR ON NATIVE AMERICANS

A. A WORLD TURNED UPSIDE DOWN

Great Britain's victory in the French and Indian War dramatically changed the balance of power in North America. The Treaty of Paris compelled France to cede Canada and its claims east of the Mississippi River to Great Britain. The British thus achieved a position of unrivalled power.

Britain's overwhelming victory posed a dire threat to Native Americans living in the Ohio River Valley and Great Lakes region. France's abrupt departure severed profitable trading networks. The French defeat also meant that Indian tribes could no longer negotiate favorable agreements by playing one European power against the other. And finally, the line of English agricultural settlements edged steadily westward, with no regard for Indian land claims or way of life.

B. PONTIAC'S REBELLION

The results of the French and Indian War made a deep impression on Native Americans. Faced with alarming threats to their independence, many Indians turned to the teaching of a Delaware spiritual leader named Neolin. Claiming to have received visions from the "Master of Life," Neolin offered hope by preaching that Indians could regain their independence if they first restored time-honored traditions. This would give them the spiritual strength and unity needed to drive the English from their lands.

Neolin's call to action inspired the Ottawa chief Pontiac to rally tribes to attack British forts in the Ohio Valley and Great Lakes. Known as Pontiac's Rebellion, the surprise raids began in 1763. Within a few months, Pontiac's warriors captured several British forts and killed hundreds of white settlers. Despite suffering initial setbacks, the British used their superior military power to regain the initiative and restore the peace.

C. THE PROCLAMATION OF 1763

Pontiac's Rebellion convinced British authorities of the need to regulate the western frontier and avoid expensive Indian wars. In October 1763 King George III signed the Proclamation of 1763, forbidding settlement west of the crest of the Appalachian Mountains. The royal order infuriated land-hungry settlers and speculators, who had expected to profit from purchasing and selling tribal lands.

The Proclamation of 1763 proved to be a fateful failure. Settlers easily evaded the British troops and poured into Tennessee and Kentucky. The expense of maintaining troops in America added to Britain's already heavy national debt. The Crown's desperate need to raise funds persuaded Parliament to enact the ill-fated Stamp Act, thus beginning the steps leading to the American Revolution.

TOPIC 13.3
NATIVE AMERICANS DURING THE JACKSONIAN ERA

A. THE INDIAN REMOVAL ACT OF 1830

Pontiac's Rebellion and later acts of armed resistance delayed but did not stop American expansion into Indian lands. When Andrew Jackson became president in 1829, just over 100,000 Native Americans lived east of the Mississippi River. Although many Americans respected the Indians, white settlers coveted their land. As noted by Missouri Senator Thomas Hart Benton, many Southern planters hoped to "convert Indian soil into slave soil."

Jackson's vision of American democracy did not include a place for Native Americans. He branded Indians "savages" standing in the way of American civilization. With Jackson's support, Congress narrowly passed the Indian Removal Act of 1830. The legislation created the Indian Territory on national lands located in present-day Oklahoma. The act thus voided half a century of treaties and enabled Jackson to force thousands of Native Americans to leave their ancestral lands.

B. THE CHEROKEE—"WE DID SO!"

The Cherokee of northern Georgia contradicted Jackson's prejudiced view of Native Americans as frontier savages. Rather than take up arms, the Cherokee chose to adapt to American culture. By the early 1830s they had developed their own written language, published a newspaper, and elected leaders to a representative government inspired by the U.S. Constitution. "You asked us to throw off the hunter and warrior state," Cherokee John Ridge told a Philadelphia audience in 1832. "We did so!"

C. *WORCESTER V. GEORGIA*, 1832

The Cherokee refused to abandon their land. Instead, they chose to legally challenge the Georgia legislature's resolution asserting the state's sovereignty over Cherokee lands within its borders. In *Worcester v. Georgia*, the Marshall-led Supreme Court upheld the Cherokee Nation's legal right to their land, declaring them a "distinct community...in which the laws of Georgia have no force." But President Jackson refused to enforce the Court's decision. He defiantly declared, "John Marshall has made his decision, now let him enforce it."

D. THE TRAIL OF TEARS

Jackson's successor Martin van Buren chose to enforce Jackson's removal policy. In 1838, about 7,000 troops led by General Winfield Scott began the forced evacuation of some 17,000 Cherokees. Historians estimate that as many as 4,000 people died on a 116-day forced relocation along routes now known as the Trail of Tears. The long ordeal finally ended when the tribes reached Indian Territory, in what is now Oklahoma.

A famous painting by Robert Lindeneux depicts a poignant scene along the Trail of Tears. Stern blue-coated soldiers escort men, women, and children, driven out of their homes with only the clothes on their backs. The troops refuse to slow the forced march to enable the ill and the elderly to recover. According to legend, a flower known as the Cherokee rose now grows on every spot where a tear fell on the tragic Trail of Tears.

TOPIC 13.4
NATIVE AMERICANS AND THE LAST WESTERN FRONTIER

A. "THE GREAT AMERICAN DESERT"

In 1840, most Americans knew very little about the land and people between the Mississippi River and the Rocky Mountains. The public assumed that savage Indian tribes occupied a region the poet Walt Whitman described as "vast, trackless spaces." Early mapmakers agreed with Whitman. Between 1825 and 1860, American maps labeled the Great Plains "The Great American Desert." Until the Civil War, most Americans seemed content to leave the region to the roaming tribes of Indians and the great herds of buffalo.

B. THE PLAINS INDIANS

About 250,000 Indians lived in the Great Plains. Their way of life depended upon the horse and the buffalo. First brought to North America by the Spanish, horses spread north into the Great Plains. By the early 1700s, the Plains Indians had learned how to capture and tame wild horses called mustangs.

The unexpected arrival of the horse enabled Plains Indians to develop a new way of life as mobile hunters. Successful hunts provided a tribe with more than just meat. As one modern historian has written, the buffalo was like a "galloping department store" that also provided food, clothing, and shelter. For example, buffalo skins made robes, blankets, and tents. Buffalo bones could be fashioned into knives, while their horns made ideal cups. Even the buffalo's tail was put to use as a handy fly swatter.

C. "AS LONG AS WATERS RUN"

During the 1850s more than 50,000 settlers and prospectors crossed the Great Plains on their way to the California gold fields and the fertile Willamette Valley in Oregon. These pioneers proved to be the beginning of a great wave of eight million people who spread across the Great Plains in the decades following the Civil War. The invading settlers disrupted the buffalo herds and spread deadly diseases such as cholera.

In an effort to prevent the outbreak of hostilities, the U.S. government invited tribal leaders to attend a conference at Fort Laramie in September 1851. After 20 days, the chiefs signed an agreement known as the Fort Laramie Treaty. Under its terms the tribes guaranteed safe passage for settlers on the Oregon Trail. In exchange, they received defined lands that would be theirs for "as long as waters flow and the grass shall grow."

D. THE TRANSCONTINENTAL RAILROADS

On May 10, 1869, railroad officials at Promontory Summit, Utah, triumphantly announced, "The last rail is laid; the last spike is driven; the Pacific Railroad is completed." The completion of the nation's first transcontinental railroad marked the beginning of a building boom across the West. By 1893, five transcontinental lines linked the east and west coasts.

The transcontinental railroads opened a new era for America. They accelerated economic growth by creating a vast integrated market for the movement of raw materials and manufactured goods. At the same time, they encouraged migrants from eastern states and immigrants from European countries to take advantage of the Homestead Act, which offered 160 acres of land to a family that would settle and maintain the land for five years.

The transcontinental railroads did not benefit the Plains Indians. The "iron horses" enabled hunters to nearly exterminate the vast herds of buffalo that once roamed across the Great Plains. This wanton slaughter struck a catastrophic blow to the core of Plains Indian life. Indian hunters rode for miles futilely searching for buffalo. The demoralized hunters returned to their tribes empty-handed. They sadly reported grim news to their hungry people, "Nothing, we found nothing."

E. FINAL BATTLES ON THE GREAT PLAINS

The construction of the transcontinental railroads, the slaughter of the buffalo, and the spread of epidemic diseases brought irrevocable changes to the Great Plains. Although young warriors engaged the U.S. Army in at least 200 battles, they faced overwhelming military forces that made resistance futile. Despite their valiant effort, the outcome always remained the same as the government confined tribes to smaller and smaller reservations.

In 1875, thousands of gold prospectors stampeded into the Black Hills in the Dakota Territory. The Sioux vowed to protect sacred ground they viewed as the center of their universe and "the heart of everything that is." The army ordered Lieutenant Colonel George Armstrong Custer to protect the prospectors and quell the rebellious Sioux warriors. Eager to win fame, Custer recklessly advanced his Seventh Cavalry along the banks of the Little Bighorn River. Instead of finding a small band of Indians, Custer stumbled on the main Sioux camp. Led by Crazy Horse, Sioux warriors resembled "bees swarming out of a hive" as they surrounded Custer and annihilated all of his men.

The Sioux's victory proved to be short-lived. News of "Custer's Last Stand" reached the East Coast on July 4, 1876, as Americans celebrated the nation's centennial. An outraged public now demanded revenge. Within a few months U.S. forces had defeated the Sioux, thus ending major warfare in the West.

F. THE GHOST DANCE

The Plains Indians suffered more than a military defeat; they also lost their independence and traditional buffalo-centered culture. Desperate and bewildered, many turned to a promise of renewal promoted by a self-proclaimed religious leader named Wovoka. Following an eclipse of the sun on January 1, 1889, Wovoka announced that an Indian Messiah would appear and restore the tribes to their former glory by resurrecting the buffalo herds and driving the white settlers back across the continent.

News of Wovoka's remarkable vision spread rapidly across the Great Plains. Wovoka persuaded his followers that they could hasten the Messiah's arrival by performing a religious ceremony known as the Ghost Dance. Male and female dancers wore white robes or "ghost-dance shirts," which some Indians believed ensured magical protection from bullets.

G. THE BATTLE OF WOUNDED KNEE, 1890

The Ghost Dance aroused unfounded fears that the Indians intended to go on the warpath. President Harrison ordered 9,000 troops into South Dakota to suppress a nonexistent Indian "uprising." Their commanding officer grimly predicted a "hungry, wild, mad horde of savages" was about to overrun the entire region. His dire warning caused panic among white settlers.

Events quickly spun out of control. Soldiers of the Seventh Cavalry, Custer's old regiment, surrounded a large group of Ghost Dancers at a trading post named Wounded Knee. On December 29, 1890, the troops attempted to disarm the Indians. But a shot suddenly rang out. The nearly 500 soldiers returned fire with repeating rifles. They randomly slaughtered about 300 of the Indians, including 200 women and children. Thirty-two soldiers died, many from their own crossfire.

Years later, an Indian survivor remembered the battle. After recalling the pitiful sight of the dead and dying, he also realized that the tragic event marked the end of an era: "And I can see that something else died there in the bloody mud and was buried in the blizzard. A people's dream died there. It was a beautiful dream."

TOPIC 13.5
FORCED ASSIMILATION

A. *A CENTURY OF DISHONOR*

Although the U.S. Cavalry could defeat the Plains Indians in battle, the U.S. government could not suppress the truth about how it had mistreated them in peace. In 1881 Helen Hunt Jackson published *A Century of Dishonor*, documenting America's long history of broken treaties and misguided Indian policies. Determined to champion reforms, Jackson sent a copy of her book to each member of Congress to urge the legislators to "redeem the name of the United States from the stain of a century of dishonor."

B. THE DAWES ACT, 1887

The accusations in *A Century of Dishonor* helped mobilize public support for a new Indian policy. Reformers believed that Indians' traditional tribal culture posed an insurmountable obstacle, preventing them from assimilating into white society. The Dawes Act aimed to "civilize" the Plains Indians by turning them into individual homeowners and farmers. Using the Homestead Act as its model, the Dawes Act subdivided tribal land into individual homesteads of 160 acres each. The government would then sell "surplus" lands to white settlers.

The government used the Dawes Act to distribute 47 million acres of land to individual Indians and their families. Unfortunately, many Indians had been nomadic hunters who knew little about farming. As a result, the Dawes Act created opportunities for opportunistic speculators to plunder Indian lands. In 1881, Indians held 155 million acres of land. Two decades later, the total had fallen to 77 million.

C. INDIAN BOARDING SCHOOLS

The Bureau of Indian Affairs (BIA) subjected Native Americans to a policy of FORCED ASSIMILATION. Reform groups and churches launched an educational assault on Indian children by isolating them in a network of boarding schools. Teachers attempted to "Americanize" their students by focusing on American culture while simultaneously forcing them to give up their indigenous cultures, languages, spiritual beliefs, and even their names.

The Carlisle Indian Industrial School in Pennsylvania became the best-known and most influential Indian boarding school. Between 1879 and 1918, over 10,000 Native American children from 140 tribes attended Carlisle. The school's stated mission was to "Kill the Indian; Save the Man." The children often left Carlisle and other boarding schools as marginal people whose new habits repelled their families, while whites continued to reject them. "I felt I was no more Indian, but would be an imitation of a white man," one Indian bitterly recalled.

D. THE TREATMENT OF NATIVE AMERICANS AND AFRICAN AMERICANS

During the period between the Civil War and World War I, deeply rooted racial prejudices affected both Native Americans and African Americans. White Americans considered the cultures of these two groups woefully deficient. In the segregated South, Redeemer governments used Jim Crow laws to legally separate African Americans from white society. In the West, Bureau of Indian Affairs officials used the Dawes Act and boarding schools to force Native Americans to adopt white ways of life.

TOPIC 13.6
CHANGE AND CONTINUITY IN INDIAN POLICIES, 1930–1980

A. THE CONTINUING PLIGHT OF NATIVE AMERICANS

The Dawes Act and the policy of forced assimilation had a devastating impact on Native American life. During the Great Depression the unemployment rate among Native Americans rose to at least three times the national average. Average life expectancy on the isolated and demoralized reservations plunged to 47 years, 20 years below the national average. By 1920, the combined effect of disease and violence sharply reduced the number of Native Americans to approximately 330,000 people. At that time, the death rate among Native Americans exceeded their birth rate.

B. JOHN COLLIER AND THE INDIAN NEW DEAL

In 1933, President Roosevelt appointed John Collier the administration's new Commissioner of Indian Affairs. A persistent and forceful critic of past Bureau of Indian Affairs actions, Collier vowed to reverse previous misguided government policies and revitalize tribal life. He began by issuing executive orders ending forced attendance in boarding schools, forbidding interference with traditional Native American religious practices, and encouraging the revival of native languages. He also successfully lobbied government agencies to include Native Americans in New Deal relief programs such as the Civilian Conservation Corps (CCC).

In 1934, Collier gained Congressional approval for the Indian Reorganization Act. Often called the Indian New Deal, the legislation reversed the Dawes Act by ending the policy of dividing Indian lands into small plots for individual families and then selling the remaining "surplus" land. The act also attempted to promote self-government by calling upon tribes to adopt written constitutions and elect representative councils.

Many provisions of the Indian Reorganization Act benefited Native Americans. Tribes regained several million acres of land lost under the Dawes Act. The law also helped awaken a new sense of hope and a renewed pride in being an American Indian.

Critics recognized the Indian Reorganization Act's positive gains. However, they pointed out that the law represented yet another attempt by non-Indians to undermine tribal traditions. For example, written constitutions and elected leaders ignored time-honored systems based upon respected chiefs working with a council of elders to reach decisions based upon a consensus.

C. THE RED POWER MOVEMENT

During the late 1960s, Native Americans joined other discontented minorities protesting against injustice. Many American Indians lived either on impoverished reservations or within urban centers often referred to as "red ghettos." Inspired by the Black Power movement, an increasingly militant generation of young Native Americans demanded better housing, more jobs, and greater educational opportunities.

On November 20, 1969, 89 Native Americans landed on Alcatraz Island in San Francisco Bay. Calling themselves Indians of All Tribes, the group declared that the island belonged to them by provisions of the Treaty of Fort Laramie of 1868, allowing American Indians to claim abandoned federal property that had once been tribal land. The 19-month occupation focused national attention on Native American grievances while also launching the Red Power movement.

The American Indian Movement (AIM) quickly became the most visible and militant Red Power group. The organization utilized civil disobedience and aggressive confrontations to publicize their grievances with the federal government. For example, in 1973 AIM members led a dramatic occupation of Wounded Knee, the site of the infamous 1890 massacre of Native Americans.

The Red Power movement fostered a growing sense of pan-Indian identity among Native Americans. Their actions also helped to mobilize public support for the Indian Education Act of 1972. The legislation provided additional funds to school districts with a high percentage of Indian children.

CHAPTER 13
PRACTICE QUESTIONS

MULTIPLE-CHOICE QUESTIONS

Questions 1–3 refer to the excerpt below.

"Europeans began to alter the landscape in ways Native Americans never had. They brought new plants and crops—rice, wheat, barley, oats—and new grasses and weeds, along with fruits such as peaches and oranges. They introduced domesticated animals such as horses, sheep, goats, and pigs, which trampled Indian cornfields and drove away wild game. Their world, quite literally, changed before Indians' eyes as European colonists transformed the forest into farmland...[But] Europe's deadliest export was invisible. Nothing hit Indian societies harder or did more to shape the subsequent course of American history than Old World diseases."

> Colin G. Calloway, historian, *First Peoples: A Documentary Survey of American Indian History*, 2012

1. **The excerpt describes effects of the**
    A. fur trade
    B. Columbian Exchange
    C. triangular trade routes
    D. First Great Awakening

2. **The pattern described in the excerpt directly led to**
    A. the emergence of food shortages among Native Americans
    B. the widespread use of white indentured servants
    C. the emergence of a racially mixed population in the English colonies
    D. the catastrophic spread of epidemic diseases among Native Americans

3. **Native American tribes in Virginia and New England responded to the changes described in the excerpt by**
    A. attempting to assimilate into Colonial societies
    B. embracing Christianity
    C. moving to new lands west of the Appalachian Mountains
    D. shifting their attitudes from guarded hospitality to open hostility

Questions 4–7 refer to the excerpt below.

"It was a fearful sight to see them thus frying in the fire, and the streams of blood quenching the same and horrible was the stink and scent thereof; but the victory seemed a sweet sacrifice, and they gave the praise to God, who had wrought so wonderfully for them, thus to enclose their enemies in their hands, and gave them so speedy a victory over so proud, insulting, and blasphemous an enemy."

> William Bradford, account of the colonists' attack on the Pequot's Mystic River Village, 1637

4. **Conflicts like the one between the Pequots and the New England colonists were primarily driven by differing**

    A. views of predestination
    B. views of the proper role of women
    C. claims to land
    D. forms of government

5. **Which of the following most directly ended conflict between Native Americans and New England colonists?**

    A. The destruction of the buffalo herds
    B. The outcome of King Philip's War
    C. The Proclamation Act of 1763
    D. The emergence of Rhode Island as a haven for dissenters

6. **The French most differed from the English in relations with Native Indians in that the French**

    A. converted more Native Indians to Protestantism
    B. imported more African slaves to harvest their cash crops
    C. opposed intermarriage with Native Americans
    D. focused on developing profitable commercial relations with Native Americans

7. **Bradford's description of the colonists' "victory" best reflects which of the following?**

    A. Assumptions about the superiority of English religion and culture
    B. A growing secularization in New England society
    C. The increasing importance of controlling the supply of maize
    D. Concerns about the economic threat posed by the Pequot's Mystic River Village

Questions 8–10 refer to the excerpt below:

"From the commencement of our government, Congress has passed acts to regulate trade and intercourse with the Indians which treat them as nations, respect their rights, and manifest a firm purpose to afford that protection which treaties stipulate…The Cherokee Nation, then, is a distinct community… in which the laws of Georgia can have no force, and which the citizens of Georgia have no right to enter but with the assent of the Cherokees themselves or in conformity with treaties and with the acts of Congress…."

Chief Justice John Marshall, majority opinion in *Worcester v. Georgia*, 1832

8. The Supreme Court decision in this excerpt was most directly a response to Andrew Jackson's

A. role in the nullification crisis
B. opposition to the national bank
C. support for the Indian Removal Act
D. opposition to recognizing the Republic of Texas

9. President Jackson's response to the Supreme Court decision in this excerpt most directly led to

A. the Trail of Tears
B. Georgia's decision to secede from the Union
C. enactment of emergency legislation guaranteeing Cherokee land titles in Georgia
D. his defeat in the presidential election of 1832

10. The Cherokee differed from other Native American tribes in the 1820s and 1830s in that the Cherokees

A. avoided contact with federal authorities by hiding in the remote parts of the Appalachian Mountains
B. refused to adopt American cultural and economic practices
C. successfully resisted the federal government's attempt to force them to move to Oklahoma Indian Territory
D. used the federal courts to defend their legal rights

Questions 11–12 refer to the excerpt below.

"Article 1: From this day forward all war between the parties to this agreement shall forever cease. The Government of the United States desires peace, and its honor is hereby pledged to keep it.

"Article 7: In order to insure the civilization of the Indians entering into this treaty, the necessity of education is admitted, especially of such as of them as are or may be settled on said agricultural reservations and they therefore pledge themselves to compel their children, male and female, between the ages of six and sixteen, to attend school.

"Article 11: In consideration of the advantages and benefits conferred by this treaty, and the many pledges of friendship by the United States, the tribes who are parties to this agreement hereby stipulate that they will relinquish all right to occupy permanently the territory outside their reservation."

> Second Treaty of Fort Laramie, agreed between the United States government and various bands of the Sioux nation, 1868

11. **During the 1860s and 1870s, which of the following was a widespread effect of the interactions between American settlers and the Plains Indians?**
    A. Decreased intensity of warfare between the two groups
    B. The emergence of racially and culturally mixed populations
    C. Confinement of the Plains Indians to ever-shrinking reservations
    D. Forced migration of Plains Indians to the Indian Territory in what is now Oklahoma

12. **Article 7 of the treaty most likely reflected which of the following goals?**
    A. Efforts to assimilate the Plains Indians into American society
    B. The destruction of the buffalo herds in order to make way for cattle ranches
    C. A desire by many Plains Indians to abandon their religious practices
    D. The importance of conservation policies designed to create new national parks

Questions 13–15 refer to the excerpt below.

"The Indian is not a 'rugged individualist;' he functions best as an integrated member of a group, clan, or tribe. Identification of his individuality with clan or tribe is with him a spiritual necessity. If the satisfaction of this compelling sentiment is denied him—as it was for half a century or more—the Indian does not, it has been clearly shown, merge into white group life. Through a modernized form of Indian organization, adapted to the needs of the various tribes (a form of organization now authorized by law), it is possible to make use of this powerful latent civic force."

> John Collier, "Indian Renaissance," from the Annual Report of the Commissioner of Indian Affairs (1935)

13. Which of the following most directly contributed to the "modernized form of Indian organization" referenced in the excerpt?

A. The Dawes Act

B. The Indian Reorganization Act

C. The curriculum of Indian boarding schools

D. The tactics of the American Indian Movement

14. The excerpt most strongly suggests that in 1935 which of the following was correct?

A. The Supreme Court's "separate but equal" doctrine was applied to both African Americans and Native Americans

B. New Deal relief programs had substantially improved economic conditions on Native American reservations

C. The plan to transform Native Americans into self-sufficient farmers had failed

D. Native Americans had become an important part of the New Deal electoral coalition

15. The ideas expressed in the excerpt emerged most directly from a larger intellectual debate over the

A. relationship between individual freedom and public order

B. relationship between religion and the federal government

C. relationship between the federal government and the states

D. relationship between minority groups and the dominant society

MULTIPLE-CHOICE ANSWERS

1.	B	5.	B	9.	A	13.	B
2.	D	6.	D	10.	D	14.	C
3.	D	7.	A	11.	C	15.	D
4.	C	8.	C	12.	A		

SHORT-ANSWER QUESTIONS

Question 1
Answer A, B, and C.

A. Briefly describe ONE specific historical difference between the treatment of Native Americans in the French and English colonies.

B. Briefly describe ONE specific historical similarity between the treatment of Native Americans in the French and English colonies.

C. Briefly describe ONE specific historical effect of the treatment of Native Americans in either the French or English colonies

Question 2
Answer A, B, and C.

A. Briefly describe ONE specific historical difference between the Dawes Act and the Indian Reorganization Act.

B. Briefly describe ONE specific historical similarity between the Dawes Act and the Indian Reorganization Act.

C. Briefly describe ONE specific historical effect of either the Dawes Act or the Indian Reorganization Act.

SHORT-ANSWER ANSWERS

Question 1

A. The French fur traders promoted generally peaceful commercial relations with Native American tribes. Over time, a gradual process of cultural interaction occurred as French traders intermarried with indigenous women. In contrast, the English colonists viewed Native Americans as "savages" who should be driven off their tribal lands. The English colonists upheld strict social boundaries that permitted little intermarriage with Native Americans.

B. Both the French and English colonists infected Native Americans with deadly diseases that decimated their population and made it much easier to capture their lands.

C. The English settlers in Virginia and New England pushed steadily westward with no regard for Indian land claims or way of life. In both areas the clash of cultures left the Native Americans a broken and defeated people.

Question 2

A. The Dawes Act attempted to "civilize" the Plains Indians by subdividing their tribal lands and transforming Native Americans into individual homeowners and farmers. In contrast, the Indian Reorganization Act reversed the Dawes Act land policy, restored tribal lands, and awakened a new sense of hope and pride in being an American Indian.

B. Both the Dawes Act and the Indian Reorganization Act have been criticized as attempts by non-Indians to undermine tribal traditions. The Dawes Act attempted to force Native Americans to become individual homeowners and farmers. The Indian Reorganization Act attempted to replace time-honored rule by respected chiefs and tribal elders with written constitutions and elected leaders.

C. The Dawes Act created opportunities for speculators to plunder Indian lands. In 1881, Indians held 155 million acres. Two decades later, the total shrank to just 77 million acres.

CHAPTER 14
THE POPULIST MOVEMENT 1880-1900

STRATEGIC IMPORTANCE

The Populist movement generates a significant cluster of questions and exam points. A careful analysis of recent APUSH exams revealed that questions about the Populist movement totaled an average of seven points per exam. Remember, you only need 75 points to earn a three, 95 points to earn a four, and 110 points to earn a five. This chapter is thus an important part of your coalition of points.

KEY POINTS AND HISTORIC GENERALIZATIONS

- During the last quarter of the nineteenth century, new machinery and fertilizers enabled American farmers to increase the number of acres under cultivation.

- As the supply of crops increased, farm prices decreased. Angry farmers blamed their distress on discriminatory freight rates charged by the railroads and the growth of corporate power in agriculture.

- The wave of agrarian discontent gave birth to the People's or POPULIST PARTY. The Populist Party platform called for a strong government role in the nation's economic system. Specific demands included government control of the railroads, free coinage of silver, a graduated income tax, and the direct election of United States senators.

- Silverites believed that the free coinage of silver would increase the supply of money and raise commodity prices, thus alleviating farm debts.

- The election of 1896 led to the collapse of the Populist Party and a new period of Republican Party dominance.

TOPIC 14.1
CAUSES OF THE POPULIST REVOLT

A. OVERPRODUCTION AND FALLING PRICES

American farmers seemed to have much to be proud of. Between 1870 and 1900 the population of the United States doubled, to just over 76 million people. New machines and fertilizers enabled farmers to increase the number of acres under cultivation. As a result, farmers were able to dramatically expand production and feed the nation's soaring population.

However, the law of supply and demand worked against farmers. As they flooded the market with more wheat, corn, and cotton, the prices of these commodities steadily fell. For example, between 1870 and 1890, Midwestern and Southern farmers nearly doubled their harvests of wheat and cotton. Yet during these two decades, increasingly frustrated farmers watched as the price of a bushel of wheat dropped from $1.04 to $0.84, while the price of a pound of cotton plunged from 24 cents to just 11 cents.

B. THE ROLE OF THE RAILROADS

Angry farmers blamed the railroads for their economic plight. Railroads were a mixed blessing. They made large-scale agriculture possible by transporting corn, wheat, cattle, and cotton to urban markets and then shipping heavy machinery and supplies to rural farms. But at the same time, farmers bitterly complained that the railroads abused their monopolies by charging exorbitant freight rates. Average freight costs increased every year between 1870 and 1893. In one particularly egregious example, the Burlington line charged its customers west of the Missouri four times what it charged customers east of the river.

C. MOUNTING DEBTS

Mounting debts provided yet another example of a powerful economic force farmers could not control. Farmers had to borrow heavily to pay for seed, fertilizers, and expensive machinery. Following the Civil War, the American economy experienced a prolonged period of deflation, as both prices and the supply of money declined. As a result, a farmer had to pay back loans with dollars that had increased in value since the time of the loan. Debt-ridden farmers accused banks of using excessively high interest rates to steal the fruits of their labor.

TOPIC 14.2
THE FIRST FARMERS' ORGANIZATIONS

A. THE GRANGER MOVEMENT

Many farmers endured a lonely existence on widely separated farms. The Granger movement began as a social and educational organization in response to the farmers' isolation. As local Grange chapters spread across the southern and western farm belts, membership rolls reached 1.5 million people by 1874.

The Grange soon became more than an organization to end the loneliness of farm life. Organizers founded cooperatives, through which farmers sold their crops and bought supplies as a group. They even tried to manufacture farm machinery. At the same time, the Grange began to fight the railroads. Led by Illinois, several states passed "Granger laws," regulating railroad freight rates.

The Grange's early success proved to be short-lived. Many of the cooperatives failed because of mismanagement. Meanwhile, the railroads won decisions in federal courts that successfully challenged the state regulations. By 1890, the Supreme Court had ruled that states could not regulate railroads engaged in interstate commerce. These setbacks led to the decline of the Grange.

B. THE FARMERS' ALLIANCE

The farmers still had much to complain about. As the Grange lost members, a new organization known as the Farmers' Alliance grew in size and significance. Founded in Texas in the mid-1870s, the new movement quickly spread through the Southern and Plains states. A growing chorus of angry farmers demanded political action to address falling commodity prices, rising freight charges, and increasing interest rates.

Alliance leaders described their surging movement as a "grand army of reform." Unlike the established Democratic and Republican parties, they welcomed women members. As a result, talented women such as Mary Elizabeth Lease embraced this opportunity and assumed key leadership roles.

Racism posed a formidable obstacle to including African Americans in the reform army. Alliance leaders such as Georgia's Tom Watson understood the importance of forging a black-white alliance. "You are kept apart," he told an interracial audience, "that you may be separately fleeced of your earnings."

Unable to overcome entrenched racial attitudes, black farmers formed the Colored Farmers' National Alliance. The organization emphasized economic justice while avoiding issues of social equality. By 1890, the Colored Farmers' National Alliance claimed over one million members.

TOPIC 14.3
THE BIRTH OF THE POPULIST PARTY

A. "RAISE LESS CORN AND MORE HELL"

America's farmers increasingly saw themselves as victims of an unjust political and economic system. As their debts continued to mount, struggling farmers became convinced that neither the Democrats nor the Republicans would address the problems caused by greedy bankers and arrogant railroad executives. They increasingly believed that a corrupt partnership between government and big business created special laws designed to benefit Wall Street financiers and unregulated monopolies.

Mary Elizabeth Lease captured the farmers' increasingly militant mood. Blessed with a deep, rich voice and a commanding presence, Lease delivered over 160 speeches as she crisscrossed the country during the winter and fall of 1890. She repeatedly lambasted predatory railroads and especially the Wall Street "money power." She passionately declared, "It is no longer a government of the people, by the people, and for the people, but a government of Wall Street, by Wall Street, and for Wall Street." Lease underscored her audience's rebellious mood by forcefully urging her listeners to "raise less corn and more hell."

B. THE POPULIST PLATFORM

The wave of agrarian discontent gave birth to the People's or POPULIST PARTY. Alliance leaders discussed plans for a third party at conventions held in Cincinnati in May 1891 and St. Louis in February 1892. Finally, in July 1892, 1,300 enthusiastic delegates met in Omaha, Nebraska, to adopt a platform and choose a candidate for the fall presidential election.

The Populist Party platform began with a grim assessment of the health of American democracy. It described a nation "brought to the verge of moral, political, and material ruin" by the growth of corporate power and economic inequality. The platform preamble emphatically concluded, "The fruits of the toil of millions are boldly stolen to build up colossal fortunes for the few."

The platform did more than offer a gloomy assessment of the nation's current condition; it also put forth an ambitious list of proposals to shift power back to the people. For example, the Constitution mandated that state legislatures choose U.S. senators. The platform addressed this elitist procedure by calling for an amendment providing for the popular election of senators.

The Populist platform devoted special attention to economic reforms. It forthrightly called for government control of the nation's railroads, declaring that "The railroad corporations will either own the people or the people must own the railroads." The Populists proposed to prevent further accumulations of wealth by supporting a graduated income tax, where rates would rise as personal income levels rose. And finally, the platform called for the free and unlimited coinage of silver. Populist leaders argued that "free silver" would put more money in circulation, thus spurring inflation and promoting growth. Rising prices for farm commodities would increase profits and reduce debts.

C. THE ELECTION OF 1892

The Populists nominated former congressman and Union general James B. Weaver of Iowa to run for president. Weaver polled over one million votes, more than any previous third-party candidate. The Populist success reminded many political observers of the 1856 election, when the Republican Party burst onto the nation's political scene. Buoyed by their success, the Populists eagerly looked forward to the 1896 presidential election.

TOPIC 14.4
THE ELECTION OF 1896

A. THE CANDIDATES—WILLIAM MCKINLEY AND WILLIAM JENNINGS BRYAN

In the spring of 1893 a panic on Wall Street touched off a severe economic depression. Within a few months, over 15,000 businesses and 600 banks closed. By the following year, one-fifth of the nation's workers had lost their jobs.

The Republicans correctly sensed that the deepening depression weakened President Cleveland and the Democrats. They confidently nominated William McKinley, the popular governor of Ohio. The Republican Party platform supported high protective tariffs and forthrightly declared, "the existing gold standard must be maintained."

Pro-silver delegates controlled the Democratic convention in Chicago. The Silverites promptly repudiated President Cleveland and wrote a platform calling for the free coinage of silver. The Democrats now had an issue but still lacked a candidate. That changed when William Jennings Bryan, a 36-year-old former congressman from Nebraska, addressed the convention.

Although already a famous orator, the youthful Bryan had not been considered a serious candidate for president. Known as the "Boy Orator," he possessed a powerful voice that reached to the farthest corners of the vast auditorium. Over 15,000 delegates listened intently as he reminded them, "We have petitioned and our petitions have been scorned." Bryan then thundered defiance as he reached his free silver conclusion: "You shall not press down upon the brow of labor this crown of thorns. You shall not crucify mankind on a cross of gold!"

Bryan's electrifying "Cross of Gold" speech galvanized the convention. Cheering delegates danced in the aisles and triumphantly hoisted Bryan onto their shoulders. Filled with conviction and pride, party leaders pledged their support for Bryan. The next day, euphoric delegates wearing silver badges and waving silver banners nominated Bryan for President.

B. THE POPULIST DILEMMA

The Democrats' surprising decision to nominate a pro-silver candidate forced the Populists to resolve an insoluble dilemma. If they chose to support Bryan, the Populists risked losing their identity as an independent third party. However, if they nominated their own candidate, the Populists risked being blamed for dividing the silver vote and helping to elect McKinley. Hoping to win a historic victory for their key issues, the deeply divided Populist delegates chose to endorse Bryan after a bitter debate.

C. AN UNPRECEDENTED CAMPAIGN

Prior to 1896, presidential candidates refrained from actively campaigning. Bryan broke with this tradition by using trains to crisscross the country. In just four months, he traveled over 18,000 miles and delivered 600 speeches to as many as five million people.

McKinley and his campaign manager Mark Hanna followed a very different strategy. Rather than barnstorm the country, McKinley remained in his home in Canton, Ohio. However, he did not sit in a rocking chair and chat with individual visitors. Instead, friendly railroad companies provided reduced fares, enabling 750,000 people to visit Canton and hear McKinley deliver carefully crafted speeches promising "good work, good wages, and good money." At the same time, a small army of 1,400 Republican speakers spread across the country. They extolled McKinley and warned of dire consequences if Bryan won the election.

McKinley's well-organized campaign won a convincing victory. He received 7,035,638 popular votes and 271 electoral votes, to 6,467,946 popular votes and 176 electoral votes for Bryan. Nearly 80 percent of the eligible voters cast their ballots in one of America's highest electoral turnouts.

D. THE DEMISE OF THE POPULIST PARTY

The election of 1896 led to the demise of the Populist Party. Bryan's defeat demoralized its supporters while dragging down hundreds of Populist state and local candidates. At the same time, the economic forces that fueled the Populist uprising unexpectedly changed. Gold strikes in South Africa, the Yukon, and Australia increased the money supply, thus ending the demand for free silver. Meanwhile, crop failures in Europe sparked increasing demand for American wheat and other farm commodities. Rising prices enabled farmers to reduce their debts and enjoy a period of prosperity that continued until the end of World War I. As the twentieth century began, the Populists and their economic causes seemed a distant memory.

TOPIC 14.5
THE IMPACT OF THE POPULIST MOVEMENT

A. ECONOMIC IMPACT

The Populists challenged the *laissez-faire* doctrine that favored minimal government interference in the economy. They argued that *laissez-faire* policies allowed the railroads and other monopolies to become too powerful. The Populists also decried the growing disparity between the great concentrations of corporate wealth and the relative weakness of organized labor.

The Populist platform addressed these economic problems by calling for the nationalization of the railroads, the unlimited coinage of silver, and a graduated income tax. However, McKinley's victory in the 1896 presidential election doomed these proposals. While the Populists failed to achieve their immediate policies, their broader critique of the American economy inspired a new generation of Progressive reformers. Supported by a growing Progressive movement, presidents Roosevelt, Taft, and Wilson all initiated campaigns to break up powerful trusts. In addition, the Sixteenth Amendment gave Congress the power to lay and collect graduated income taxes.

B. POLITICAL IMPACT

The Populists produced a remarkable group of articulate leaders who championed a variety of reforms designed to promote more direct democracy. For example, the Populist platform called for the direct election of senators by voters instead of state legislatures. The Seventeenth Amendment successfully implemented this reform.

Despite their long-term political influence, the Populists failed to create an enduring political party. The strength of white supremacy in the South prevented the Populists from uniting poor white and black farmers. At the same time, northern laborers believed that the Populist demand for inflation would erode the value of their paychecks. And finally, the McKinley campaign successfully broadened the Republican coalition to include the majority of northern urban workers and Catholic immigrants.

CHAPTER 14
PRACTICE QUESTIONS

MULTIPLE-CHOICE QUESTIONS

Questions 1–2 refer to the excerpt below.

"When the [Civil] War ended the colored people had nothing much on which to live….They had to get the local merchant or someone else to supply the food for the family to eat while the first crop was being made. For every dollar's worth of provisions so advanced the local merchant charged from 12 to 30 percent interest. In order to be sure that he secured his principal and interest a mortgage or lien was taken on the crop….Of course the farmers could pay no such interest and the end of the first year found them in debt—the 2nd year they tried again, but there was the old debt and the new interest to pay, and in this way the 'mortgage system' has gotten a hold on everything that it seems impossible to shake off."

> Booker T. Washington, letter to novelist George Washington Cable, October 8, 1889

1. **Which of the following most directly followed from Washington's description of the problems faced by African American farmers?**

    A. The election of 17 African Americans to Congress
    B. The industrialization of some segments of the Southern economy
    C. The formation of the Colored Farmers' National Alliance
    D. The federal government's new campaign to fight poverty in the Deep South

2. **The plight of Southern sharecroppers most closely resembles the economic conditions faced by**

    A. small town bankers
    B. Midwestern farmers
    C. urban machine politicians
    D. settlement house workers

Questions 3–5 refer to the excerpt below.

"Wall Street owns the country. It is no longer a government of the people, by the people, and for the people, but a government of Wall Street, by Wall Street, and for Wall Street. The great common people of this country are slaves, and monopoly is the master. The West and South are bound and prostrate before the manufacturing East....The [political] parties lie to us and the political speakers mislead us....We want money, land, and transportation. We want the abolition of the National Banks, and we want the power to make loans direct from the federal government. We want the foreclosure system wiped out."

Mary Elizabeth Lease, speech given in 1890

3. **Lease's accusations in the excerpt best reflect which of the following?**
   A. Anxieties about the influx of immigrants to Northern cities
   B. Concerns about the decline of the Democratic Party
   C. Outrage at the failure of Congress to extend voting rights to women
   D. Anger at the growth of corporate power in agriculture and the economy

4. **Which of the following groups would be most likely to agree with Lease's accusations?**
   A. Labor leaders
   B. Wall Street bankers
   C. Catholic immigrants
   D. *Laissez-faire* economists

5. **Lease's speech suggests that she would strongly support**
   A. the feminist movement
   B. the Dawes Act
   C. a stronger government role in the economy
   D. a new network of transcontinental railroads

Questions 6–9 refer to the excerpt below.

"Nothing has done more to injure the [Western] region than these freight rates. The railroads have retarded its growth as much as they first hastened it. The rates are often four times as large as Eastern rates....These freight rates have been especially burdensome to the farmers who are far from their selling and buying markets....Another fact which has incited the farm against corporations is the bold and unblushing participation of the railways in politics....[The] railroads have secured an iron grip upon legislatures."

F.B. Tracy, "Why the Farmers Revolted," *Forum*, October 1893

6. **The author most directly expresses an economic perspective that would support**
   A. the use of federal power to redistribute wealth
   B. government subsidies for transportation
   C. efforts by workers to organize local and national unions
   D. increased government regulation of railroads

7. **Problems associated with the conditions described in this excerpt most directly led to**
   A. the growth of utopian communities
   B. the formation of the Populist Party
   C. the formation of new labor unions to confront the railroads
   D. the enactment of government subsidies to support struggling farmers

8. **Which of the following best describes the Supreme Court's ruling on state laws limiting freight rates?**
   A. The Supreme Court deferred to the Interstate Commerce Commission as the final authority on establishing freight rates
   B. The Supreme Court used the Sherman Anti-Trust Act to justify its support for state laws limiting freight rates
   C. The Supreme Court reversed its *laissez-faire* philosophy toward corporations
   D. The Supreme Court ruled regulation of interstate commerce an "exclusive" federal right

9. **Which measure did the Populists embrace as a way to address the railways' "iron grip upon legislatures?"**

   A. The unlimited coinage of silver
   B. The use of federal power to redistribute wealth
   C. The passage of a constitutional amendment providing for the direct election of U.S. senators
   D. The passage of a constitutional amendment permitting a graduated income tax

Questions 10–11 refer to the excerpt below.

"[We] seek to restore the government of the Republic to the hands of 'the plain people,' with which class it originated….Our country finds itself confronted by conditions for which there is no precedent in the history of the world;… We pledge that if given power we will labor to correct these evils by wise and reasonable legislation, in accordance with the terms of our platform. We believe that the power of government—in other words, of the people—should be expanded (as in the case of the postal service) as rapidly and as far as the good sense of an intelligent people and the teaching of experience shall justify, to the end that oppression, injustice, and poverty shall eventually cease in the land."

   People's (Populist) Party platform, 1892

10. **Which of the following later groups held ideas closest to those expressed in the Populist Party platform?**

   A. New Deal reformers
   B. Social Darwinists
   C. Nativists
   D. Supporters of Senator Joseph McCarthy

11. **The activism advocated in the Populist Party platform most directly inspired reform programs by**

   A. American Indians
   B. Environmentalists
   C. Progressives
   D. Christian evangelicals

Questions 12–15 refer to the excerpt below.

"If they dare to come out in the open field and defend the gold standard as a good thing, we will fight them to the uttermost. Having behind us the producing masses of this nation and the world, supported by the commercial interests, the laboring interests, and the toilers everywhere, we will answer their demand for a gold standard by saying to them: You shall not press down upon the brow of labor this crown of thorns; you shall not crucify mankind upon a cross of gold."

William Jennings Bryan, speech at the Democratic convention, 1896

12. Bryan's Cross of Gold speech was primarily an expression of his

A. fundamentalist religious beliefs
B. advocacy of free and unlimited coinage of silver
C. anti-imperialist convictions
D. opposition to teaching the theory of evolution in public schools

13. Which of the following groups would most likely agree with Bryan's main claim?

A. urban workers
B. Wall Street financiers
C. western farmers
D. white-collar and professional workers

14. The excerpt is best understood as a direct response to which of the following economic developments?

A. The first Red Scare
B. The prevalence of sharecropping in the South
C. The increasing usage and exploitation of western landscapes
D. The growing debts of farmers

15. The sentiment expressed in this excerpt best reflects

A. the growing conflict between rural and urban interests
B. the nativist resistance to the wave of immigrants from Southern and Eastern Europe
C. the need to recognize labor unions and collective bargaining
D. the efforts by Southern leaders to promote greater industrial development

MULTIPLE-CHOICE ANSWERS

1. C	5. C	9. C	13. C
2. B	6. D	10. A	14. D
3. D	7. B	11. C	15. A
4. A	8. D	12. B	

SHORT-ANSWER QUESTIONS

Question 1
Using the excerpts below, answer A, B, and C.

"Of course, the farmer who has overtraded, or expanded his operation beyond his means, in a time of commercial depression is affected just as anyone else is in like conditions.

"The simple fact that we produce more wheat than we consume, and that, consequently, the price of the whole crop is determined, not by the markets within this country, but by the world-markets, is sufficient to put wheat, as regards its price, in a different class from those articles whose markets are local….And it need not be said that many wheat-growing farmers make little or no allowance for events beyond their limited range of local information….

"The sudden enlargement of the supply without any corresponding increase of demand produced that alarming fall in the price of wheat which has been made the farmer's excuse for thinking that silver is the magic panaceas for all his ills…."

> J. Laurence Laughlin, "Causes of Agricultural Unrest," *Atlantic Monthly* (November, 1896)

"It is clear that trusts are contrary to public policy and hence in conflict with the Common law. They are monopolies organized to destroy competition and restrain trade….Once they secure control of a given line of business, they are masters of the situation and can dictate to the two great classes with which they deal—the producer of the raw material and the consumer of the finished product. They limit the price of the raw material so as to impoverish the producer, drive him to a single market, reduce the price of every class of labor connected with the trade, throw out of employment large numbers of persons who had been before engaged in a meritorious calling and finally…

they increase the price to the consumer....The main weapons of the trusts are threats, intimidation, bribery, fraud, wreck, and pillage."

James B. Weaver, *A Call to Action: An Interpretation of the Great Uprising, Its Sources and Causes* (1892)

A. Briefly describe ONE major difference between Laughlin's and Weaver's historical interpretations of the causes of the Populist revolt.

B. Briefly explain how ONE specific historical event or development from the period 1880–1896 that is not specifically mentioned in the excerpts could be used to support Laughlin's argument.

C. Briefly explain how ONE specific historical event or development from the period 1880–1896 that is not specifically mentioned in the excerpts could be used to support Weaver's argument.

Question 2

Using the table below, answer A, B, and C.

Agricultural Prices in Dollars per Unit, 1865–1900

Year	Wheat		Cotton		Corn	
	Price Per Buschel	Millions of Bushels Produced	Price Per Pound	1,000 Bales Produced	Price Per Buschel	Millions of Bushels Produced
1865	2.16	NA	.83	2,094	NA	NA
1870	1.04	254	.24	4,352	.52	1,125
1875	1.01	314	.15	4,631	.42	1,450
1880	.95	502	.12	6,606	.39	1,707
1885	.77	400	.11	6,576	.32	2,058
1890	.84	449	.11	8,653	.50	1,650
1895	.51	542	.07	7,162	.25	2,535
1900	.62	599	.10	10,124	.35	2,662

Source: Historical Statistics of the United States

A. Briefly explain ONE specific historical development that accounts for the change in agricultural production and prices between 1865 and 1900.

B. Briefly explain ONE specific historical effect of the changes in agricultural production and prices between 1865 and 1900.

C. Briefly explain a SECOND specific historical effect of the changes in agricultural production and prices between 1865 and 1900.

SHORT-ANSWER ANSWERS

Question 1

A. Laughlin argues that farmers are to blame for their economic plight. They overproduce crops and pay little attention to fluctuations in demand from world markets. In contrast, Weaver argues that monopolies are the central reason for the economic plight of American farmers. Monopolies destroy competition, restrain trade, and limit the price of raw materials.

B. American farmers used new machinery and chemical fertilizers to dramatically increase the number of acres under cultivation. This had the inevitable effect of increasing supply, lowering prices, and raising debt levels.

C. The railroads abused their monopolies by charging exorbitant freight rates. Average rates increased every year between 1870 and 1893.

Question 2

A. Improved farm machinery, irrigation, and chemical fertilizers led to the increased production of wheat, cotton, and corn. As the supply of these commodities increased, prices steadily decreased.

B. Distress among farmers led to the emergence of movements such as the Grange, Farmer's Alliance, and Populists.

C. The wave of agrarian discontent gave birth to the People's or Populist Party. The Populist platform called for government control of the railroads, free coinage of silver, a gradual increase in tax rates, and the direct election of U.S. Senators.

CHAPTER 15
THE COLD WAR
1945–1953

STRATEGIC IMPORTANCE

The Cold War movement generates a significant cluster of questions and exam points. A careful analysis of recent APUSH exams revealed that questions about the origins and early stages of the Cold War totaled an average of seven points per exam. Remember, you only need 75 points to earn a three, 95 points to earn a four, and 110 points to earn a five. This chapter is thus an important part of your coalition of points.

KEY POINTS AND HISTORIC GENERALIZATIONS

- The United States emerged from World War II as the world's foremost military, economic, and technological superpower.

- The COLD WAR was a prolonged period of economic and political rivalry between the United States and the Soviet Union. It began with the announcement of the Truman Doctrine in 1947 and ended with the fall of the Berlin Wall in 1989 and the collapse of the Soviet Union in 1991.

- CONTAINMENT was America's Cold War strategy of blocking the expansion of Soviet influence. George Kennan first articulated the policy in his famous Long Telegram and article in *Foreign Affairs*.

- COLLECTIVE SECURITY is a principle of mutual support in which all nations in an alliance pledge to consider an attack on one as an attack on all.

- The Truman Doctrine committed the United States to use its military and economic strength to block the expansion of Soviet influence in strategic areas such as Greece, Turkey, and Western Europe.

- The Marshall Plan committed the United States to provide a massive program of economic assistance to help the nations of Western Europe recover from the devastation caused by World War II.

- The Berlin Blockade marked the first great Cold War test of containment. The Berlin Airlift successfully thwarted the Soviet attempt to cut off supplies to West Berlin.

- The United States, Canada, and ten Western European nations formed the NATO Alliance as a military bulwark to block Soviet expansion. The alliance operates on the principle of collective security.

- The United States emerged from World War II as a global superpower. Led by President Truman, the United States abandoned its traditional isolationist policies and pledged to come to the aid of democratic governments throughout the world.

- Historian John Lewis Gaddis argues that the Cold War emerged from an "interactive system" in which the actions and responses of the United States and the Soviet Union produced an escalating spiral of mutual distrust and antagonism. For example, the Soviet's Berlin Blockade prompted the Berlin Airlift. These actions helped convince the United States and its allies to form the NATO Alliance. The Soviet Union then responded by forming the Warsaw Pact.

- The North Korean surprise invasion of South Korea precipitated the Korean War. President Truman did not want to be accused of "losing" South Korea. He did not ask Congress for a declaration of war. Instead, American troops fought under the auspices of the United Nations.

- The costly limited war in Korea provided a source of frustration that contributed to the rise of a period of paranoia and unsubstantiated accusations of disloyalty known as McCARTHYISM.

TOPIC 15.1
FROM COOPERATION TO CONFRONTATION

A. THE YALTA CONFERENCE

On February 3, 1945, the leaders of the victorious Grand Alliance—Franklin D. Roosevelt, Winston Churchill, and Josef Stalin—met at the Black Sea resort city of Yalta. The Allied leaders toasted the imminent defeat of Germany. With World War II nearly over, Churchill optimistically looked forward to "the broad sunlight of victorious peace."

Victorious peace, however, meant different things to each of the three leaders. For Churchill, it meant a free and democratic Europe that Britain would lead thanks to its centuries-old parliamentary tradition and its mighty empire. For Stalin, victorious peace meant increased Soviet power and a chance to protect the USSR from any further German invasion. Finally, for Roosevelt, victorious peace meant a world in which democracy could thrive under American leadership.

The discussions held during the next eight days reflected these differences. The Yalta conference produced a series of compromises. Churchill and Roosevelt agreed to a temporary division of Germany. Meanwhile, Stalin agreed to permit free elections in Poland and other Eastern European countries then occupied by the Red Army. He also agreed to participate in an international conference to take place in April in San Francisco. There, FDR's dream of a United Nations would become a reality. "We really believed in our hearts," one Roosevelt advisor later recalled, "that this was the dawn of the new day we had all been praying for and talking about for so many years." Yet within a short time this optimistic spirit vanished, and the United States and the Soviet Union became bitter rivals in a long postwar period of confrontation and rivalry known as the COLD WAR.

B. THE IRON CURTAIN

Stalin believed he had compelling reasons for trying to dominate Eastern Europe. World War II had seriously weakened the Soviet Union. It had suffered 20 million casualties and lost about one-fourth of its capital assets. In contrast, the United States emerged from World War II as the world's strongest military and economic power. It possessed a monopoly over nuclear weapons and an industrial economy that produced almost half of the world's manufactured goods.

Acutely aware of America's strength and his own weakness, Stalin wanted only friendly countries as neighbors. He interpreted America's insistence upon free elections as a poorly concealed attempt to push the Soviet Union out of Eastern Europe. "A freely elected government in any of the Eastern European countries would be anti-Soviet," Stalin admitted, "and that we cannot allow."

Stalin's determination to dominate Eastern Europe became a reality following the defeat of Nazi Germany. The process of creating communist dictatorships began with the installation of pro-Soviet coalition governments. Since the Soviets always retained control over the military and police in each country, they easily dominated the government. Communist officials censored all books, newspapers, and radio broadcasts and strictly controlled all houses of worship.

Churchill recognized that the creation of Soviet-dominated puppet governments violated the principle of national self-determination and posed a threat to Western Europe. In a speech delivered on March 6, 1947, at Westminster College in Fulton, Missouri, he warned that "an Iron Curtain has descended across the Continent." Churchill insisted that this was "certainly not the liberated Europe we fought for."

Churchill predicted that the Soviets would try to avoid war. "What they desire," he said, "is the fruits of war and the indefinite expansion of their power and doctrines." Since the Russians admired strength and scoffed at military weakness, Churchill urged the United States to take a strong stand against Soviet expansion.

C. GEORGE KENNAN AND CONTAINMENT

Stalin's aggressive postwar actions did not surprise George Kennan. A leading U.S. State Department expert on Russian history, he believed that Soviet hostility toward the capitalist nations would remain a constant factor for years to come. In an influential Long Telegram and subsequent essay published in *Foreign Affairs*, Kennan argued that Communist ideology led Soviet leaders to believe that "the outside world was hostile and that it was their duty eventually to overthrow the political forces beyond their borders." Given this antagonism, Kennan urged the United States to adopt a policy of "long-term, patient but firm, and vigorous containment of Soviet expansive tendencies." By CONTAINMENT, he meant adopting a strategic policy of blocking the expansion of Soviet military power and Communist ideology.

Kennan acknowledged that containment would place a tremendous burden upon American resources. He also predicted, however, that containment would ultimately produce changes within the Soviet Union. He reasoned that if the United States blocked the Soviet Union's expansionist drive, its leaders would be forced to turn inward and reform their totalitarian system.

D. THE TRUMAN DOCTRINE

Stalin did not limit his ambitious program of expansion to Eastern Europe. In early 1947, the lengthening shadow of Soviet pressure threatened to undermine the independence of both Turkey and Greece. Conditions were particularly perilous in Greece, where a civil war raged between Communist insurgents and supporters of the pro-Western Greek monarchy.

Almost one year after Churchill delivered his Iron Curtain speech, Britain announced it could no longer afford to give aid to Greece and Turkey. An American official later noted, "Great Britain within the hour handed the job of world leadership with all its burden and all its glory to the United States." President Truman decided he had to act. On March 12, 1947, he asked a joint session of Congress for $400 million in economic and military assistance for Greece and Turkey.

Truman did not stop with a request for money. The United States, he declared, could survive only in a world in which freedom flourished. He then articulated what became known as the Truman Doctrine: "I believe that it must be the policy of the United States to support free people who are resisting attempted subjugations by armed minorities or outside pressures."

Congress responded by approving Truman's request for economic aid to assist Greece and Turkey. The Truman Doctrine thus marked a turning point in American history. After the First World War, America had withdrawn into isolation, leaving Europe to contend with its own problems. As the leader of the Free World, the United States now recognized a responsibility to protect Europe, defend freedom, and use its power to limit the spread of Communism throughout the world. "The free people of the world look to us for support in maintaining their freedom," declared Truman. "If we falter in our leadership, we may endanger the peace of the world."

TOPIC 15.2
CONTAINMENT IN EUROPE

A. THE MARSHALL PLAN

World War II devastated large parts of Europe. Desperate Europeans faced acute shortages of food, fuel, and industrial raw materials. In both 1946 and 1947, agricultural and industrial production in all European countries fell below pre-war levels. Economic weakness threatened political instability, making Europe vulnerable to Soviet influence. For example, the Communist Party enjoyed growing support among French and Italian industrial workers.

The Truman administration recognized that the shattered European economy required a massive infusion of economic aid. In a commencement address at Harvard University on June 5, 1947, Secretary of State George C. Marshall outlined a bold plan of economic assistance to all of Europe, including the Soviet Union. He pledged, "Our policy is directed not against a country or doctrine but against hunger, poverty, desperation, and chaos." Marshall's assurances did not assuage Stalin's deep suspicions of American actions. He refused American aid and claimed the Marshall Plan represented a hostile act against the Soviet Union and Eastern Europe.

Stalin's rejection did not deter Congress from enacting the Marshall Plan. American economic aid began flowing into Europe in 1948. During the next four years, 16 Western European countries received $13 billion, the equivalent of about $200 billion in 2019. The Marshall Plan helped to alleviate food shortages, stimulate industrial production, and forge new bonds of friendship between the United States and Western Europe. The program thus started the process of economic integration that led to the Common Market and ultimately the European Union.

B. THE BERLIN AIRLIFT

At the end of World War II, the Allies divided Germany into four separate occupation zones. As Soviet-American relations deteriorated, Cold War tensions increasingly focused on Berlin. As Germany's largest city and former capital, Berlin had a tremendous political and psychological significance. The Allies recognized this fact when they divided Berlin into four separate zones controlled by the United States, Britain, France, and the Soviet Union. The city itself, however, lay in East Germany, 110 miles inside the Soviet-occupied zone.

Stalin viewed the presence of the Western powers in Berlin as an obstacle to his plan to dominate East Germany. On June 24, 1948, he cut all the roads, rail lines, and canals linking the city to West Germany. Stalin knew that the vulnerable and now isolated city only had about a 30-day supply of food to feed its population of 2.2 million people. He believed that the blockade would convincingly demonstrate that the United States had neither the power nor the will to support Berlin.

Truman recognized that the Berlin Blockade represented a direct challenge to America's new policy of containment. He rejected the options of ordering a discreet withdrawal or provoking a military confrontation by sending an armed convoy through East Germany. At the same time, Truman refused to withdraw. "We are going to stay, period!," he firmly declared.

Truman surprised Stalin by choosing to supply West Berlin by air. Although this risky strategy avoided a military confrontation, it required a massive and unprecedented airlift to supply the 4,500 tons of food, coal, and medicine the people of West Berlin needed every day. To guard against any Soviet attempt to intercept the airlift, Truman transferred 60 strategic bombers to bases in Great Britain.

The Berlin Airlift proved to be an inspiring success. American, British, and French aviators flew 277,804 missions and delivered 2.3 million tons of supplies in just 321 days. In addition, American pilots raised the spirits of West Berlin children by parachuting thousands of toys and candy bars.

Stalin realized that he had been outwitted. The constant roar of planes over Berlin provided a vivid demonstration of American determination. The crisis changed the relationship between Germany and the Western Allies from that of occupiers and occupied to partners in a joint struggle to defend the Free World. Faced with these strategic and psychological realities, Stalin lifted the blockade on May 12, 1949.

The airlift underscored Berlin's importance as a visible symbol of the Cold War in Europe. In 1961, the Soviets surrounded the city with a 28-mile concrete wall, designed to prevent East Germans from escaping to freedom in West

Berlin. The Berlin Wall quickly became the supreme symbol of the Iron Curtain in Europe.

C. RIVAL ALLIANCES

The Berlin Airlift convinced American leaders of the need to organize an alliance to protect Western Europe against possible Soviet aggression. On April 4, 1949, ten European countries joined the United States and Canada in signing the North Atlantic Treaty Organization (NATO). The pact operated on the principle of COLLECTIVE SECURITY. Article 5 stipulated "an armed attack against one or more of the signatories in Europe or North America shall be considered an attack against them all."

NATO represented an example of a permanent alliance that George Washington warned against in his Farewell Address. America's decision to join a peacetime alliance based on collective security marked a decisive break from the country's long-standing isolationist past. The Truman administration thus positioned the United States as a superpower, ready to accept its global responsibilities.

The Soviet Union did not view NATO as a defensive alliance. Instead, its leaders criticized NATO as an example of how America's demand for new markets and additional raw materials turned it into an expansionist power, threatening Soviet security. In 1955, the Soviets responded by forming a rival military alliance with their Eastern European satellites called the Warsaw Pact. Within less than a decade, the United States and the Soviet Union went from being allies to being leaders of hostile alliances, facing each other across a tense and divided Europe.

TOPIC 15.3
COLD WAR SHOCKS AND RESPONSES

A. "THIS IS NOW A DIFFERENT WORLD"

The Senate's ratification of America's participation in the NATO Alliance and the successful end of the Berlin Airlift marked great achievements for the Truman administration. However, in the fall of 1949, alarming events in Siberia and China shocked the United States and dramatically escalated Cold War tensions.

Stalin responded to America's nuclear monopoly by launching a massive program to build a Soviet atomic bomb. On August 29, 1949, Russian scientists successfully tested a nuclear device in a remote area of Siberia. Within days, American high-altitude reconnaissance flights detected unusual levels of radiation in the lower stratosphere. After carefully studying the data, Atomic

Energy Commission scientists reported their findings to President Truman. Shocked by the news, Truman repeatedly asked, "Are you sure?"

Truman revealed the news to the American public on September 23, 1949. In a terse official statement he announced that the Russian detonation of an atomic explosion had ended America's nuclear monopoly. Although the Soviet success did not surprise American physicists, it stunned the public. Senator Vandenberg captured the nation's sense of anxiety and dread when he declared, "This is now a different world."

Vandenberg's appraisal proved to be accurate. The Soviet bomb accelerated the nuclear arms race. Within a short time, both superpowers began testing thermonuclear or hydrogen bombs hundreds of times more powerful than the bombs that destroyed Hiroshima and Nagasaki. The nuclear arms race became a defining feature of the Cold War as the United States and the Soviet Union devoted enormous resources to produce fearsome weapons of mass destruction.

B. THE FALL OF CHINA

While Americans began to absorb the implications of the Soviet atomic bomb, shocking events in China rocked the Truman administration. During the years following World War II, a bitter civil war raged between the Nationalists led by Chiang Kai-shek and the Communists led by Mao Zedong. As the recognized leader of China, Chiang appeared to have the upper hand. His army outnumbered Mao's forces by about two to one. In addition, the United States supported the Nationalists with about $2 billion in aid.

Despite Chiang's seemingly formidable advantages, Mao's disciplined forces steadily gained ground. Corrupt, incompetent officers weakened the Nationalist army. As a result, Chiang's demoralized troops often turned and fled rather than fight the enemy. Almost 75 percent of the military supplies sent by the United States fell into Communist hands. A soaring inflation that doubled prices 67 times in less than three years ruined the Chinese middle class. An American military advisor summed up the rapidly deteriorating situation when he reported that the Nationalist losses were due to "the world's worst leadership" and "a complete loss of will to fight."

On October 1, 1949, 300,000 cheering people gathered in Beijing's Tiananmen Square to witness Mao triumphantly proclaim the birth of the People's Republic of China. A few months later, Mao signed a Treaty of Friendship with the Soviet Union. Meanwhile, Chiang and the remnants of his defeated army fled to Formosa (present-day Taiwan), an island 110 miles east of the the Chinese mainland. The United States refused to establish diplomatic relations with Mao's new government and instead continued to recognize Chiang.

The Communist victory in China had far-reaching consequences. It triggered a wave of criticism that played an important role in the rise of a Red Scare and the success of Joseph McCarthy. At the same time, Mao's victory caused a major shift in America's policy toward Japan.

C. THE RECONSTRUCTION OF JAPAN

World War II devastated Japan and caused high casualties and widespread destruction. About three million Japanese lost their lives, including more than half a million civilians. America's intensive strategic bombing left Tokyo in ruins and damaged industrial facilities throughout the country. Japan capitulated after nuclear attacks on Hiroshima and Nagasaki caused the deaths of 210,000 civilians.

Truman recognized the importance of transforming Japan from a defeated enemy into a supportive Cold War ally. He therefore refused to divide Japan into multinational zones like those in Germany. He appointed General Douglas MacArthur Supreme Commander of the Allied Powers of occupation. MacArthur promptly implemented policies designed to both demilitarize and democratize the defeated country. He began by disbanding the Japanese armed forces and removing their military equipment. Under his direction, Japan adopted a new constitution that created a parliamentary government, renounced war, and allowed women to vote and own property.

The fall of China convinced the Truman administration to view Japan as a bulwark against the spread of communism in Asia. United States economic aid helped to revive Japan's shattered economy. In September 1951, the U.S. signed a treaty ending America's military occupation while also retaining key military bases. Japan thus became an important American ally and a noteworthy example of the success of democracy and free-market economics.

TOPIC 15.4
THE KOREAN WAR

A. THE COLD WAR TURNS HOT

The Korean peninsula is no stranger to war. It shares a long border with China and extends to a point just 100 miles from Japan. As a result, both of these powers have vied for control of the mountainous peninsula. At the same time, Korean nationalists resented foreign domination and wanted to unify their country.

At the end of World War II, American and Soviet troops arbitrarily divided the Korean peninsula at the 38th parallel. Although this began as a temporary arrangement, the chill of the Cold War soon froze the boundary, thus creating two rival Korean states—a Soviet-sponsored Communist government in the north and an American-supported, pro-Western government in the south.

The communist dictator of North Korea, Kim Il Sung, persuaded Stalin to approve an invasion of South Korea. The North Korean army suddenly roared to life on the morning of June 25, 1950. Hundreds of cannon unleashed a thunderous artillery barrage. Spearheaded by 150 modern Soviet T-34 tanks, over 80,000 North Korean soldiers smashed through the overmatched South Korean defenses and rolled south. Within a few days, the North Korean forces overran Seoul, the South Korean capital, and seemed certain to conquer the entire Korean peninsula.

The surprise invasion stunned the Truman administration. As the military situation in South Korea deteriorated, Truman held urgent meetings with his senior advisors. They grimly recalled how the Western powers appeased Hitler's aggression at the Munich conference in 1938. Determined to avoid this mistake, they argued that the invasion posed a threat to the security of Japan and to America's leadership of the Free World. "We've got to stop these sons of bitches no matter what," Truman forcefully declared.

Truman did not ask Congress for a declaration of war. Instead, he called upon the United Nations to intervene. Taking advantage of a temporary Soviet boycott, the UN Security Council voted unanimously to send troops to defend South Korea. This marked the first time in history that a world organization mobilized to stop aggression.

B. DARING AND MISCALCULATION

The United States contributed the major portion of the UN military forces. Truman named Douglas MacArthur the commander of the multinational army. At first, MacArthur's outnumbered soldiers failed to stop the North Korean drive down the peninsula. But by August, American reinforcements had halted the Communist advance near the vital port of Pusan.

Having secured Pusan, MacArthur boldly launched a daring counterattack. On September 15, 1950, U.S. Marines stormed ashore at Inchon, a port some 150 miles behind the North Korean lines. At the same time, MacArthur ordered the forces protecting Pusan to attack. The strategic gamble paid off. The two armies crushed the shocked North Koreans. By the end of September, MacArthur's victorious armies successfully recaptured all of South Korea.

The entire Korean peninsula now seemed within Truman and MacArthur's grasp. Rather than accept a return to the status quo of restoring the 38th parallel, Truman agreed to allow MacArthur to invade North Korea and reunify the peninsula by force. In October, UN forces crossed the 38th parallel and confidently advanced toward the Yalu River, Korea's northern border with China.

The Chinese ominously warned that they would not "stand idly by" and allow North Korea's defeat. MacArthur assured Truman that the Chinese were too weak to pose a real danger. He was wrong. On November 26, 1950, blaring bugles and shrieking whistles announced the beginning of massive human wave attacks by over 200,000 Chinese soldiers. Caught completely by surprise, the UN forces retreated along icy roads in sub-zero weather. "We face an entirely new war," MacArthur grimly admitted.

C. TRUMAN VERSUS MACARTHUR

The Chinese intervention confronted Truman with a dangerous new reality. After a costly retreat, American commanders reversed the Communist drive and reestablished a strong defensive position near the 38th parallel. Faced with a costly stalemate, Truman abandoned his goal of unifying Korea and now chose to fight a limited war to defend only South Korea. The President argued that this strategy would prevent a major war with China and the Soviet Union. He therefore ordered MacArthur to solidify a defensive position along the 38th parallel.

MacArthur expressed great dissatisfaction with these restrictions. He forcefully argued that the United States should blockade China and bomb its military bases and industrial centers. In a letter to Joe Martin, the Republican Minority Leader in the House, MacArthur wrote, "We must win. There is no substitute for victory."

Truman could not permit MacArthur to publicly question his orders. On April 11, 1951, he relieved MacArthur of his command. "I could do nothing else and still be President," Truman explained. Although his decisive action protected the principle of civilian control over the military, it outraged the American public. Huge crowds welcomed MacArthur home. In New York City, seven million people showered him with ticker tape. On the same day, baseball fans in Washington booed Truman when he threw out the ceremonial game ball.

Despite enormous public pressure, Truman stood his ground. At a special congressional hearing, his administration struck back. Military officials warned that MacArthur's plan would require too many soldiers and thus expose Europe to Soviet attack. A showdown with China, General Omar Bradley firmly declared, would be "the wrong war, at the wrong place, at the wrong time, and with the wrong enemy." After these hearings the American people gradually came to accept MacArthur's recall.

D. STALEMATE AND ARMISTICE

The Korean War's first year of combat featured astonishing and rapid reversals of fortune as the rival armies marched up and down the peninsula. In contrast, the next two years settled into a bloody stalemate near the original boundary along the 38th parallel. In fighting reminiscent of the trench warfare in World War I, American soldiers lost their lives fighting dangerous patrols and repelling enemy raids.

Peace talks began in July 1951. While the talks dragged on, the fighting continued. After 25 months and 158 separate meetings, the warring sides finally signed an armistice or cease-fire agreement. Although the armistice established a truce, it was not a peace treaty. Without saying a single word, the military commanders signed the agreement. The South Korean representative refused to attend the meeting.

E. CONSEQUENCES OF THE KOREAN WAR—ASIA

The Korean War has cast a long shadow over events in Asia. The conflict left the Korean peninsula permanently divided between a brutal dictatorship in North Korea and a prosperous democracy in South Korea. A heavily fortified, 160-mile long and 2.5-mile wide Demilitarized Zone (DMZ) separates the two Koreas. About 28,000 American soldiers remain stationed along the DMZ. Backed by America's overwhelming military power, these troops help deter North Korean aggression while reassuring South Korea that America will stand by its ally.

The Korean War also had important consequences for Japan and China. By creating a tremendous demand for industrial goods, the war played a key role in reviving the Japanese economy. At the same time, the Korean War ended any chance that the United States might recognize the People's Republic of China. As relations with China deteriorated, the United States pledged to protect Taiwan. This commitment enabled Taiwan to survive and ultimately prosper.

As the Korean War turned into a prolonged stalemate, President Truman began to focus his attention on other possible targets of Communist aggression. During the early 1950s, he linked France's attempt to regain its colonies in Indochina with the larger global struggle against Communism. This little-noticed commitment began the fateful process of America's growing involvement in Vietnam.

F. CONSEQUENCES OF THE KOREAN WAR FOR THE UNITED STATES

American historians often call the Korean War the "Forgotten War." It took place after America's triumphant victories in World War II and before the nation's traumatic experience in Vietnam. Its seesaw battles and long stalemate took place in a period just before television became a ubiquitous part of American life. While the Korean War failed to generate either ardent supporters or outraged protestors, it nonetheless had far-reaching consequences for American life.

The Korean War marked the first major military engagement of the Cold War. At least 36,000 U.S. troops lost their lives, and some 103,000 suffered battle-related wounds. The costly limited war provided a source of frustration that contributed to the rise of a period of paranoia and unsubstantiated accusations of disloyalty known as McCARTHYISM.

The war provided the justification for a massive American military build-up. Defense spending rose from over $13 billion in 1949 to $50 billion in 1953. These expenditures helped fuel a period of sustained economic growth. Defense spending played an important role in spurring economic growth in parts of the South and West Coast.

Prior to the Korean War, American soldiers fought in segregated units. In July 1948, President Truman ordered the racial desegregation of the U.S. armed forces. The Korean War marked the first time American forces fought in integrated units.

And finally, President Truman chose to fight the war under the auspices of the United Nations, rather than ask Congress for a declaration of war. This established a precedent for America's escalation of the war in Vietnam.

CHAPTER 15
PRACTICE QUESTIONS

MULTIPLE-CHOICE QUESTIONS

Questions 1–3 refer to the excerpt below.

"At the present moment in world history nearly every nation must choose between alternate ways of life. The choice is too often not a free one. One way of life is based upon the will of the majority, and is distinguished by free institutions, representative government, free elections, guarantees of individual liberty, freedom of speech and religion, and freedom from political oppression. The second way of life is based upon the will of a minority forcibly imposed upon the majority. It relies upon terror and oppression, a controlled press and radio; fixed elections, and the suppression of personal freedoms. I believe it must be the policy of the United States to support free peoples who are resisting attempted subjugation by armed minorities or by outside pressures."

President Harry S. Truman, Address before a joint session of Congress, March 12, 1947

1. **The Truman Doctrine was most directly a response to Soviet pressure in**
   A. Latin America
   B. Greece and Turkey
   C. Berlin
   D. Korea

2. **Truman's address inaugurated a new American foreign policy known as**
   A. containment
   B. massive retaliation
   C. flexible response
   D. détente

3. **The ideas expressed in the excerpt most directly represent a departure from the position taken in**

   A. Washington's Farewell Address
   B. the Roosevelt Corollary
   C. Wilson's Fourteen Points
   D. the Atlantic Charter

Questions 4–5 refer to the except below.

"Our policy is directed not against any country or doctrine but against hunger, poverty, desperation, and chaos. Its purpose should be the revival of a working economy in the world so as to permit the emergence of political and social conditions in which free institutions can exist….Any government that is willing to assist in the task of recovery will find full cooperation, I am sure, on the part of the United States government."

> George C. Marshall, Secretary of State, Commencement speech at Harvard University, June 5, 1947

4. **The policy advocated in this excerpt was intended to**

   A. address the need to contain the Soviet Union through military action
   B. dispel anxieties caused by the Cold War
   C. promote the economic reconstruction of Western Europe
   D. refine the Soviet model of economic planning and rapid industrialization

5. **Statistics on which of the following could best be used to support the success of the Marshall Plan?**

   A. A comparison of the military budgets in Western and Eastern Europe between 1948 and 1953
   B. A comparison of welfare benefits in Western and Eastern Europe between 1948 and 1953
   C. A comparison of per capita income in Western and Eastern Europe between 1948 and 1953
   D. A comparison of membership in labor unions in Western Europe and Eastern Europe between 1948 and 1953

Questions 6–7 refer to the excerpt below.

PRAGUE, Wednesday, Feb. 25—"The 'action committees' of Communist Premier Klement Gottwald were taking over authority in the capital and throughout Czechoslovakia yesterday in what looked like a revolution. The country was rapidly turned into a 'People's Front' nation of the typical Eastern European variety. Ministries of the Government were brought under control of the Communists, the army was told to 'remain true to the Soviet Union,' the free press was being suppressed and the Gottwald forces apparently gained the support they needed to form a majority regime."

The New York Times, February 25, 1948

6. **The excerpt best serves as evidence of which of the following trends in Europe in the years immediately following World War II?**
   A. The Soviet Union's commitment to fulfill the promises Stalin made at the Yalta and Potsdam conferences
   B. The Soviet Union's decision to create a sphere of influence in Eastern Europe
   C. The Soviet Union's decision to use the processes of negotiation, compromise, and consensus-building to protect its strategic interests
   D. The Soviet Union's attempt to stave off an economic crisis predicted by Marxist analysis of post-war conditions in Europe.

7. **The event described in this excerpt most directly persuaded**
   A. America to adopt a more conciliatory policy toward the Soviet Union
   B. America to adopt a strategy designed to liberate Eastern Europe from Soviet domination
   C. CIA officials to implement a secret plan to destabilize the Soviet Union
   D. President Truman to support a military alliance to defend Western Europe

Questions 8–10 refer to the excerpt below.

"Have received a peremptory letter from Soviet Deputy Commander requiring on 24 hours notice that our military and civilian employees proceeding thru Soviet Zone to Berlin will submit to individual documentation and also will submit their personal belongings to Soviet inspection. Likewise a permit is required from Soviet Commander for all freight brought into Berlin by military trains for the use of our occupation forces. Obviously these conditions would make impossible travel between Berlin and our zone by American personnel except by air. Moreover, it is undoubtedly the first of a series of restrictive measures designed to drive us from Berlin....A retreat from Berlin at this moment would, in my opinion, have serious if not disastrous political consequences in Europe."

> General Lucius D. Clay, Military Governor of the American zone of occupation in Germany, March 31, 1948

8. The excerpt best serves as evidence of which of the following trends during the late 1940s?

A. The weakening of the Truman Doctrine

B. The escalation of Cold War tensions

C. The use of proxy states to fight Cold War battles

D. The use of collective military action to deter Soviet aggression

9. Truman's strategic response to the Berlin Blockade drew most heavily from

A. Mohandas Ghandhi's strategy of nonviolence

B. Karl Marx's strategy of class struggle

C. Neville Chamberlain's strategy of appeasement

D. George Kennan's strategy of containment

10. Which of the following is a continuation of the "series of restrictive measures" sanctioned by the Soviet Union in Berlin?

A. Constructing the Berlin Wall

B. Shooting down an American U-2 spy plane

C. Refusing to accept Marshall Plan aid

D. Forming the Warsaw Pact

Questions 11–12 refer to the excerpt below.

"The unfortunate but inescapable fact is that the ominous result of the civil war in China was beyond the control of the government of the United States. Nothing that this country did or could have done within the reasonable limits of its capabilities could have changed the result; nothing that was left undone by this country has contributed to it. It was the product of the internal Chinese forces, forces which this country tried to influence but could not. A decision was arrived at within China, if only a decision by default. And now it is abundantly clear that we must face the situation as it exists in fact. We will not help the Chinese or ourselves by basing our policy on wishful thinking."

Secretary of State Dean Acheson, U.S. Position on China, August 1949

11. The excerpt was written in response to

A. China's intervention in the Korean War
B. Mao Zedong's decision to sign a Treaty of Friendship with the Soviet Union
C. Mao Zedong's victory in the Chinese civil war
D. McCarthy's accusations about alleged Communist sympathizers working in the U.S. State Department

12. Acheson's analysis suggests that the political events in China were most directly shaped by

A. America's inept policies
B. China's internal balance of forces
C. Japan's invasion of Manchuria
D. Stalin's military assistance

Questions 13–15 refer to the excerpt below.

"It seems strangely difficult for some to realize that here in Asia is where the Communist conspirators have elected to make their play for global conquest, and that we have joined the issue thus raised on the battlefield; that here we fight Europe's war with arms while the diplomats there still fight it with words; that if we lose the war to Communism in Asia the fall of Europe is inevitable, win it and Europe most probably would avoid war and yet preserve freedom. As you point out we must win. There is no substitute for victory."

General Douglas MacArthur, Letter to Joseph Martin, House Republican Leader, March 20, 1951

13. **President Truman responded to General MacArthur's public statement that "there is no substitute for victory" by**

    A. threatening to bomb China with tactical nuclear weapons
    B. asking Congress for a declaration of war
    C. abandoning containment as a viable foreign policy
    D. firing MacArthur for insubordination

14. **MacArthur's argument in the excerpt best reflects which of the following?**

    A. Resistance to the concept of limited war
    B. Anxiety about Soviet influence in Europe
    C. Support for greater American involvement in Indochina
    D. Support for methods to identify Communists and other radicals in the United States

15. **The Korean War contributed to**

    A. the decline in public confidence and trust in government during the 1950s
    B. the reelection of President Truman in 1952
    C. the climate of frustration and paranoia that led to the rise of McCarthyism
    D. the establishment of diplomatic relations between the United States and the People's Republic of China

MULTIPLE-CHOICE ANSWERS

1. B	5. C	9. D	13. D
2. A	6. B	10. A	14. A
3. A	7. D	11. C	15. C
4. C	8. B	12. B	

SHORT-ANSWER QUESTIONS

Question 1
Using the excerpts below, answer A, B, and C.

"Betraying the hopes of the world, breaking treaties and commitments, the Soviet government after World War II embarked on a new course of forcible expansion and aggression. In 1945 and 1946 Russia's neighbors in Europe and the Far East, their territory occupied by the Red Army at the end of the fighting, were transformed into a new kind of dependencies, so-called satellites with the Communist Party in power. Although the United States and her Western allies protested this course, Moscow remained adamant, fully aware of the inability of the Western allies to prevent this process of expansion."

David J. Dallin, "Cold War and Containment," 1956

"Aggressive American plans to shape the postwar international economic structure along the lines of free trade and capitalist supremacy led to attempts to create a global American empire, and this in turn, caused the deterioration of relations with Communist Russia and the beginnings of the Cold War between East and West. American economic policy since 1947 has been tied primarily and increasingly to military aid to those governments concerned with containing, repelling, or protecting themselves from Communist aggression."

Lisle A. Rose, *Dubious Victory*, 1973

A. Explain ONE major difference between Dallin's and Rose's interpretations of the causes of the Cold War.

B. Provide ONE piece of evidence from the period between 1945 and 1953 that supports Dallin's interpretation, and explain how it supports his interpretation.

C. Provide ONE piece of evidence from the period between 1945 and 1953 that supports Rose's interpretation, and explain how it supports her interpretation.

Question 2
Answer A, B, and C.

A. Briefly describe ONE specific historical difference between the effectiveness of containment in Europe and Asia in the period 1945–1953.

B. Briefly describe ONE specific historical similarity between the effectiveness of containment in Europe and Asia in the period 1945–1953.

C. Briefly explain ONE specific historical effect of containment in either Europe or Asia in the period 1945–1953.

SHORT-ANSWER ANSWERS

Question 1

A. The traditional school of historians dominated American scholarly discussion of the Cold War during the decade after World War II. Like other traditional historians, Dallin blamed the Cold War on Soviet expansion in Eastern Europe. In contrast, the revisionist school of historians blamed the Cold War on American economic policies. Like other revisionists, Rose argued that America's drive for "capitalist supremacy" turned the United States into an expansionist power that posed a threat to the Soviet Union.

B. Dallin's argument is supported by Soviet policy in Poland. Soviet leader Joseph Stalin broke his Yalta pledges by forbidding free elections in Poland and by installing a puppet or satellite communist regime. This intrusion into Eastern and Central Europe violated the principle of national self-determination and posed a real threat to Western Europe. As the leader of the Free World, the United States had to implement a policy of containment to block Soviet expansion.

C. Rose's argument is supported by America's economic and military policies, implemented by the Marshall Plan and the NATO alliance. Although America claimed it funded the Marshall Plan to fight poverty, it also transformed Western Europe into a lucrative market for American products. At the same time, the NATO alliance enabled the United States to encircle the Soviet Union with military bases manned by American forces backed up by B-52 bombers armed with nuclear weapons. This policy forced the Soviet Union to develop its own nuclear weapons, thus triggering the Cold War arms race.

Question 2

A. The NATO alliance and the Marshall Plan implemented America's policy of containment in Europe. These policies revived the Western European economy and protected the region from Soviet invasion or Communist subversion. In contrast, containment in Asia proved to be a partial success. Japan recovered and became an American ally. However, the Korean War ended in a stalemate, which left the peninsula divided between a communist dictatorship in North Korea and an American ally in South Korea.

B. Germany and Japan were both members of the Axis Powers in World War II. America's containment policy transformed West Germany and Japan into successful democracies allied with the United States.

C. The policy of containment left a divided Berlin deep inside a divided Germany. It also left Europe split into two hostile alliances—NATO and the Warsaw Pact.

CHAPTER 16
IMMIGRATION AND NATIVISM 1750–2010

STRATEGIC IMPORTANCE

Immigration and nativism generate a significant cluster of questions and exam points. A careful analysis of recent APUSH exams revealed that questions about the causes and consequences of immigration trends and nativist movements totaled an average of six points per exam. Remember, you only need 75 points to earn a three, 95 points to earn a four, and 110 points to earn a five. This chapter is thus an important part of your coalition of points.

KEY POINTS AND HISTORIC GENERALIZATIONS

- Anglo-Protestants placed their stamp upon America's core culture during the colonial period.

- Three waves of immigrants have settled in America between 1830 and the present. Each wave has featured distinctive groups from Europe, Asia, and Latin America.

- NATIVISM, or anti-immigrant agitation, has been a recurring response to each wave of immigrants.

- Crop failures in Ireland and failed revolutions in Germany sparked the first great wave of immigration. America's emerging industrial economy offered jobs for both groups. The majority of Irish and German immigrants settled in the Northeast and Midwest. Very few settled in the South.

- Anti-Catholic and anti-immigrant passions sparked the formation of the Know-Nothing Party. Although the Know-Nothings soon disappeared, the party marked the beginning of a recurring pattern of nativist backlash against immigrants.

- The Chinese Exclusion Act of 1882 barred Chinese from entering the United States. The act marked America's first legislation targeting a specific racial group of immigrants.

- Beginning in the 1890s, a wave of NEW IMMIGRANTS from Southern and Eastern European countries, such as Italy and Poland, began to pour into America. Booming industries offered plentiful jobs, while America's constitutional freedoms offered hope for new lives.

- Jacob Riis's photographs captured the daily grind of poverty and overcrowding in New York City's Lower East Side. His book *How the Other Half Lives* marked the beginning of the MUCKRAKER movement, in which reform-minded journalists exposed urban and industrial problems. Inspired by Riis and other muckrakers, Progressive reformers attempted to address the worst abuses of America's industrial society.

- A combination of religious prejudice, economic competition, and scientific racism fueled a revival of nativist sentiment directed at the new immigrants. Madison Grant's influential but racist book, *The Passing of the Great Race*, helped justify the efforts of the Immigrant Restriction League to mobilize public support for restrictive immigration laws.

- A nationwide fear of aliens known as the RED SCARE raised public anxieties and fears of radicals who allegedly sought to overthrow the government.

- Congress responded to the fears that immigrants were dangerous radicals by passing the National Origins Act of 1924. The act limited annual immigration to two percent of a country's population in the United States at the time of the 1890 census.

- The Immigration and Naturalization Act of 1965 abolished the national origins quotas. This legislation has set in motion far-reaching demographic changes that are reshaping American society.

TOPIC 16.1
INTRODUCTION—THE BIG PICTURE

A. THE ANGLO-PROTESTANT FOUNDATION

The process of settling North America began about 25,000 years ago when nomadic hunters crossed a land bridge connecting Asia to what is now Alaska. Although the Spanish began the European colonization of North America, the English became the first sizeable European group to settle in what became the United States. The 1790 census revealed that English and Scottish Protestants and their descendants comprised 75 percent of the new nation's white population. (It is important to remember that enslaved Africans comprised about 20 percent of America's total population.)

The Anglo-Protestant majority placed their stamp upon America's core culture. The overwhelming majority of people spoke English, worshipped in

Protestant churches, and accepted republican principles of government. This cultural dominance shaped responses to the waves of non-English groups who immigrated to America during the nineteenth and twentieth centuries.

B. "THEY'RE COMING TO AMERICA"—THREE WAVES OF IMMIGRATION

In his popular song "America," Neil Diamond repeatedly stresses the stirring refrain, "They're coming to America." Diamond's verse underscores the important and enduring role immigration has played in American history. However, the rate of immigration has not been constant. Historians have identified three major waves of immigration.

The first great wave of immigration took place between 1840 and 1860. During this period, almost five million people immigrated to America. While many came from England and Scandinavia, over two-thirds of the total came from Ireland and Germany. The overwhelming majority of the antebellum immigrants chose to settle in Northeastern cities and on Midwestern farms. Most immigrants avoided the South, because they did not want to compete for jobs with enslaved laborers.

The second great wave of immigration began in the 1890s and lasted until the passage of restrictive immigration acts in the early 1920s. This wave featured millions of "new immigrants" from Southern and Eastern Europe. The overwhelming majority of these immigrants arrived in New York City and then settled in urban enclaves in the Northeast and Midwest.

A third wave of immigration began in the mid-1960s, when the Immigration and Naturalization Act of 1965 abolished the restrictive quotas imposed during the 1920s. The new law has sparked a significant and growing wave of immigrants from Latin America and Asia. In addition, this period has witnessed a contentious controversy over the status of illegal immigrants from Mexico and Central America.

C. WAVES OF NATIVISM

America's religious freedom, political liberties, and economic opportunities have served as powerful magnets for immigrants from around the world. The Statue of Liberty's glowing torch symbolized America's role as a great beacon of hope. Unfortunately, not all Americans welcomed the flood of newcomers.

Known as NATIVISM, anti-immigrant agitation has deep roots in American history. For example, Ben Franklin frowned upon the wave of German immigrants settling in Pennsylvania. He openly complained, asking, "Why should Pennsylvania, founded by the English, become a Colony of Aliens, who will shortly be so numerous as to Germanize us instead of our Anglifying them?"

Franklin's question expressed a nativist sentiment that did not fade away. In the late 1790s, leaders of the Federalist Party became alarmed by the influx of "dangerous" radicals who supported the French Revolution. In 1798, the Federalist-controlled Congress passed the Alien and Sedition Acts. The legislation raised the eligibility requirement for citizenship from five years to fourteen. Another law gave the president the power to arrest or expel all aliens "dangerous to the peace and safety of the United States." Although Jefferson's Democratic-Republicans allowed the laws to expire, they established a precedent for nativist laws passed during the nineteenth and twentieth centuries.

TOPIC 16.2
THE FIRST WAVE, 1840-1860

A. THE IRISH IMMIGRANTS

During the 1830s and early 1840s, Anglo-Protestants, enslaved Africans, and Native Americans comprised America's most significant ethnic and racial groups. However, unforeseen events in Ireland suddenly changed this demographic pattern. In 1845 a blight swept across Ireland's farms and ruined the nation's entire potato crop. At that time, Ireland's impoverished peasant farmers relied upon potatoes as a staple food they ate for lunch, dinner, and even breakfast. Famine and contagious diseases soon claimed over one million lives.

Faced with misery and death, about 1.7 million Irish men, women, and children abandoned their homeland in a mass exodus to America. The desperate refugees packed into cramped cargo ships on a perilous 3,000-mile voyage lasting four to six weeks. In 1847, about one-fourth of the 85,000 passengers perished on the aptly named "coffin ships."

The Irish immigrants poured into fast-growing port cities along the Northeast coast. Lacking job skills and financial resources, they performed menial and dangerous work. Irish men dug canals, laid railroad tracks, and unloaded cargo ships, while Irish women cleaned homes and toiled in New England textile mills. For example, the percentage of Irish workers employed in the Lowell textile mills jumped from 8 percent in 1845 to 50 percent in 1860.

B. THE GERMAN IMMIGRANTS

A wave of over 1.5 million Germans immigrated to America between 1840 and 1860. German immigrants formed a diversified group that included exiled political refugees and farmers displaced by industrial development. The majority of Germans attended Protestant churches. However, about one-third were Catholics, and a significant number were Jewish. Unlike the Irish, the Germans settled on farms and in Midwestern cities such as Milwaukee, St. Louis, and Chicago. Because the Germans included such a varied group, they were difficult to stereotype. As a result, the Germans experienced less prejudice than did the Irish.

C. THE NATIVIST BACKLASH

During the 1840s and 1850s, the Northeast's booming cities experienced both rapid population growth and industrialization. The sudden flood of Irish immigrants added religious tensions to this volatile mix. The Catholic Church's ornate ceremonies contrasted with the simple services in Protestant churches. At the same time, black-robed priests and nuns seemed strange and threatening.

Lawless mobs soon exploited the anxieties and fears of native-born Americans. In Washington, D.C., nativists seized a marble block given by Pope Pius IX for construction of the Washington Monument and tossed it into the Potomac River. Vandalism escalated to violence in Louisville, Kentucky. On August 6, 1855 nativists attacked German and Irish Catholic neighborhoods. The Bloody Monday riot left 22 dead, scores injured, and many homes and businesses in ruins.

The anti-Catholic and anti-immigrant passions did more than give rise to acts of vandalism and violence; they also sparked the formation of a nativist political party. During the early 1850s, nativists formed secret organizations complete with special handshakes and passwords. When outsiders questioned members about their purpose, they usually replied, "I know nothing." The suspicious nativists were popularly known as "Know-Nothings."

The Know-Nothings soon formed a political party that directed its hostility toward Catholic immigrants from Ireland and Germany. The party platform forcefully declared, "Americans must rule America!" The Know-Nothings demanded laws that would allow only native-born Americans to hold political office. Know-Nothing candidates enjoyed initial success. The party captured over 40 congressional seats in the 1854 election. Its 1856 presidential candidate, Millard Fillmore, won 21 percent of the popular vote and eight electoral votes.

The Know-Nothings' electoral success proved to be fleeting. The anti-Catholic fervor subsided as immigration declined, and the country shifted its focus to the great national debate over slavery. Although the Know-Nothing Party soon disappeared, it marked the beginning of a recurring pattern of nativist backlash against immigration.

TOPIC 16.3
CHINESE IMMIGRATION, 1849-1882

A. THE "GOLD MOUNTAIN"

The electrifying news that gold had been discovered in California quickly spread to China. Between 1849 and 1852, about 25,000 Chinese traveled across the Pacific to seek their fortunes in a land they optimistically called the "Gold Mountain." Not all Chinese immigrants sought wealth panning for gold. When the gold fields became less profitable, the transcontinental railroads offered a new source of employment. Lured by high wages, 12,000 Chinese workers helped build the Central Pacific line. Although they comprised 90 percent of the company's workforce, officials carefully excluded Chinese workers from the ceremony celebrating the completion of the transcontinental railroad.

The completion of the transcontinental railroad in 1869 did not end the Chinese presence in California. During the 1870s, thousands of Chinese laborers returned to the West Coast to seek work. Many settled in San Francisco, where they formed a close-knit community. Chinese laborers earned a livelihood working in factories where they helped manufacture boots, shoes, cigars, and woolens. At the same time, businessmen opened restaurants and laundries that dotted Chinatown's crowded streets.

B. THE ANTI-CHINESE FUROR

More than 200,000 Chinese arrived in the United States between 1851 and 1881. West Coast residents originally welcomed the Chinese newcomers as hardworking members of their communities. However, as the number of Chinese immigrants steadily increased, the white settlers' attitude shifted from acceptance to antagonism. Uniting under the slogan "California for Americans," nativists began demanding legislation to restrict Chinese miners. In 1852, the California legislature enacted a discriminatory tax requiring all foreign miners to pay a $3.00 monthly license fee.

The United States economy endured a painful depression during the 1870s. Labor leaders, newspapers, and politicians accused Chinese workers of driving down wages and taking jobs away from whites. Inflamed by anti-Chinese fervor, mobs burned Chinese homes and shops.

C. THE CHINESE EXCLUSION ACT OF 1882

The Workingman's Party in California expressed the growing anti-Chinese sentiment gripping the West Coast when they proclaimed the slogan, "The Chinese Must Go!" During the early 1880s, Chinese exclusionists successfully turned their alleged California problem into a national issue. Although the Chinese constituted just 0.002 percent of the U.S. population, nativists demanded that Congress enact a law prohibiting Chinese immigration.

Congress responded to the growing nativist pressure by passing the Chinese Exclusion Act of 1882. Signed into law by President Arthur, the law barred Chinese from entering the United States. It also forbade legal Chinese residents from becoming citizens. The Chinese Exclusion Act marked America's first legislation targeting a specific racial group of immigrants. Congress did not rescind the law until 1943, when it became a source of embarrassment between the United States and China.

TOPIC 16.4
THE SECOND WAVE, 1890-1924

A. THE "HUDDLED MASSES"

During 1907 a daily flotilla of transatlantic steamships, flying flags from a number of European nations, criss-crossed New York City's crowded harbor. The ships did not carry raw materials or finished industrial goods. Instead, they brought thousands of newcomers, anxiously waiting for ferries to carry them to Ellis Island, America's busiest immigration receiving station. The view of the Statue of Liberty lifting her torch of freedom filled the new arrivals with a sense of hope. At the same time, the towering office buildings of lower Manhattan filled them with a sense of apprehension.

The "huddled masses" arriving in New York harbor in 1907 were part of a tidal wave of 20 million immigrants who settled in America between 1890 and 1924. This surge in immigration caused a dramatic change in America's ethnic mix. Prior to the 1890s, most new Americans came from Western European countries such as England, Ireland, and Germany. But beginning in the 1890s, ethnic groups known as NEW IMMIGRANTS began to arrive from countries in Southern and Eastern Europe such as Italy, Poland, and Russia. The overwhelming majority of the new immigrants practiced the Roman Catholic and Jewish faiths.

The new immigrants fled violent religious persecution, oppressive governments, and hopeless poverty. Pushed by intolerance and hardship, the new immigrants were pulled by America's booming industrial economy. Pennsylvania coal mines, Pittsburgh steel mills, Chicago slaughterhouses, and New York City garment-making sweatshops all offered plentiful jobs for unskilled workers.

The new immigrants were pulled to America by more than just jobs; they also coveted America as a land offering a new life. "At Ellis Island I was born again," recalled Emmanuel Goldenberg, a Jewish immigrant whose family fled anti-

Semitic mobs in Romania. He later achieved fame and fortune as a Hollywood actor named Edward G. Robinson.

B. "A GRAY, STONE WORLD"

The harsh realities of life and work in America soon tempered the new immigrants' initial optimism. The overwhelming majority of newcomers gravitated to ethnic enclaves in Northern and Midwestern cities. Lacking financial resources, one-third stayed in New York City.

New York City posed a particularly challenging urban environment. Landlords squeezed families into rows of tenement buildings. According to one report, 1,231 Italians lived in 120 rooms in a neighborhood known as "Little Italy." A single square mile in the Lower East Side contained 334,000 people, making it one of the most densely populated places in the world. One resident described his depressing neighborhood as "a grey, stone world of tall tenements, where even on the loveliest spring day there was not a blade of grass."

C. JACOB RIIS AND *HOW THE OTHER HALF LIVES*

Jacob Riis understood how poverty's sharp edge could challenge even the most resilient immigrant family. After arriving from Denmark in 1870, Riis lived in one of New York City's dark, overcrowded tenement buildings. Unwilling to accept defeat, he taught himself how to use the recent invention of flash photography. As a police reporter for *The New York Tribune*, Riis covered some of the city's most crime-ridden districts.

Riis used his pioneering photographic skills to document the hardship of life in Lower East Side tenements, streets, and alleys. His black-and-white images captured the daily grind of poverty and overcrowding. His poignant photographs of children opened New Yorkers' eyes to a world they had previously ignored.

In 1890, Riis compiled his photographs and graphic commentary into an influential book, *How the Other Half Lives*. The powerful work galvanized a new generation of Progressive reformers to demand more careful building inspections and slum clearance projects. In addition, *How the Other Half Lives* marked the beginning of the MUCKRAKER movement, in which reform-minded investigative journalists wrote hard-hitting articles exposing urban poverty, unsanitary food processing plants, and examples of corporate greed and corruption.

TOPIC 16.5
CLOSING THE GOLDEN DOOR

A. THE REVIVAL OF NATIVIST SENTIMENT

America's seemingly insatiable demand for unskilled labor fueled a rising wave of new immigrants. "I thought it was a stream that would never end," reported one exhausted official as he watched endless lines of immigrants pass through the great Registry Hall in Ellis Island. But the great wave did come to an end. A combination of religious prejudice, economic competition, and scientific racism fueled a revival of nativist sentiment.

The late nineteenth century witnessed a rise in prejudice directed at Catholics and Jews. In 1887 working-class Protestants in states throughout the Rocky Mountains and far West formed the American Protective Association. Members opposed the so-called Roman menace by organizing boycotts of Catholic merchants and vowing to never vote for Roman Catholic political candidates. At the same time, Jews faced growing social and economic discrimination, supported by negative stereotypes portraying them as cunning and greedy merchants who exploited trusting Americans.

Economic competition reinforced the fears and suspicions bred by religious intolerance. In 1893, a panic on Wall Street touched off a severe economic depression. A worried advisor warned President Cleveland, "We are on the eve of a very dark night." Within a year, one-fifth of the nation's workers lost their jobs. Alarmed labor leaders blamed immigrant workers for taking American jobs and working for low wages. They also accused ruthless corporate officials of using immigrants as strikebreakers.

The Immigrant Restriction League (IRL) took advantage of the country's growing climate of anxiety and suspicion. Formed in Boston in 1894, the IRL advanced the pseudo-scientific theory that each ethnic group had its own inborn characteristics. For example, Anglo-Saxons possess courage and leadership skills, placing them at the top of the ethnological pyramid. In contrast, Italians were a violent and undisciplined ethnic group, incapable of assimilating American culture. The IRL pointed to scores from newly developed IQ tests as evidence proving that new immigrants had inferior intelligence compared with native, white Anglo-Saxon Protestants.

The IRL played a critical role in shaping public opinion to support new laws designed to restrict immigration. In 1917, the IRL successfully lobbied Congress to pass an Immigration Act, including a literacy test, banning immigrants over sixteen who could not read a language. But the IRL's mission was not completed. Led by Madison Grant, they pushed for quotas to limit immigration from Southern and Eastern Europe. In his influential book, *The Passing of a Great Race*, Grant offered alleged historic evidence to support his view that the influx of new immigrants threatened to undermine America's superior Anglo-Saxon civilization.

B. WORLD WAR I AND "AMERICA FOR AMERICANS"

Before asking Congress for a declaration of war, President Wilson predicted: "Once lead this people into war, and they'll forget there was ever such a thing as tolerance...the spirit of ruthless brutality will enter into the very fibre of our national life." The President was right. A special propaganda agency, the Committee on Public Information, enlisted 75,000 "Four-Minute Men" to deliver brief patriotic speeches at gatherings across the country. Former president Theodore Roosevelt captured the national spirit of conformity when he demanded that all immigrants become "100 percent Americans." He insisted that everyone follow "the simple and loyal motto, America for Americans."

C. THE RED SCARE

Peace did not bring a return to tolerance. The nativism unleashed by World War I reached a new high in a short but intense Red Scare. In November 1917, Bolsheviks led by Vladimir Lenin seized power in Russia and promptly created a communist dictatorship. The revolutionary upheaval in Russia alarmed many Americans who believed that communist sympathizers and other radicals secretly planned to undermine the United States government.

The fear of subversives escalated in late April 1918 when the post office intercepted 38 packages containing bombs addressed to prominent citizens. A wave of labor strikes and race riots further intensified public anxiety, adding to calls for action. Zealous patriots branded anyone appearing different or foreign as "un-American" and therefore a "Red."

The RED SCARE, a nationwide fear of aliens, prompted Attorney General A. Mitchell Palmer to act. Although no more than one-tenth of one percent of adult Americans actually belonged to the domestic communist movement, Palmer launched a massive roundup of foreign-born radicals. The Department of Justice released most of the 4,000 people it arrested. However, the agency deported about 500 aliens without hearings or trials.

The Palmer Raids marked the end of the Red Scare. But they did not mark the end of the postwar drive for "one hundred percent Americanism." Led by a revived Ku Klux Klan, nativists linked foreigners and militant radicals with all immigrants from Southern and Eastern Europe.

A. RESTRICTIVE QUOTAS

The fears and suspicions ignited by World War I and the Red Scare strengthened a growing anti-immigrant coalition of voters. Congress responded to the nativist push for restrictive measures by passing the National Origins Act of 1924. The law limited annual immigration to two percent of a country's population in the United States at the time of the 1890 census. Since the wave of new immigrants began in 1890, the quotas favored immigrants from Northern and Western Europe while sharply reducing the flow of immigrants from Southern and Eastern Europe. For example, England received a generous quota of 65,721, while Italy received a mere 3,845 per year.

The new QUOTA SYSTEM provided for 153,714 immigrants from Europe while continuing to ban immigration from Asia. However, the law placed no restrictions on the Western Hemisphere. As a result, Canadians and Mexicans were free to enter into the United States. For example, approximately 500,000 Mexican workers came to the United States during the 1920s.

TOPIC 16.6
THE THIRD WAVE, 1965-2015

A. LOW TIDE, 1924-1965

The quota system caused a dramatic decline in immigration to America. Just 4.1 million newcomers entered the United States between 1930 and 1960. While foreign-born people represented 15 percent of the population in 1930, they comprised only 4.7 percent in 1960. Given the sharp decline in immigration, authorities closed Ellis Island in 1954. The abandoned facility provided a striking symbol of the dramatic change in American immigration policy.

B. THE IMMIGRATION AND NATURALIZATION ACT OF 1965

A combination of factors created political support for meaningful immigration reform. President Kennedy believed that immigration contributed to national strength. The Democratic Party platform condemned quotas as "a policy of deliberate discrimination" that "contradicts the founding principles of this nation." The coalition of liberal activists that supported the Civil Rights Act of 1964 also supported immigration reform as a measure to eliminate racism.

President Johnson embraced the cause of immigration reform. The Democratic Party's landslide victory in the 1964 presidential election gave LBJ a mandate for Great Society programs that included a plan to revise the nation's immigration policy.

The Immigration and Naturalization Act of 1965 abolished the national origins quotas. The law created a new system of hemispheric caps, permitting 170,000 immigrants from nations in the Eastern Hemisphere and 120,00 from nations in the Western Hemisphere. Later legislation raised these limits to just below 700,000 people.

The new law also included a critical exemption for all immigrants with immediate family members living in the United States. The heightened emphasis on family unification led to a phenomenon known as chain migration. The naturalization of a single immigrant opened the door to his or her brothers and sisters and their spouses. They in turn could sponsor their own family members. By the 1990s, family reunions accounted for two-thirds of all immigrants coming to the United States.

C. UNINTENDED CONSEQUENCES

President Johnson signed the Immigration and Naturalization Act of 1965 in a ceremony held on Liberty Island. The president promised Americans that "The bill we sign today is not a revolutionary bill. It does not affect the lives of millions. It will not reshape the structure of our daily lives." Johnson's reassurances proved to be wrong. Neither LBJ nor the legislation's supporters anticipated the new law's sweeping long-term effects.

The new legislation set in motion far-reaching demographic changes that are reshaping American society. By the beginning of the 21st century, about one million immigrants entered the United States each year. The foreign-born population rose from 9.6 million in 1965 to a record high of 45 million in 2015. As a result, immigrants now comprise about 14 percent of the U.S. population.

The dramatic rise in immigration is altering America's ethnic and racial composition. Since 1965 more than half of American's newcomers have immigrated from Latin America, while another fourth have come from Asia. In 1965 whites of European descent comprised 84 percent of the U.S. population, while Hispanics accounted for four percent and Asians for less than one percent. Fifty years later, the white percentage fell to 62 percent, while the Hispanic percentage rose to 18 percent, and the Asian percentage increased to six percent. Latinos have now overtaken African Americans as America's largest minority.

D. ILLEGAL IMMIGRATION

Approximately 11 million illegal or undocumented immigrants now live in the United States. Historians trace the roots of this problem to 1964. In that year Congress ended the Bracero program, which allowed Mexican agricultural workers to work in the United States and then return to their homeland. The program's repeal, combined with the Immigration and Naturalization Act's cap on immigration from the Western Hemisphere, led to a sharp rise in undocumented workers who illegally remained in the United States.

E. A RAINBOW SOCIETY

The changes in American immigration patterns have produced a "rainbow society" that includes a rich diversity of people. Supporters of this change argue that immigration is infusing America with talented and energetic people who contribute to economic growth. However, critics argue that the high rate of immigration creates competition for low-skilled jobs while shattering America's cultural homogeneity.

CHAPTER 16
PRACTICE QUESTIONS

MULTIPLE-CHOICE QUESTIONS

Questions 1–4 refer to the graph below.

Annual Number of New Legal Permanent Residents, 1820-2017

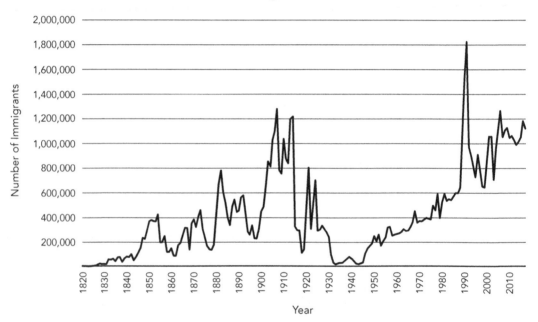

Source: Migration Policy Institute (MPI) tabulation of the U.S. Department of Homeland Security

1. **Which of the following most directly contributed to the waves of immigration from 1840 to 1860 and from 1890 to 1920 shown on the graph?**

    A. An American policy encouraging chain migration
    B. Incentives offered by U.S. companies hoping to hire skilled migrant workers
    C. Economic hardships and political oppression in Europe
    D. Fluctuations in American credit and stock markets

2. **Which of the following was a direct effect of the waves of immigration from 1840 to 1860 and from 1890 to 1920 shown on the graph?**

   A. A series of protest strikes by American labor unions

   B. An upsurge in nativist activity

   C. The displacement of Native Americans to reservations in the West

   D. The establishment of settlement houses by Progressive reformers

3. **The immigrants from 1890 to 1920 most typically settled in which of the** following areas of the United States?

   A. Cities in the Far West

   B. Cities in the Northeast

   C. Farms in the Southwest

   D. Small towns in the South

4. **Which of the following most directly contributed to the trend depicted in the graph after 1970?**

   A. The influence of nativist political parties

   B. Strict regulations on immigrants from Southern and Eastern Europe

   C. A decline in internal migration in the United States

   D. A new immigration system stressing family unification

Questions 5–8 refer to the excerpt below.

"I would like the members of the Senate to read the book just recently published by Madison Grant, *The Passing of the Great Race*. Thank God we have in America perhaps the largest percentage of any country in the world of pure unadulterated Anglo-Saxon stock; certainly the greatest of any nation in the Nordic breed. It is for the preservation of that splendid stock that has characterized us that I would make this not an asylum for the oppressed of all countries, but a country to assimilate and perfect that splendid type of manhood that has made America the foremost Nation in her progress and in her power, and yet the youngest of all the nations."

> Address by Senator Ellison D. Smith, South Carolina, April 9, 1924, *Congressional Record*

5. **Which of the following would most directly fulfill Senator Smith's goal to make America "not an asylum for the oppressed of all countries?"**

    A. The Alien and Sedition Acts of 1798
    B. The Chinese Exclusion Act of 1882
    C. The National Origins Act of 1924
    D. The Immigration and Naturalization Act of 1965

6. **Which of the following most directly contributed to Senator Smith's fear that America's Anglo-Saxon stock was threatened?**

    A. The revival of the Ku Klux Klan
    B. The failure of the Know-Nothing Party
    C. The wave of new immigrants from Southern and Eastern Europe
    D. The Red Scare following World War I

7. **Senator Smith's purpose in the excerpt was to**

    A. gain support for restrictive immigration quotas
    B. propose expanded privileges for Nordic Americans
    C. reduce sectional tensions between the North and the South
    D. Support poll taxes and literacy tests to deter African Americans from voting

8. **Senator Smith's positive reference to Madison Grant's book, *The Passing of the Great Race*, indicates that he would most strongly endorse the tenets of**

    A. *Laissez-faire* capitalism
    B. Progressivism
    C. Scientific racism
    D. Perfectionism

Questions 9–10 refer to the excerpt below.

"Here is a woman. In the Old Country she had lived much of her life, done most of her work, outdoors. In America, the flat confines her. She divides up her domain by calico sheets hung on ropes, tries to make a place for her people and possessions. But there is no place and she has not room to turn about. It is true, everything is in poor repair, the rain comes through the ceilings, the wind blows dirt through the cracks in the wall. But she does not even know how to go about restoring order, establishing cleanliness. She breaks her back to exterminate the proliferating vermin. What does she get? A dozen lice behind her collar."

Oscar Handlin, historian, *The Uprooted*, 1951

9. **Conditions like those described in the excerpt contributed most directly to which of the following?**

    A. Calls for a return to an agrarian economy and society
    B. An increase in Progressive reform activity
    C. The migration of African Americans to cities in the Northeast
    D. The acceptance of immigrants by native-born Americans

10. **Which of the following would have been most likely to expose the conditions described in this excerpt?**

    A. Populists such as Mary Lease
    B. Anti-imperialists such as William Jennings Bryan
    C. Industrialists such as Andrew Carnegie
    D. Muckrakers such as Jacob Riis

Questions 11–12 refer to the excerpt below.

In the second reign year of Haamfong [1852] a trip
        to Gold Mountain was made.
With a pillow on my shoulder, I began my perilous
        journey:
Sailing a boat with bamboo poles across the sea,
Leaving behind wife and sisters in search of money,
No longer lingering with the woman in the bedroom,
No longer paying respect to parents and home.

A Chinese folk song, quoted in Ronald Takaki, *A Different Mirror*, 2008

11. **The excerpt is best understood as a response to which of the following historical developments?**

    A. The discovery of gold in California
    B. The construction of the first transcontinental railroad
    C. The Union's victory in the Civil War
    D. The Supreme Court's decision in *Plessy v. Ferguson*

12. Which of the following was a direct effect of the migration described in this excerpt?

A. The improvement of relations between the United States and China
B. The formation of a political party that promoted nativism
C. The emergence of an industrial economy in California
D. The total exclusion of immigration from China

Questions 13–15 refer to the excerpt below.

"Article 3: Americans must rule America; and to this end native-born citizens should be selected for all State, Federal, and municipal offices and government employment.

"Article 9: A change in the laws of naturalization, making a continual residence of twenty-one years…an indispensable requirement for citizenship hereafter…

"Article 10: Opposition to any union between Church and State; no interference with religious faith or worship, and no test oaths for office…"

American Party Platform, 1856

13. Article 10 of the platform most likely reflected which of the following sentiments?

A. Nativist backlash directed against Catholic immigrants from Ireland and Germany
B. Nativist backlash directed against Jewish immigrants from Poland and Russia
C. Nativist backlash directed against radicals who supported the Bolshevik Revolution
D. Nativist backlash directed against illegal immigrants crossing the American border with Mexico

14. Which of the following contributed to reducing the concerns raised in the American Party platform?

A. The implementation of strict immigration quotas
B. The discovery of gold in California
C. A shift in public focus to the national debate over slavery
D. A striking growth in the power of urban political machines

15. Sentiments similar to those expressed in the excerpt were most effective in prompting a change in federal immigration policy during the

   A. 1890s
   B. 1920s
   C. 1950s
   D. 1960s

MULTIPLE-CHOICE ANSWERS

1. C	5. C	9. B	13. A
2. B	6. C	10. D	14. C
3. B	7. A	11. A	15. B
4. D	8. C	12. D	

SHORT-ANSWER QUESTIONS

Question 1
Using the image below, answer A, B, and C.

THE ONLY WAY TO HANDLE IT.

The Literary Digest, May 7, 1921, Library of Congress

A. Briefly describe ONE perspective expressed by the artist about the future direction of American immigration policy.

B. Briefly explain how ONE event or development led to the historical situation depicted in the image.

C. Briefly explain ONE specific outcome of the debates about immigration policy in the early 1920s.

Question 2
Answer A, B, and C.

A. Briefly describe ONE specific historical difference between the National Origins Act of 1924 and the Immigration and Naturalization Act of 1965.

B. Briefly describe ONE specific historical similarity between the National Origins Act of 1924 and the Immigration and Naturalization Act of 1965.

C. Briefly explain ONE specific historical effect of either the National Origins Act of 1924 or the Immigration and Naturalization Act of 1965.

SHORT–ANSWER ANSWERS

Question 1

A. The artist supports quotas as "The only way to Handle" the wave of Southern and Eastern European immigrants clamoring to enter the United States.

B. A tidal wave of 20 million immigrants settled in America between 1890 and 1924. The overwhelming majority of these new immigrants were Catholics and Jews from Southern and Eastern Europe.

C. The American public feared that immigration was having a deleterious impact upon the nation's culture. Congress responded by passing the National Origins Act of 1924. The act limited annual immigration to two percent of a country's population in the United States at the time of the 1890 census.

Question 2

A. The National Origins Act of 1924 established quotas deliberately designed to sharply restrict the number of immigrants entering the United States from Southern and Eastern Europe. In contrast, the Immigration and Naturalization Act of 1965 abolished national origins quotas.

B. Both the National Origins Act of 1924 and the Immigration and Naturalization Act of 1965 established limits on the number of immigrants who could legally enter the United States. The National Origins Act used quotas, while the Immigration and Naturalization Act used a system of hemispheric caps.

C. The Immigration and Naturalization Act of 1965 had the unintended consequence of allowing a dramatic increase in immigration from Latin America and Asia. This wave of immigration is altering America's ethnic and racial composition.

CHAPTER 17

FROM THE CONSERVATIVE REVIVAL TO GLOBALIZATION 1964–2010

STRATEGIC IMPORTANCE

Chapter 12 features the following five recent topics: the rise of the conservative movement, Reaganomics, the end of the Cold War, the digital revolution, and globalization. These topics are drawn from Periods 8 and 9 in the APUSH Framework.

College Board test writers have focused special attention on these five historical developments. Each APUSH exam has included one or even two sets of multiple-choice questions that test recent historic trends and events. In addition, the topics covered in Chapter 12 have generated one DBQ and portions of two long-essay questions.

Chapter 12 is an important part of the coalition of points you need to score a three. APUSH exams have devoted an average of 18 points to the topics covered in this chapter. Remember, you only need 75 points to earn a three, 95 points to earn a four, and 110 points to earn a five. This chapter is thus a particularly important part of your coalition of points.

KEY POINTS AND HISTORIC GENERALIZATIONS

- Inexpensive air conditioning, low taxes, and aerospace projects encouraged many Americans to move to the South and West. Known as the SUNBELT, this growing region emerged as an increasingly significant political and economic force.

- The rapid growth of evangelical Christian churches and organizations spurred greater political and social activism by religious conservatives.

- A resurgent conservative movement enabled Ronald Reagan to defeat Jimmy Carter in the 1980 presidential election.

- Reagan's victory enabled Republicans to enact significant tax cuts and the deregulation of many industries. However, the Reagan administration did not make cuts in Social Security, Medicare, or veteran's benefits.

- Reagan's SUPPLY-SIDE program of tax cuts helped restore economic prosperity. However, his massive defense budgets also led to dramatic increases in the national debt.

- Reagan used forceful speeches to condemn the Soviet Union as an "evil empire." U.S. defense spending placed pressure on Russia's faltering command economy. Gorbachev's "new thinking" contributed to the fall of the Berlin Wall and the collapse of the Soviet Union.

- Technological innovations in computing, the Internet, and digital mobile smartphones increased access to information and transformed daily life.

- GLOBALIZATION increased American participation in a world that became more interconnected and interdependent.

- Employment decreased in manufacturing, causing a decline in union membership.

- Real wages stagnated for the working and middle classes amid growing economic inequality.

TOPIC 17.1
THE CONSERVATIVE RESURGENCE

A. THE ELECTION OF 1964

The 1964 presidential election featured a historic choice between liberal and conservative candidates. The Democratic nominee, President Lyndon Johnson of Texas, ran on a liberal platform promising to wage war on poverty, extend medical care to the elderly, and support a landmark voting rights bill. In contrast, the Republican nominee, Senator Barry Goldwater of Arizona, ran on a conservative platform promising to cut taxes, shrink the federal government, and restore American military strength.

The election appeared to produce definitive results. Johnson won 61 percent of the vote and crushed Goldwater in the Electoral College. LBJ's overwhelming victory seemed to usher in a new age of liberal dominance and conservative retreat. But surface appearances proved to be misleading. An unanticipated combination of Sunbelt conservatives, Christian evangelicals, and blue-collar workers forged an increasingly powerful political coalition that won the White House in 1980.

B. DISCONTENTED SUNBELT CONSERVATIVES

Political commentators noted that both President Johnson and Senator Goldwater hailed from states in a region they named the SUNBELT. The coincidence was not a surprise. The Sunbelt comprised a booming region of

14 states, stretching from North Carolina through Florida and Texas to Arizona and California. During the 1970s, these states experienced unprecedented growth.

A number of factors combined to make the Sunbelt America's fastest growing region. Affordable air-conditioning cooled homes and offices during the region's hot summers. Low taxes and weak labor unions attracted businesses. And finally, the federal government awarded Sunbelt states a host of defense and space contracts. For example, Florida and Texas became centers of huge aerospace complexes.

The historic migration of people and businesses translated into growing political power. As their population increased, Sunbelt states claimed more seats in the House of Representatives and thus more votes in the Electoral College. In the 1960 presidential election, California, Texas, and Florida had a total of 66 electoral votes. Twenty years later, these three states commanded 88 electoral votes.

The prosperous suburbs surrounding Los Angeles, Phoenix, Dallas, and Atlanta quickly became conservative strongholds. White middle class suburbanites opposed Great Society programs. Instead, they embraced a conservative philosophy favoring reductions in expensive government welfare programs and burdensome business regulations. The Sunbelt conservatives formed what historian Lisa McGirr called "the ground forces of the conservative revival."

C. ALARMED CHRISTIAN EVANGELICALS

The 1960s and 1970s produced a number of social and cultural changes that alarmed Christian evangelicals. Hippies experimented with drugs and celebrated premarital sex. Feminists challenged traditional family roles and enthusiastically endorsed the Equal Rights Amendment (ERA). At the same time, the newly vocal gay community demanded recognition and equal civil rights.

Outraged Christian evangelicals did not limit their opposition to hippies, feminists, and gays; they also directed special outrage at liberal Supreme Court decisions. Rulings prohibiting officially sponsored prayer and Bible readings in public schools deeply offended devout Christians, who believed these activities played an important role in the development of moral values. The Supreme Court's 1973 decision in *Roe v. Wade* legalizing abortion aroused outrage among both Protestants and Catholics who defended the unborn infant's right to life.

Sexual permissiveness, the ERA, school prayer, and abortion galvanized a determined group of conservative Christians known as the RELIGIOUS RIGHT. For example, Phyllis Schlafly successfully marshaled opposition to the ERA, while Beverly LaHaye founded the Concerned Women for America (CWA) to link groups of local activists.

The Religious Right became a significant force in American politics when Jerry Falwell, a Baptist minister and popular religious broadcaster from Lynchburg, Virginia, founded the Moral Majority. Launched in 1979, the organization advanced a "pro-life, pro-family, pro-morality, and pro-American" agenda. The Moral Majority's four million members and two million donors played a key role in mobilizing evangelical Christians into a powerful political force.

D. DISCONTENTED BLUE–COLLAR WORKERS

During the 1970s, millions of Americans watched *All in the Family*, a humorous but culturally relevant television program about a working class family living in Queens, New York. Most episodes revolved around the outspoken views of Archie Bunker, a World War II veteran who worked as a foreman on a loading dock. Although he was a fictional character, Archie's frustrations accurately reflected the growing discontent among American blue-collar workers.

Beginning with the New Deal, working-class voters formed a core group of the Democratic Party coalition. However, during the late 1970s, unsettling economic and social issues prompted many of these voters to rethink their loyalty to the Democratic Party. Slowing wage growth, rising prices, and growing tax burdens threatened their standard of living. At the same time, court-ordered busing of school children to achieve racial balance fueled a growing sense of resentment.

As the 1980 presidential election approached, real-life Archie Bunkers felt increasingly alienated from Democratic Party policies and candidates. They searched for a new leader who promised to roll back expensive social welfare programs, support traditional family values, and restore economic confidence.

E. THE ELECTION OF 1980

During the fall of 1980, millions of concerned Americans felt squeezed by double-digit inflation, crippling mortgage rates, and an unemployment rate of nearly eight percent. Overseas, 53 American hostages languished in an Iranian prison despite months of futile negotiations by the Carter administration. Opinion polls reported that less than 25 percent of the American people approved of President Carter's leadership. For many, it seemed as if America had lost its way.

Sensing victory, the Republicans nominated Ronald Reagan as their presidential candidate. A one-time movie actor, television host, and two-term governor of California, Reagan refused to listen to dire forecasts predicting an increasingly dismal future. "There are those in our land," he declared, "who would have us believe that the United States, like the other great civilizations of the past, has reached the zenith of its power." Reagan then confidentially insisted, "I don't believe that."

During the 1980 presidential campaign, Reagan repeatedly asked the American people to answer one question: "Are you better off now than you were four years ago?" On election day, a resurgent coalition of conservative Republican voters answered *no*. Reagan and his running mate, George H.W. Bush, won a convincing victory.

TOPIC 17.2
THE REAGAN REVOLUTION

A. "GOVERNMENT IS NOT THE SOLUTION TO OUR PROBLEMS"

President Reagan inherited a struggling economy. However, he was not discouraged by the nation's formidable economic problems. Reagan used his inaugural address to urge Americans to "believe in ourselves." He confidently predicted, "We can and will resolve the problems which now confront us."

Unlike New Deal and Great Society reformers, Reagan did not propose a package of expensive government programs. Instead, he reversed generations of liberal economic practice by declaring, "Government is not the solution to our problems. Government is the problem."

B. SUPPLY–SIDE ECONOMICS

Reagan championed a new approach known as SUPPLY-SIDE ECONOMICS. According to this theory, high tax rates discourage economic activity and thus reduce the nation's tax revenue. Supply-side economists argued that significant reductions in personal and corporate tax rates would encourage private investment and innovation. America's ailing economy would spring back to life as consumers bought more goods and corporations hired more workers.

President Reagan expressed confidence that supply-side economic principles would restore America's economic vitality. Declaring that the American people "expect us to act," Reagan proposed a Program for Economic Recovery that reporters promptly labeled "REAGANOMICS."

The president's economic plan included three fundamental goals. First and foremost, it called for a significant reduction in personal and corporate tax rates. Second, Reagan pledged to eliminate unnecessary and inefficient federal regulations. And finally, the president's plan asked Congress to cut $41 billion from 83 federal programs.

Reagan's proposals included two key exceptions. Yielding to strong public support, he promised to make no cuts in Social Security, Medicare, or veteran's pensions. In addition, Reagan called for a massive program of military spending to deter Soviet aggression.

C. THE GREAT COMMUNICATOR

Enacting his economic proposals required a range of political skills. Reagan deftly used television speeches to build public support for his program. Enthusiastic voters responded by flooding Congress with telephone calls and telegrams supporting the President. Reagan's success earned him the nickname "The Great Communicator."

Winning congressional support required more than great television speeches, however. Reagan used his personal charm to win support from individual members of Congress. During his first few months in office, he met 96 times with senators and representatives and spent many additional hours talking with them on the phone. He even invited 11 hesitant congressmen to a barbecue at the Camp David presidential retreat.

Reagan's persuasive speeches and artful personal lobbying worked. The final bill reduced all individual tax rates by about 25 percent. As a result, the top tax rate fell from 70 to 50 percent.

D. "IT'S MORNING AGAIN IN AMERICA"

At first, Reaganomics failed to revive the economy. In late 1981 America entered a severe recession, with the unemployment rate peaking at 10.3 percent, the highest since the Great Depression. Critics labeled the economic downturn the "Reagan Recession."

Despite the difficult beginning, Reagan remained optimistic. He urged the public to "stay the course." The President's confidence proved to be justified. The recession soon faded, and America entered a long period of growth and prosperity. Between late 1982 and 1988, the economy added more than 17 million new jobs, inflation fell to single digits, and the gross national product showed the biggest percentage increase in three decades.

Reagan's supporters pointed to the nation's rapidly improving economy as evidence that it was "morning again in America." With inflation under control and more people at work, a new spirit of confidence spread across the country. In one popular ad, the narrator asked voters, "Why would we ever want to return to where we were less than four short years ago?" In 1984 voters overwhelmingly endorsed President Reagan's leadership with a landslide victory over his Democratic rival, former Vice President Walter Mondale.

E. TROUBLING LONG–TERM PROBLEMS

Although good times seemed to have returned, they masked troubling long-term problems. Despite deep cuts in social programs, federal spending continued to escalate as military spending soared. Because of the deep tax cuts, the federal government took in less money, causing a dramatic increase in the national debt. During Reagan's presidency, the United States added $1.8 trillion to the debt. Once the world's biggest lender, the United States became its largest debtor.

TOPIC 17.3
THE END OF THE COLD WAR

A. THE COLLAPSE OF DÉTENTE

President Nixon and Soviet leader Leonid Brezhnev initiated a policy known as DÉTENTE during a series of highly publicized summit meetings held during the early 1970s. Détente represented an attempt to ease superpower tensions through increased diplomacy, trade, cultural exchanges, and joint missions in space. Although détente sought to create a spirit of peaceful coexistence, it did not end the Cold War. The Berlin Wall still stood as a seemingly permanent symbol of the ongoing Cold War between the Communist and Free World.

Détente failed to deter Soviet military aggression. In late 1979, 100,000 Russian troops invaded Afghanistan to support a pro-Soviet puppet government. President Carter denounced the invasion and announced that the United States would boycott the Moscow Olympics. Nonetheless, the Soviet invasion of Afghanistan and the continuing hostage crisis in Iran created an impression of American weakness and growing Soviet strength.

B. THE "EVIL EMPIRE" AND STAR WARS

President Reagan dismissed détente as a failed policy that created an illusion of peaceful coexistence. In his first news conference, the new president criticized détente as a "one-way street." He underscored his point by bluntly asking, "Isn't détente what a farmer has with his turkey—until Thanksgiving day?"

Reagan did more than just reject détente; he also refused to accept the widespread belief that the Soviet Union was an indestructible adversary. Instead, he called communism a "temporary aberration which will one day disappear from the earth because it is contrary to human nature."

The collapse of détente chilled relations between the United States and the Soviet Union. In a speech delivered in 1982 to members of the British Parliament, Reagan confidently predicted, "The march of freedom and democracy...will leave Marxism-Leninism on the ash heap of history." Less than a year later he branded the Soviet Union an "evil empire," responsible for the renewal of Cold War tensions.

Reagan believed the world had reached a "historic turning point" in the struggle between freedom and tyranny. In order to defend America's allies, he launched a massive military build-up, funded by increasing annual defense budgets from $144 billion to $295 billion. In addition, Reagan proposed to create an orbiting weapons system designed to detect and destroy incoming Soviet missiles. A skeptical press dubbed the plan "Star Wars," after a popular science fiction movie.

C. GORBACHEV AND NEW THINKING

America's growing military strength alarmed Soviet leaders. They recognized that their faltering economy could not match America's scientific and technological advantages. Soviet leaders from Lenin to Brezhnev had created a totalitarian state that controlled the mass media and restricted human rights. Soviet citizens lived in a climate of fear that rewarded silence and discouraged individual initiative.

On March 10, 1985, members of the Politburo, the Communist Party's top decision-making group, unexpectedly chose Mikhail Gorbachev as their new General Secretary. At 54, Gorbachev was the youngest Soviet leader since Stalin. The cautious party officials who chose Gorbachev knew that reforms were needed to revitalize the Soviet economy. However, they did not foresee that Gorbachev's rise to power marked the beginning of a fateful series of revolutionary events.

Gorbachev soon pledged a program of "new thinking" designed to shatter Russia's stagnant status quo. His policy of *glasnost*, or openness, encouraged Soviet citizens to freely discuss ways to reform their society. Russians had much to complain about. At that time only 23 percent of urban homes and 7 percent of rural homes had telephones. At the same time, Gorbachev's ambitious policy of *perestroika*, or economic restructuring, attempted to reform the Soviet Union's inefficient command economy.

Gorbachev's new thinking also extended to the Soviet satellites in Eastern Europe. He encouraged East Bloc leaders to try new strategies to strengthen their lagging economies, thus lessening their dependence upon Soviet aid. However, the aging leaders of East Germany, Czechoslovakia, and Romania stubbornly rejected implementing reform measures.

D. "MR. GORBACHEV, TEAR DOWN THIS WALL"

Popular discontent and the declining appeal of communist ideology prepared Eastern Europeans for change. Although these forces had been present for some time, the threat of Soviet military intervention had always kept them in check.

President Reagan believed that the "last pages" of Soviet history "are even now being written." Determined to push events forward, Reagan came to West Berlin, long the symbolic center of the Cold War. On June 12, 1987, over 200,000 West Berliners gathered to hear the American president. From a platform beside the brick, stone, concrete, and razor wire of the Berlin Wall, Reagan challenged Gorbachev to begin a new era of freedom in Eastern Europe: "General Secretary Gorbachev, if you seek peace, if you seek prosperity for the Soviet Union and Eastern Europe, if you seek liberalization, come here to this gate. Mr. Gorbachev, open this gate. Mr. Gorbachev, tear down this wall!"

President Reagan's stirring words marked a turning point in the Cold War. His clarity of vision bolstered the morale of the pro-democracy movement throughout Eastern Europe. His commitment to freedom put relentless pressure on Gorbachev and the East German government to open the barrier that had divided Berlin since 1961.

E. "THE WALL IS GONE!"

President Reagan predicted that "The wall cannot withstand freedom." His prediction proved to be true. Protests within East Germany soon gained momentum. On November 9, 1989, a new East German leader opened the Berlin Wall. The long-divided city of Berlin erupted in joyous celebration. Once-feared border guards smiled as huge crowds climbed on top of the wall to celebrate. Many slammed hammers into the wall, smashing the despised symbol of Communist oppression into small concrete souvenirs. Jubilant Berliners danced, sang, and chanted, "The wall is gone! The wall is gone!"

The fall of the Berlin Wall marked the beginning of a series of once unimaginable events. Inspired by the destruction of the most visible symbol of Soviet authority, demonstrators overthrew communist dictators throughout Eastern Europe. Less than one year later, the United States, Soviet Union, and the members of the North Atlantic Treaty Organization accepted German reunification within the NATO alliance.

F. THE BEGINNING OF A NEW WORLD ORDER

The tidal wave of change in Eastern Europe soon swept into the Soviet Union. As the Communist Party's iron grip weakened, nationalist groups within the fourteen republics surrounding the Russian Republic demanded greater control over their internal affairs. Gorbachev watched helplessly as his authority vanished. A former colleague pointedly observed, "He tried to reform the unreformable."

On December 25, 1991, Gorbachev resigned his position as leader of a country that ceased to exist. Fifteen independent republics, the largest of which was Russia, replaced the nonexistent Soviet Union. The United States now stood alone as the world's sole superpower. President Bush proclaimed this historic development as the beginning of a "new world order."

TOPIC 17.4
THE DIGITAL REVOLUTION

A. A NEW ELECTRONIC ORDER

During the 1970s and 1980s, a relatively small group of scientists, innovators, and entrepreneurs led a digital revolution that began to transform American life. As the Cold War ended, corporate leaders at Apple, IBM, Intel, and Microsoft launched a far-reaching computer revolution. However, breathtaking changes still awaited America and the world. In 1989 no one had purchased a book on Amazon, played a videogame on a Sony PlayStation, looked for information on Google, researched a report on Wikipedia, liked a friend's picture on Facebook, watched a video on YouTube, or sent a text message on an iPhone. Within 20 years of the fall of the Berlin Wall, all of these activities became indispensible parts of a historic digital revolution.

B. ENIAC, THE "GIANT BRAIN"

On February 14, 1946, the War Department unveiled a top secret machine called ENIAC, an acronym for Electronic Numerical Integrator and Computer. ENIAC's size and complexity awed the public. The $487,000 room-size computer contained almost 18,000 vacuum tubes and several miles of wiring. It weighed 30 tons and took up 3,000 cubic feet of space in a climate-controlled room. Heralded by the press as the "Giant Brain," ENIAC required only 30 seconds to calculate the trajectory for an artillery shell. The same process required 20 human hours.

C. THE INTEL 4004 MICROPROCESSOR

Mainframe computers like ENIAC soon became commonplace in American military bases, universities, and corporate research centers. They guided the flights of intercontinental missiles, predicted weather patterns, and tabulated data for scholarly research projects. However, their size and cost posed insurmountable barriers for private individuals.

The move from mainframe computers to small personal computers began in November 1971, when Intel introduced its 4004 microprocessor. A microprocessor is a single integrated circuit or computer chip that merges all the central processing functions of a computer into a single component. Incredibly, the 4004 microprocessor contained as much processing power as the room-filling ENIAC.

Intel proudly boasted that its 4004 microprocessor opened "a new era in integrated electronics." The new era raced ahead as Intel engineers successfully doubled computing power every 18 to 24 months. As a result, microprocessors became the heart of a new generation of small but powerful computers.

D. THE PERSONAL COMPUTER REVOLUTION

Rapid advances in inexpensive Intel microprocessors enabled engineers and entrepreneurs to create the first generation of what they called microcomputers. In 1977, Steve Wozniak and his friend Steve Jobs founded Apple Computer. Their groundbreaking Apple II computer included a keyboard, extensive memory, and software that supported a wide range of functions. Revenue from sales of the new Apple II soared from $800,000 in 1977 to $48 million in 1979.

IBM had long dominated the mainframe market. Startled IBM executives took note of Apple's stunning success. During the summer of 1980, they created a special task force to create a rival computer. The IBM team secured their software from Microsoft, a small Seattle-based company founded by Bill Gates.

IBM released its new Personal Computer, or PC, in August 1981. The IBM PC soon dominated a booming computer market. By the early 1990s, computers had become an integral part of American life and work.

E. THE EMERGENCE OF THE INTERNET

The personal computer revolution enabled individual users to create word documents, spreadsheets, photographs, and a host of other digital representations. However, while users could create and shape digital information, they could not share it with others.

The process of creating an interconnected computer network began following the launch of Sputnik in 1957. Stunned by the Soviet success, the Eisenhower administration established the Advanced Research Projects Agency (ARPA) to facilitate scientific research at various laboratories across the country. ARPA constructed a network called Arpanet that originally linked computers at four universities. Within a short time, the rapidly expanding network became known as the Internet.

Finding documents on the Internet became an increasingly difficult problem. However, a brilliant British programmer named Tim Berners-Lee solved this problem by devising a common computer language that enabled every network user to easily access and post information. Berners-Lee named his new product the World Wide Web.

Released to the public in August 1991, the World Wide Web helped transform the Internet into an "information superhighway." The final breakthrough in connectivity came in August 1998, when Netscape launched its Navigator web browser. Soon Navigator, American Online, Yahoo! and the Microsoft Internet Explorer enabled computer users to shop, do research, listen to music, or surf the Internet for interesting webpages.

F. THE SMARTPHONE REVOLUTION

On January 9, 2007, Apple CEO Steve Jobs excitedly told his Macworld 2007 audience, "I have been looking forward to this for two and a half years." He then forcefully declared, "Today, Apple is going to reinvent the phone." Jobs then proceeded to introduce the iPhone. The device offered a number of features including email capability, high-speed Internet access, a built-in camera, and a high-definition touchscreen.

The iPhone more than lived up to Jobs' prediction. It marked the beginning of a far-reaching and still unfolding revolution. Within a decade after Job's famous presentation, over 225 million Americans and 2 billion people worldwide owned a smartphone. These pocket-size computers facilitated almost instantaneous communication that ushered in an era of constant connectivity.

TOPIC 17.5
GLOBALIZATION

A. THE ACCELERATING ADVANCE OF GLOBALIZATION

The 1980s marked the beginning of a revolutionary series of technological advances that promoted a global movement of people, products, and ideas. GLOBALIZATION refers to the process by which technological, economic, political, and cultural exchanges are making the world more interconnected and interdependent.

In 1492, distance and superstition isolated the people and products of Europe and the Americas. The process of globalization began when Columbus's small fleet of three ships began exploring the Caribbean islands. The interaction between the Spanish and the inhabitants of the Americas set in motion a complex movement of people, foods, animals, and germs known as the Columbian Exchange (See Chapter 1).

The Columbian Exchange generated an Atlantic trading community linking Europe, Africa, and the Americas. For example, in the mid-1700s American colonists sipped tea brewed from leaves imported by the British East Company. They sweetened their tea with Jamaican sugar grown by African slaves.

The period between the end of the Civil War and World War II witnessed a surge in globalization. Steam-powered ships brought a massive wave of Southern and Eastern Europeans to America (See Topic 11.4). The transatlantic telegraph enabled rapid exchanges of news between Europe and America. The telegraph set the stage for telephone and wireless communication. However, the spread of a severe depression from Europe to America and Japan illustrated the downside of globalization.

The fall of the Berlin Wall combined with the digital revolution to create a global market characterized by the free flow of money, goods, people, and information. Multinational companies play an increasingly prominent role in the global economy. For example, coffee is now second to oil as the most traded commodity in the world. Headquartered in Seattle, Washington, Starbucks is the world's largest chain of coffee stores. Just over half of the company's 30,000 stores are located outside the United States. Customers in Seattle, Beijing, and Seoul enjoy drinking blends from coffee beans grown in Columbia, Indonesia, Brazil, and many other countries.

B. THE LOSS OF MANUFACTURING JOBS

America dominated the Industrial Revolution. Its pioneering industrialists showed the world how to mass-produce everything from cars to suburban homes. American workers built planes, tanks, and ships that crushed Germany and Japan.

Manufacturing jobs constituted the core of America's industrial economy from the 1950s to the 1980s. However, employment in manufacturing peaked in 1979. During the next four decades, the nation lost over seven million manufacturing jobs.

Economists point to a number of reasons why the United States lost so many manufacturing jobs. Many argue that today's workforce no longer consists entirely of people. Instead, companies increasingly use sophisticated machines to execute tasks traditionally performed by human workers. This trend began in the 1980s, when automobile companies first used robots to automate their assembly lines. Manufacturers found that the robots were efficient, cost-effective, and safe.

While they do not deny the importance of automation, a growing number of economists point to globalization as a primary cause of the loss of American manufacturing jobs. Globalization has intensified a worldwide competition for low-cost labor. Industry after industry has felt the pressure of competing in a ruthlessly efficient international marketplace.

The iPhone provides a particularly vivid example of how the global marketplace is causing the loss of American manufacturing jobs. Highly paid engineers at Apple's headquarters in Cupertino, California, design the iPhone. However, the device is assembled by several hundred thousand poorly paid workers in massive Chinese factories. This system lowers the price of iPhones for consumers but causes the loss of manufacturing jobs for Americans.

C. THE DECLINE OF UNION MEMBERSHIP

The lure of cheap labor has encouraged American companies to relocate their production facilities in countries such as China and Mexico. This has caused a sharp decline in union membership. The percentage of employed union members peaked in 1945 at 33.4 percent of the employed labor force. This figure fell to just 10.7 percent in 2017.

D. THE RISING IMPORTANCE OF THE SERVICE SECTOR

The digital revolution and globalization are transforming the American economy. As the manufacturing sector has declined, employment in the service sector has steadily risen. More than three out of four jobs in the United States economy are now included in a broad category that ranges from the 1.5 million employees at Walmart to the 57,000 employees who work at the "Googleplex" in Mountain View, California.

Global competition has benefited and harmed different segments of the U.S. economy. Competition with workers across the globe has produced relentless downward pressure on American wages. At the same time, the shift to a service economy has benefited corporate executives and highly skilled professionals. As a result of these trends, wages have stagnated for working-class and middle-class Americans but have risen for employees in the high-tech and financial sectors.

CHAPTER 17
PRACTICE QUESTIONS

MULTIPLE-CHOICE QUESTIONS

Questions 1–4 refer to the excerpt below.

"It was in suburbs such as Garden Grove, Orange County, [California]...that small groups of middle-class men and women met in their new tract homes, seeking to turn the tide of liberal dominance. Recruiting the like-minded, they organized study groups, opened 'Freedom Forum' bookstores, filled the rolls of the John Birch Society, entered school board races, and worked within the Republican Party, all in an urgent struggle to safeguard their particular vision of freedom and the American heritage. In doing so, they became the ground forces of a conservative revival—one that transformed conservatism from a marginal force preoccupied with communism in the early 1960s into a viable electoral contender by the decade's end."

> Lisa McGirr, historian, *Suburban Warriors: The Origins of the New American Right*, 2015

1. **The "middle-class men and women" referenced in the excerpt were part of which broader historical movement?**
   A. The emergence of a counterculture
   B. The rise of radical feminists
   C. The protests of the Civil Rights movement
   D. The growth of the conservative movement

2. **The "tide of liberal dominance" refers to all of the following EXCEPT**
   A. Great Society programs
   B. The emergence of environmental activism
   C. The increasing participation of women in the labor force during the Second World War
   D. Supreme Court decisions prohibiting officially sponsored prayer and Bible readings in the public schools

3. **Which of the following best supports McGirr's assertion about how conservatism became "a viable electoral contender"?**

   A. The election of Barry Goldwater
   B. The election of Lyndon Johnson
   C. The election of Jimmy Carter
   D. The election of Ronald Reagan

4. **Which of the following ultimately became political allies of the Orange County conservatives?**

   A. Discontented blue-collar workers in the North
   B. Environmental activists in the Pacific Northwest
   C. Black Power protestors in urban ghettos
   D. Native American activists in South Dakota

Questions 5–7 refer to the excerpt below.

"I will not stand by and watch this great country destroying itself under mediocre leadership that drifts from one crisis to the next, eroding our national will and purpose…I will not accept the excuse that the Federal Government has grown so big and powerful that it is beyond the control of any President, any administration or Congress. We are going to put an end to the notion that the American taxpayer exists to fund the Federal Government. The Federal Government exists to serve the American people…We are taxing ourselves into economic exhaustion and stagnation, crushing our ability and incentive to save, invest and produce. This must stop."

   Ronald Reagan, speech accepting the Republican Party nomination for President, July 17, 1980

5. **The excerpt most strongly suggests that in 1980 which of the following was correct?**

   A. The Vietnam War remained a divisive issue
   B. The United States was entering a period of unprecedented peace and prosperity
   C. The Federal Government exercised too much control over the American economy
   D. The Republican Party overwhelmingly endorsed stringent environmental regulations

6. **The ideas expressed in the excerpt contributed most directly to Reagan's support for**

    A. supply-side economic policies
    B. the withdrawal of American forces from Vietnam
    C. campaigns by moral reformers to promote temperance
    D. legislation to promote the interests of organized labor

7. **Which of the following would have been most likely to support the views expressed in this excerpt?**

    A. Progressive Democrats living in the South
    B. White homeowners living in the Sunbelt
    C. Gay rights activists living in New York City
    D. Social Security recipients living in Florida

Questions 8–9 refer to the excerpt below.

"They [Soviet leaders] preach the supremacy of the state, declare its omnipotence over individual men, and predict its eventual domination of all peoples on Earth, they are the forces of evil in the modern world….I believe that communism is another sad, bizarre chapter in human history whose last pages are even now being written."

> President Ronald Reagan, speech to the National Association of Evangelicals, March 8, 1983

8. **Based upon the excerpt, President Reagan would most likely support**

    A. a return to President Nixon's policy of détente
    B. increases in American military budgets
    C. greater global economic integration under American leadership
    D. a decrease in American intervention in Latin America and the Middle East

9. **Which of the following contributed most directly to the fulfillment of President Reagan's prediction that communism's "last pages are even now being written?"**

    A. The spread of computer technology and Internet use
    B. The implementation of protective tariffs by America and its NATO allies
    C. The need for Mikhail Gorbachev's program of political and economic reforms
    D. The successful deployment of America's Strategic Defense Initiative or "Star Wars"

Questions 10–12 refer to the following graph.

US Manufacturing Jobs: On the Decline Since the 1960s
Percent of workers employed in manufacturing

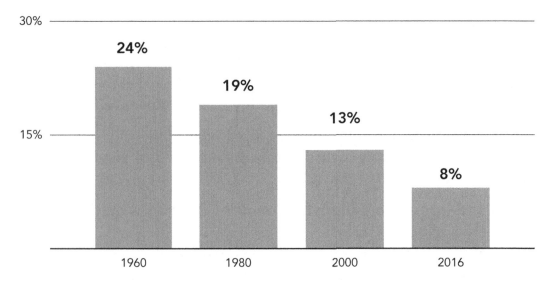

Source: United States Bureau of Labor Statistics

10. **The overall trend from 1960 to 2016 depicted on the graph was most directly caused by the**

    A. end of the Cold War
    B. impact of federal tax cuts
    C. increasing integration of female workers into the U.S. labor force
    D. increasing integration of the United States into the world economy

11. The overall trend from 1960 to 2016 depicted in the graph most directly led to a decline in

   A. union membership
   B. Social Security payments
   C. global trade
   D. environmental activism

12. The overall trend from 1960 to 2016 depicted in the graph contributed to

   A. intense cultural debates over gender roles
   B. an increase in digital communications
   C. expansion of the war on terrorism
   D. wage stagnation among the working and middle class amid growing economic inequality

Questions 13–15 refer to the excerpt below.

"Today, millions of transistors, each costing far less than a staple, can be etched on wafers of silicon. On these microchips, all the world's information and entertainment can be stored in digital form, processed and zapped to every nook of a networked planet....The microchip has become—like the steam engine, electricity, and the assembly line—an advance that propels a new economy."

   Walter Isaacson, historian and biographer, *TIME Magazine*, December 29, 1997

13. Which of the following earlier trends was most similar to the transformation described in the excerpt?

   A. The reforms implemented by Radical Reconstruction
   B. The attacks on labor activists and radical immigrants during the First Red Scare
   C. The development of national political parties during the early 1800s
   D. The Industrial Revolution in the latter half of the 1800s

14. The excerpt most directly reflects which of the following trends in the 1980s and 1990s?

   A. The expanding political participation of Christian groups
   B. The growing impact of the digital revolution
   C. The deregulation of industry
   D. The continuing cost of Great Society welfare programs

15. All of the following played key roles in propelling the "new economy" referenced in this excerpt EXCEPT the

A. ENIAC computer
B. Personal Computer (PC)
C. Internet
D. Smartphone

MULTIPLE-CHOICE ANSWERS

1. D	5. C	9. C	13. D
2. C	6. A	10. D	14. B
3. D	7. B	11. A	15. A
4. A	8. B	12. D	

SHORT-ANSWER QUESTIONS

Question 1
Using the excerpts below, answer A, B, and C.

"It is important to remember, though, that the peaceful end to the Cold War we have just witnessed is not the only conceivable way the Cold War could have ended. In adding up that conflict's costs, we would do well to recognize that the time it took to conclude the struggle was not time entirely wasted. That time—and those costs—appear to us excessive in retrospect, but future historians may see those expenditures as long-term investments in ensuring that the Cold War ended peacefully. For what we wound up doing with nuclear weapons was buying time—the time necessary for the authoritarian approach to politics to defeat itself by nonmilitary means. And the passage of time, even if purchased at an exorbitant price has at last begun to pay dividends."

John Lewis Gaddis, "The Cold War, The Long Peace, and the Future," 1992

"The United States emerged from the Cold War over-armed, burdened by debt and poverty, and carrying numerous scars from self-inflicted wounds to cherished institutions—all for the sake of the superpower competition. In forging itself into a hard-line Cold War warrior, the U.S. ultimately undermined its 'best traditions' more than it measured up to them. Had its leaders and citizens demonstrated greater faith in the strength of the nation's founding principles, the U.S. might have emerged from the Cold War contest economically leaner, brighter of spirit, and with its democratic institutions and values far stronger."

Wade Huntley, "Who Won the Cold War," 1993

A. Briefly describe ONE major difference between Gaddis's and Huntley's historical interpretations of the consequences of the Cold War for the United States.

B. Briefly describe ONE specific historical event or development from the period 1947–1991 that is not explicitly mentioned in the excerpts that could be used to support Gaddis's argument.

C. Briefly describe ONE specific historical event or development from the period 1947–1991 that is not explicitly mentioned in the excerpts that could be used to support Huntley's argument.

QUESTION 2:
Answer (a), (b), and (c). Confine your answer to the period from 1964 to 1980.

A. Briefly describe ONE specific historic difference between the reasons why Christian evangelicals and blue-collar workers became discontented with aspects of American life in the period from 1964 to 1980.

B. Briefly describe ONE specific historic similarity between the reasons why Christian evangelicals and blue-collar workers became discontented with aspects of American life in the period from 1964 to 1980.

C. Briefly explain ONE historic impact of the discontent felt by either Christian evangelicals or blue-collar workers in the period 1964 to 1980.

SHORT–ANSWER ANSWERS

Question 1

A. Gaddis argues that Cold War expenditures were a necessary investment that ensured that the long struggle between the United States and the Soviet Union ended peacefully. In contrast, Huntley argues that the Cold War inflicted unnecessary economic and cultural costs on America's democratic institutions and traditions.

B. The 1957 launch of Sputnik led to the creation of the Advanced Research Projects Agency (ARPA). ARPA constructed a computer network called Arpanet that evolved into the Internet. The Internet became a key part of the digital revolution and the process of globalization.

C. The Cold War encouraged an anti-Communist crusade during the early 1950s. Senator McCarthy's unsubstantiated accusations created an unnecessary climate of fear and paranoia that ruined careers and damaged America's traditions of free speech and due process.

Question 2

A. Christian evangelicals became discontented by social issues such as liberal Supreme Court decisions that prohibited school prayer and legalized abortion. In contrast, blue-collar workers became discontented by economic issues such as slowing wage growth, rising prices, and growing tax burdens.

B. Both Christian evangelicals and blue-collar workers were part of a backlash against the Great Society's liberal policies, the counterculture's permissive lifestyle, and the Vietnam War's protests and costs.

C. Many Christian evangelicals became members of the Moral Majority. The Moral Majority's four million members became a powerful political force that played a key role in the conservative movement and the election of Ronald Reagan in 1980.

PART V

MINI-CHAPTERS ON KEY TOPICS

CHAPTER 18
THE SECOND GREAT AWAKENING AND THE SOCIAL GOSPEL MOVEMENT

LOCATION AND STRATEGIC IMPORTANCE

The Second Great Awakening occurred in Period 4 (1800 –1848) while the Social Gospel movement occurred in Period 6 (1865 – 1898) and Period 7 (1890 – 1945). This chapter can stand alone as part of a topical review of the impact of religion on American reform movements.

The information in Chapter 18 has generated a significant number of answers on multiple-choice and short-answer questions. In addition, DBQs have regularly asked students to evaluate the impact of Second Great Awakening ideas on the abolition, temperance, and women's rights movements.

TOPIC 18.1
THE SECOND GREAT AWAKENING

1. The Second Great Awakening was a wave of religious fervor that swept across America between 1800 and 1830.

2. Thousands of people attended emotionally charged camp meetings featuring appeals to faith and conversion by charismatic preachers. Passionate worshippers pledged to renounce worldly sins and strive to lead more godly lives.

3. Intense religious revivals were especially widespread in central and western New York. This region became known as the "Burned-Over District" because of the particularly enthusiastic revivals that crisscrossed the area.

4. The Burned-Over District was the birthplace of the Church of Jesus Christ of Latter-Day Saints, or the Mormons. Founded in the 1820s by Joseph Smith, Mormonism attracted a number of loyal followers. In 1847, Brigham Young led more than 2,000 Mormons on an arduous journey to the shores of the Great Salt Lake in Utah.

5. Puritan ministers taught that God controlled each individual's destiny. In contrast, Charles Grandison Finney delivered inspiring sermons stressing

that Christians are not doomed by original sin. Instead, he emphasized humanity's inherent goodness and each individual's potential for self-improvement.

6. Finney and other Second Great Awakening preachers stressed that each individual was a "moral free agent" who could improve his or her life.

7. It was a short step from the Second Great Awakening emphasis upon spiritual progress to a belief in the possibility of social progress. The Second Great Awakening thus inspired a commitment to PERFECTIONISM –faith in the human ability to build a just society.

8. The optimistic belief that Christians have an obligation to improve their society generated a number of reform movements. In his essay "Man the Reformer," Ralph Waldo Emerson observed that "in the history of the world the doctrine of Reform had never such scope as the present hour." Emerson had a point. The Second Great Awakening inspired reformers to promote better care for the mentally ill, combat alcoholism, reform public education, abolish slavery, and expand women's rights.

9. Middle-class women played an especially important role in the Second Great Awakening. They boosted church membership and also spearheaded a number of reform movements. For example, Dorothea Dix urged humane treatment for the mentally ill while Lucretia Mott and Elizabeth Cady Stanton worked tirelessly to fight for women's rights.

10. The close link between religion and reform awakened America to the evils of slavery. For example, the call for moral reform influenced William Lloyd Garrison's demand for the immediate emancipation of all enslaved people.

TOPIC 18.2
THE SOCIAL GOSPEL MOVEMENT

1. The end of Reconstruction marked the beginning of a new era in American economic history. As the Second Industrial Revolution gathered momentum, millions of rural Americans and Southern and Eastern European immigrants flooded into factories to earn wages. At the same time, American cities began to rapidly grow. For example, the population of Chicago soared from 300,000 in 1870 to 1.1 million in 1890.

2. The rapidly changing world of industrial and urban America produced a range of new social problems. A small but influential group of journalists known as muckrakers wrote widely read articles calling attention to urban slums, the exploitation of child labor, and dangerous and often unsanitary conditions in American factories.

3. In 1896, pastor Charles Sheldon published a collection of his Sunday night services. Titled *In His Footsteps*, the book described how a fictitious midwestern pastor challenged his congregation to confront social issues by asking them to answer one question: "What would Jesus do?" The book quickly became a huge success and ranks as one of the best-selling books of all time.

4. Sheldon's book played an important role in mobilizing Protestant churches to apply Christian values to modern social problems. Known as the Social Gospel, the movement focused on building a just society by addressing pressing urban and industrial problems.

5. Walter Rauschenbusch was a theologian and Baptist pastor who emerged as one of the key figures in the Social Gospel movement. Rauschenbusch's sermons and books urged his followers to use direct social action to rectify the social sins plaguing American society.

6. Rauschenbusch strongly opposed the core beliefs of Social Darwinism. Influenced by Charles Darwin's theory of natural selection, Social Darwinists argued that there is a natural evolutionary process by which the fittest will survive and prosper while the unfit and lazy deserve their fate and should not receive help from society. In contrast, Rauschenbusch insisted that society has a moral responsibility to help the poor and less fortunate.

7. The Social Gospel movement added energy and a sense of urgency to the Progressive movement. Inspired by the Social Gospel message, Jane Addams transformed a decaying mansion located in the heart of one of Chicago's poorest immigrant neighborhoods into a thriving settlement house that offered services such as day care, English lessons, and personal hygiene. Hull House became a model that inspired the founding of over 400 similar facilities in cities across America.

8. The Social Gospel movement also played an important role in supporting the growth of Young Men and Women's Christian Associations (YMCA and YWCA). Both organizations were founded to help urban youth respond to urban environments without losing their religious faith.

9. Many historians argue that the Social Gospel movement constitutes a distinctive Third Great Awakening. They point out that the First Great Awakening focused largely on redeeming the souls of individual sinners. The Second Great Awaking focused on both individual salvation and social sins such as alcoholism and slavery. In contrast, the Third Great Awakening galvanized American Protestants to address the plight of impoverished people living in urban slums.

10. The Social Gospel movement became closely intertwined with the Progressive movement. Like the Progressive movement, the Social Gospel movement reached its peak in the years before the First World War. The horrors of the war created a mood of public disillusionment with social reform and a widespread desire to enjoy the material prosperity and frivolous entertainment of the Roaring Twenties.

CHAPTER 19

MARKET REVOLUTION AND THE RISE OF INDUSTRIAL CAPITALISM

LOCATION AND STRATEGIC IMPORTANCE

The MARKET REVOLUTION occurred in Period 4 (1800–1848), while the rise of industrial capitalism occurred in Period 6 (1865–1898). This chapter can stand alone as part of a topical review. Another option would be to use it after Chapter 8 as part of a chronological review of Periods 4 and 6.

The information in Chapter 17 has generated a significant number of answers on multiple-choice and short-answer questions. For example, both the 2015 and 2016 APUSH exams included short-answer questions. The 2015 question asked students to assess the economic impact of both the Market Revolution and the rise of industrial capitalism. The 2016 question asked students to compare how two noted historians evaluated Gilded Age business leaders.

TOPIC 19.1

THE MARKET REVOLUTION, 1820–1860

1. During the Era of Good Feelings, most Americans produced goods for local markets. Farmers and merchants in the Old Northwest lacked efficient and inexpensive access to markets along the East Coast. For example, farmers surrounding Pittsburgh were forced to use the Ohio and Mississippi rivers to ship their products to New Orleans, where their goods were then loaded onto cargo ships headed for East Coast ports.

2. Canals, steamboats, and railroads revolutionized American economic life during the antebellum period between 1820 and 1860.

3. Steamboats carried bulky farm products such as wheat, corn, and flour far more cheaply than covered wagons. By the 1840s, steamboats opened the Ohio and Mississippi river valleys to two-way traffic.

4. The Erie Canal connected Albany on the Hudson River with Buffalo on Lake Erie. When it opened in 1825 the 363-mile-long waterway created an all-water route that cut travel time from New York City to Buffalo from 20

days to six and reduced the cost of moving a ton of freight between these two cities from $100.00 to $5.00. The Erie Canal sparked the rapid growth of Buffalo while helping transform New York City into America's greatest commercial center.

5. Railroads connected cities, encouraged settlement, and reduced the cost of transporting goods. The number of miles of railroad track soared from just 13 when the Baltimore and Ohio opened in 1829 to 30,626 in 1860.

6. The Market Revolution had a significant economic impact on life in the Northeast. It created close trade ties with the Old Northwest, hastened the shift from hand-made to machine-made goods, and accelerated a transition to a wage-based economy. A group of ambitious entrepreneurs emerged as a new class of wealthy urban capitalists.

7. The Market Revolution had a significant impact on economic life in the Midwest. It accelerated the migration of settlers into the region, transformed Chicago into an important transportation hub, and closely linked the economies of the Midwest and the Northeast.

8. The South failed to keep up with the pace of industrialization and urbanization in the Northeast and Midwest. A Cotton Kingdom based upon slave labor extended across the Deep South. Led by a wealthy group of planters, the South produced a distinctive regional identity.

9. Innovations including textile machinery, steam engines, the telegraph, and agricultural inventions such as the steel plow and mechanical reaper increased the efficiency of production methods. The creation of profitable regional and interregional markets led to an American system of manufacturing that utilized machines with interchangeable parts to mass produce standardized low-cost goods.

10. As the Market Revolution gained momentum, it encouraged a division of labor between home and work. While men held jobs in a competitive market economy, the home became the special "sphere" for women.

TOPIC 19.2
THE RISE OF INDUSTRIAL CAPITALISM, 1865-1900

1. America's railroad network increased from 35,000 miles in 1865 to 193,000 miles in 1900. Railroad construction stimulated industrial growth by consuming vast quantities of iron, steel, coal, and lumber. The enormous expansion of rail lines facilitated the unprecedented movement of people, products, and ideas.

2. Prior to the Civil War, wood provided about half of America's energy. However, during the postwar period coal played a key role in the rise of industrial capitalism. American railroads and steamships took the lead in replacing wood with coal. In addition, steel mills used vast quantities of coal to fire their furnaces.

3. Railroads, steel companies, and oil refineries all faced intense competition from ambitious rivals. During the 1880s and 1890s, corporate executives consolidated their businesses into huge trusts and holding companies. By 1900, enormous corporations dominated the steel, oil, sugar, and meat packing industries.

4. Industrial capitalism produced a number of significant benefits. Efficient mass production methods reduced prices and gave consumers access to cheaper commodities. Growing corporations hired thousands of foremen, managers, and engineers who became part of a rising middle class.

5. The mechanization of production transformed many factories into places where low-paid workers performed simple and repetitive tasks.

6. America's booming economy concentrated unprecedented wealth in the hands of a small but powerful group of industrial titans. By 1900, the richest two percent of American households owned over one-third of the nation's physical wealth.

7. SOCIAL DARWINISM is the belief that there is a natural evolutionary process by which the fittest will survive and prosper. During the Gilded Age, wealthy business and industrial leaders embraced Social Darwinism to justify their success as both appropriate and inevitable. Social Darwinism provided a convenient explanation for the growing disparity of wealth between the rich and poor during the late nineteenth century.

8. Andrew Carnegie urged wealthy Americans to use their financial resources to help the less fortunate and improve society. Known as the GOSPEL OF WEALTH, this view inspired many wealthy industrialists to support colleges, museums, and public libraries.

9. Industrial workers formed new labor unions to confront managerial power. During the 1880s and 1890s, labor and management battled over wages and working conditions. Over 23,000 strikes disrupted the American economy during these two decades.

10. A new generation of Southern leaders strove to build a more diversified regional economy. New textile mills in the Carolinas and steel mills in Birmingham, Alabama, helped lead the process. However, the dream of a New South remained elusive. In 1900, two-thirds of all Southern men still worked as sharecroppers and tenant farmers.

CHAPTER 20
MANIFEST DESTINY AND IMPERIALISM

LOCATION AND STRATEGIC IMPORTANCE

MANIFEST DESTINY occurred during Period 5 (1844–1877), while IMPERIALISM occurred during Period 7 (1890–1945). This chapter can stand alone as part of a topical review. Another option would be to use it after Chapter 9 as part of a chronological review of Periods 5 and 7.

The information in Chapter 18 has generated a significant number of answers to multiple-choice questions. Manifest Destiny is often used as the answer to multiple-choice questions linked to a map depicting America's westward expansion. Test writers have used imperialism as a central concept for DBQ questions about America's expanding role in world affairs during the late 1890s.

TOPIC 20.1
MANIFEST DESTINY

1. As he left the White House in 1837, Andrew Jackson confidently predicted Providence chose Americans to be "the guardians of freedom to preserve it for the benefit of the human race." The American people wholeheartedly agreed with Jackson. Convinced of the superiority of their customs and institutions, the public enthusiastically supported territorial expansion.

2. MANIFEST DESTINY is associated with the territorial expansion of the United States from 1815 to 1860. During this time, the United States expanded to the Pacific Ocean.

3. John O'Sullivan coined the term Manifest Destiny in 1845. An influential journalist and proponent of Jacksonian democracy, O'Sullivan believed that the United States had a right to claim the entire Oregon Territory. He argued that America's claim to these lands "is by the right of our Manifest Destiny to overspread and to possess the whole of the continent which Providence has given us for the development of the great experiment of liberty and federated self-government entrusted to us."

4. Manifest Destiny assumed that from its earliest beginnings America embarked upon a special experiment in freedom and democracy. The phrase successfully captured the linkage between territorial expansion and America's self-proclaimed mission to spread the blessings of liberty and progress across the continent.

5. Illinois Representative John Wentworth expressed the optimistic sense of America's special destiny when he told Congress that the original States had a divinely sanctioned mission to become the "great center from which civilization, religion, and liberty should radiate and radiate until the whole continent should bask in their blessings."

6. The issue of Manifest Destiny dominated the 1844 presidential election. As the campaign began, Texas still remained independent, California still belonged to Mexico, and America and Great Britain still shared the Oregon Territory.

7. President Polk and other leaders used Manifest Destiny to justify the annexation of Texas and the Mexican War.

8. Whigs criticized Manifest Destiny as an excuse for justifying the war with Mexico. New England abolitionists forcefully argued that the slogan "extending the area of freedom" really meant extending the institution of slavery.

9. Mexico lost the Mexican War and ceded New Mexico and California to the United States while also accepting the Rio Grande as the Texas border. At that time, New Mexico included what is now Arizona, Nevada, Utah, and parts of Colorado and Wyoming.

10. Manifest Destiny transformed the United States into a transcontinental republic. Instead of giving rise to a new era of harmony, the postwar spirit of nationalism quickly faded as a sectional struggle over the territorial expansion of slavery began to dominate American political life.

TOPIC 20.2
IMPERIALISM

1. America emerged from the age of Manifest Destiny as a continental republic that stretched from the Atlantic to the Pacific. During the three decades following the Civil War, the nation focused its energies on Reconstruction, industrial development, and settling the West.

2. IMPERIALISM is the policy of extending a nation's power through military conquest, economic domination, and/or annexation. Imperialism gained support in the United States in the late 1890s.

3. Advocates of imperialism argued that compelling economic interests required America to play a more aggressive role in world affairs. Imperialists pointed out that the Depression of 1893 dealt a severe blow to the American economy. Industrial leaders insisted that America needed new foreign markets and sources of raw materials in order to restore prosperity and ensure the nation's economic leadership.

4. Proponents of imperialism argued that America's status as a great nation required it to project naval power into the Pacific Ocean. In his book *The Influence of Sea Power upon History*, Captain Alfred T. Mahan maintained that the United States should view the Pacific Ocean as a commercial highway that required the presence of a powerful navy. The United States therefore had a strategic interest in obtaining bases and coaling stations in the Pacific to facilitate and defend its Asian interests. Theodore Roosevelt, Henry Cabot Lodge, and other influential expansionists championed Mahan's recommendations.

5. Advocates of imperialism argued that the United States had a moral responsibility to bring the blessings of its civilization to less advanced peoples. Often called "The White Man's Burden," this idea justified a new national mission to "elevate backward peoples." For example, President McKinley believed that the Filipinos "were unfit for self-government." He concluded "that there was nothing left for us to do but to take them all, and to educate the Filipinos, and uplift and civilize and Christianize them."

6. The Anti-Imperialist League strongly opposed the annexation of the Philippines. League members argued that imperialism violated America's long-established commitment to the principles of self-determination and anti-colonialism. William Jennings Bryan argued that "Imperialism is the policy of empire....A republic cannot be an empire because a republic rests upon the theory that the government derived its power from the consent of the governed and colonialism violates this theory."

7. Leading pacifists warned that imperialism would encourage militarism. For example, Jane Addams feared that imperialism would encourage a "barbaric instinct" that would overwhelm America's traditional "humane instinct."

8. Like the Whigs before them, the anti-imperialists opposed a policy of territorial expansion that betrayed America's democratic institutions.

9. Both Manifest Destiny and imperialism justified military conflicts. The war with Mexico resulted in the acquisition of California and the New Mexico territory. The war with Spain resulted in the acquisition of Puerto Rico, Guam, and the Philippines.

10. The acquisition of the Philippines provoked a bloody guerilla war. After three years of fighting, America's overwhelming military power finally crushed the rebels.

CHAPTER 21
POPULISTS AND PROGRESSIVES

LOCATION AND STRATEGIC IMPORTANCE

The Populist and Progressive movements both occurred during Period 7 (1890–1945). This chapter can stand alone as part of a topical review. Another option would be to use it after Chapter 9 as part of a chronological review of Period 7.

The information in Chapter 19 has generated a significant number of multiple-choice and short-answer questions. For example, test writers have asked students to interpret an anti-Populist cartoon and a political cartoon about the linkage between muckraking and the Meat Inspection Act.

TOPIC 21.1
THE POPULISTS

1. During the last quarter of the nineteenth century, new machinery and fertilizers enabled American farmers to increase the number of acres under cultivation. But as the supply of crops increased, farm prices decreased, and farmers faced mounting debts.

2. Debt-ridden farmers blamed the railroads and the nation's economic system for their problems. They accused the railroads of abusing their monopoly by charging exorbitant freight rates. They assailed government economic policies that limited the money supply by mandating that the nation's currency had to be backed by gold. This limited America's supply of money and benefitted the banks and wealthy creditors.

3. America's farmers increasingly saw themselves as victims of an unjust political and economic system. As their debts mounted, struggling farmers became convinced that neither the Democratic nor the Republican parties would address the problems caused by greedy bankers and arrogant railroad executives.

4. In 1892 the wave of agrarian discontent gave birth to the People's or Populist Party. The Populists hoped to build a coalition of Western and Southern

farmers and Eastern industrial workers that would replace the Democrats as a major political party.

5. The Populist Party platform put forth an ambitious list of proposals to shift power back to the people. They demanded a graduated income tax, whereby individuals earning higher incomes paid a higher percentage in taxes. The list of political reforms called for the direct election of senators, the secret ballot, and a one-term limit for the president. And finally, the Populist Party platform called for the free and unlimited coinage of silver. Populist leaders argued that "free silver" would put more money into circulation, thus spurring inflation and promoting growth. Rising prices for farm commodities would increase profits and reduce debts.

6. The Populists achieved surprising success in the 1892 election. Their presidential candidate, James B. Weaver, polled over one million votes, more than any previous third-party candidate. The Populist goal of replacing the Democrats as a major political party now seemed possible.

7. The Democrats surprised the Populists by repudiating President Cleveland and writing a platform endorsing the free coinage of silver. The Democrats now had an issue but still lacked a candidate. That changed when William Jennings Bryan, a 36-year-old former congressman from Nebraska, addressed the convention. Bryan's famous "Cross of Gold" speech electrified the convention. The next day, euphoric delegates nominated Bryan for President.

8. The Democrats' surprise decision to nominate a pro-silver candidate forced the Populists to confront a difficult choice. They could support Bryan and surrender their identity as an independent party. Or they could nominate their own candidate and divide the pro-silver vote. After a bitter debate, the Populists reluctantly chose to endorse Bryan.

9. The 1896 presidential campaign proved to be an epic contest. Nearly 80 percent of the eligible voters cast their ballots in one of America's highest election turnouts. The voters gave the Republican candidate William McKinley a convincing victory.

10. The election of 1896 led to the demise of the Populist Party. However, their reform message did not die. A new generation of Progressive reformers endorsed constitutional amendments calling for a graduated income tax and the direct election of senators.

TOPIC 21.2
THE PROGRESSIVES

1. After the collapse of the Populist Party the reform spirit shifted to the cities where a new generation of well-educated middle- and upper-middle-class reformers focused on a broad range of problems caused by industrialization and urbanization. Unlike the Populists, the Progressives did not initially form a third party. Instead, Progressivism embraced a widespread multifaceted movement to build a more democratic and just society. The Progressive Era is usually dated from 1890 to America's entry into World War I in 1917.

2. Both the Populists and the Progressives rejected *laissez-faire* or "hands off" government policies. Instead, they wanted government to play an active role in public life. The Progressives believed that complex social problems required a broad range of governmental responses. "The real heart of the movement," declared one Progressive, "was to use the government as an agency of human welfare."

3. The Progressives were idealists who believed that conflict and ruthless competition would not improve society. Instead, they optimistically believed that informed citizens could create a just society that would confront the plight of the urban poor, regulate corporations, protect the environment, address consumer issues, and elect honest leaders.

4. MUCKRAKERS were journalists who exposed corruption and social problems through investigative reporting. For example, Upton Sinclair's *The Jungle* used nauseating details to describe unsanitary practices in the meatpacking industry. His description of rats running across piles of warehouse meat provoked a national outcry. Congress responded to public pressure by enacting the Pure Food and Drug Act and the Meat Inspection Act to restore proper sanitation standards. These two acts illustrate the relationship between muckraking and reform legislation.

5. The Progressive Era marked a significant turning point in the history of American women. When the era began, men ran the nation's businesses and cast all of its votes. The prevailing belief in the cult of domesticity restricted women to their homes. During the Progressive Era a generation of middle-class "New Women" extended their role as guardians of the home to include becoming activists who fought to improve their communities. Women became a driving force behind many Progressive Era reforms. They joined clubs, founded settlement houses, and successfully fought for constitutional amendments prohibiting the sale of alcoholic beverages and granting women the suffrage.

6. Women's commitment to aggressively join the Progressive battle for social reform sparked a nationwide settlement house movement. Jane Addams founded Hull House, the first and best-known American settlement house. The facility provided day care nurseries, English lessons, and a number of courses on cooking, dressmaking, and personal hygiene. Hull House served as a model for other middle-class women, who founded over 400 settlement houses in cities across America.

7. Theodore Roosevelt quickly became a major voice in the Progressive movement. Like other Progessives, TR believed that government should be used to solve the nation's pressing problems. The dynamic force of his personality revitalized the presidency and established the White House as the focal point of American life. During his administration, TR launched antitrust action against the Northern Securities Company and secured passage of the Hepburn Act to regulate the railroads.

8. The wanton exploitation of western forests, wildlife, and scenic areas outraged Progressives. PRESERVATIONISTS believed that government policies should preserve wilderness areas in their natural state. In contrast, CONSERVATIONISTS believed that government policies should promote the management of natural resources in a responsible and sustained manner. TR embraced both views. He set aside more Federal land for natural parks and wildlife preserves than all of his predecessors combined. As a Conservationist he signed the Newlands Reclamation Act that funded irrigation projects throughout the West.

9. Woodrow Wilson successfully implemented his Progressive New Freedom program by reducing tariffs, creating the Federal Reserve System, and strengthening antitrust laws.

10. Progressive Era reforms devoted little attention to the plight of African Americans. However, the era did witness the formation of the National Association for the Advancement of Colored People (NAACP) and the emergence of W.E.B. Du Bois as an influential black leader.

CHAPTER 22
NEW DEAL AND GREAT SOCIETY

LOCATION AND STRATEGIC IMPORTANCE

The New Deal occurred during Period 7 (1890–1945), while the Great Society occurred during Period 8 (1945–1980). This chapter can stand alone as part of a topical review. Another option would be to use it after Chapters 9 and 19 as part of a chronological review.

The information in Chapter 20 has generated a significant number of multiple-choice and short-answer questions. For example, test writers recently asked students to compare how two historians viewed the New Deal's achievements and shortcomings.

TOPIC 22.1
THE NEW DEAL

1. When Franklin D. Roosevelt took the oath of office on March 4, 1933, the United States faced a grave economic crisis. During the previous three years 86,000 businesses closed their doors, 9,000 banks declared bankruptcy, stocks lost 89 percent of their value, and the unemployment rate rose to a staggering 24.9 percent. Poverty had become a way of life for one-fourth of the nation.

2. America's collapsing banking system posed the first test of FDR's leadership. The week before his inauguration, millions of panicky depositors had withdrawn their assets in cash. Within four days, Congress passed a new banking act. On March 12, FDR broadcast the first of his famous radio fireside chats to describe the measures that had been taken to resolve the banking crisis. His confidence reassured the American public. The next morning long lines of people formed to redeposit their money into the bank.

3. FDR promised and quickly delivered a "New Deal for the American people." In just one hundred days from March 9 to June 16, 1933, Congress approved

fifteen major pieces of social and economic legislation. Unlike either the Progressive Era presidents or his predecessor Herbert Hoover, Roosevelt recognized that America's millions of unemployed workers needed direct federal relief. For example, the Civilian Conservation Corp (CCC) created a jobs program for two million unemployed men aged 18 to 25. The men lived in camps and worked on a variety of conservation projects in the nation's parks and recreation areas.

4. The New Deal did more than provide immediate relief. It also attempted to promote economic recovery, institute long-term reforms, and restore public confidence in the nation's banking system. For example, the Glass-Steagall Banking Act established the Federal Deposit Insurance Corporation (FDIC) to guarantee bank deposits up to $5,000. The FDIC successfully calmed the public's fear of losing their hard-earned savings.

5. In 1934 and 1935 the Democratic majorities in Congress enacted a series of far-reaching programs known as the Second New Deal. The Social Security Act created a federal pension system funded by taxes on a worker's wages and by an equivalent contribution by employers. The Wagner Labor Relations Act recognized labor's right to bargain collectively. The new law created the National Labor Relations Board (NLRB) to protect workers from unfair practices and to arbitrate labor-management disputes.

6. The New Deal did not directly confront racial injustice. For example, CCC camps were often racially segregated. Nonetheless, the New Deal programs did create employment opportunities that helped African Americans survive the Great Depression. Despite the New Deal's limitations, African Americans overwhelmingly switched their allegiance from the Republican Party to FDR and the Democratic Party.

7. African Americans became an important part of the New Deal coalition of voters that formed during the 1930s. The coalition also included urban Progressives, members of labor unions, ethnic minorities, and white Southerners. This coalition enabled the Democratic Party to win the White House in six of the eight presidential elections between 1936 and 1964.

8. New Deal programs were only partially successful in reducing unemployment and reviving the economy. The United States finally emerged from the Great Depression when the federal government sharply increased military spending at the beginning of World War II.

9. The New Deal accelerated the process first begun during the Progressive Era of expanding the federal government's role in American life. Under the New Deal the federal government accepted responsibility for addressing a wide range of social problems previously left to individuals, states, and local

governments. By the end of the 1930s, the federal government became America's largest single employer.

10. The New Deal did NOT integrate the armed forces, sponsor the ERA, nationalize basic industries, or provide recognition for migrant workers.

TOPIC 22.2
THE GREAT SOCIETY

1. President Lyndon B. Johnson plunged into his presidential duties in the dark days following the assassination of President Kennedy. In May 1964 he delivered a speech challenging America to build a "Great Society" that would use the power of the federal government to end racial injustice, fight poverty, and promote the social welfare. Unlike FDR, Johnson did not face an economic crisis. Instead, he conceived the Great Society during a period of great economic prosperity.

2. LBJ understood that the fight against Jim Crow segregation posed the nation's most urgent social problem. He proudly signed the landmark 1964 Civil Rights Act into law on July 2, 1964. The act barred discrimination in public facilities such as hotels, restaurants, and theaters. The legislation authorized the attorney general to bring suits to accelerate school desegregation. In addition, the act outlawed discrimination in employment on the basis of race, religion, national origin, or sex.

3. President Johnson and civil rights leaders next turned to the issue of voting rights. The Fifteenth Amendment gave black males the right to vote. However, a combination of literacy tests and poll taxes effectively nullified the amendment. The Voting Rights Act of 1965 made the Fifteenth Amendment an operative part of the Constitution. The law ended literacy tests and other devices used to prevent African Americans from voting.

4. President Johnson believed that his landslide victory in the 1964 election gave him a mandate to pursue his dream of waging an "unconditional War on Poverty." Congress supported the President's bold initiative by passing a host of new federal programs to help the poor. For example, high school dropouts learned new skills in over 50 Job Corps camps.

5. The Great Society also dealt with the pressing health care needs of America's senior citizens. The Social Security Amendments of 1965 created Medicare and Medicaid. These programs established government health insurance coverage for elderly and poor Americans.

6. The Great Society included legislation designed to improve the quality of American education. The Elementary and Secondary Education Act of 1965

provided over one billion dollars to fund preschool programs, support school libraries, purchase textbooks, and provide special education services.

7. The Immigration Act of 1965 abolished the system of national quotas established by the National Origins Act of 1924. Although it was not recognized at the time, the new law had the unintended consequence of permitting a new wave of immigration from Latin America and Asia.

8. The Great Society did not ignore the environment. For example, the Water Quality Act of 1965 set national water quality standards.

9. The escalating costs of the Vietnam War forced President Johnson to divert funds from the War on Poverty to the war in Vietnam. In 1968, the United States spent $322,600 to kill each Communist soldier. In that year, Great Society programs received just $53,000 for each American in the War on Poverty.

10. The Great Society did NOT establish the Peace Corps, create Social Security, guarantee employment, or place new restrictions on immigration.

CHAPTER 23
THE 1920S AND THE 1950S

LOCATION AND STRATEGIC IMPORTANCE

The 1920s occurred during Period 7 (1890–1945), while the 1950s occurred during Period 8 (1945–1980). This chapter can stand alone as part of a topical review. Another option would be to use it after Chapters 10 and 20 as part of a chronological review.

The information in Chapter 21 has generated a significant number of multiple-choice and short-answer questions. For example, test writers often ask students to compare aspects of American culture in the 1920s and 1950s.

TOPIC 23.1
THE 1920S

1. The 1920s began with a wave of anticommunist hysteria known as the RED SCARE. On January 2, 1920, Attorney General A. Mitchell Palmer ordered Department of Justice agents to arrest thousands of suspected anarchists, Communists, and radical leftists in more than 30 cities. The Palmer raids violated civil liberties by breaking into homes and union offices without arrest warrants. Although most of those arrested were released, the Department of Justice deported about 500 alleged radicals without holding hearings or trials.

2. The Palmer Raids marked the end of the Red Scare. However, they did not mark the end of intolerance and nativism. During the early 1920s, membership in the Ku Klux Klan swelled to as many as four million people. The revived Klan endorsed white supremacy and immigration restriction. Congress responded to this nativist pressure by passing the National Origins Act of 1924. The law established quotas that sharply reduced the flow of immigrants from Southern and Eastern Europe.

3. The Republican Party controlled the White House during the 1920s. Presidents Harding, Coolidge, and Hoover all rejected Wilson's vision of

American leadership in the League of Nations. They also largely ignored the zealous idealism of reform-minded Progressives. Instead, Harding began the decade by promising the nation an escape from complex problems and a return to "normalcy." For Harding, Coolidge, and Hoover, normalcy meant pursuing pro-business policies and avoiding troublesome domestic issues.

4. The 1920s witnessed the mass production of a new generation of affordable consumer products. Labor-saving devices such as refrigerators, washing machines, electric irons, and vacuum cleaners made household chores easier, thus creating time to enjoy leisure activities. The mass production of automobiles had the greatest impact upon American society. Surging car sales stimulated the growth of companies that produced steel, rubber tires, glass, and gasoline. Within a few years the automobile transformed America from a land of isolated farms and small towns into a nation of cities and suburbs connected by paved roads.

5. During the 1920s Hollywood movies emerged as America's fifth largest industry. Moviegoers purchased 100 million tickets a week to watch Rudolph Valentino, Clara Bow, Charlie Chaplin and other popular screen idols. The movie boom gained additional momentum when Hollywood producers released the first "talkies" in 1927. Within a year Walt Disney put a sound track on an animated cartoon featuring a mouse he named Mickey.

6. On November 2, 1920, radio station KDKA of Pittsburgh, Pennsylvania turned on its new transmitter and broadcast the news that American voters had elected Warren Harding as the nation's new president. KDKA's reign as America's only operating radio station did not last long. By the middle of the decade over 600 new stations broadcast a mix of news, weather forecasts, sports scores, music, comedy routines, and most of all commercials to an audience of 50 million listeners.

7. The radio boom and the mass production of automobiles and consumer goods fueled a spectacular economic boom. Materialism flourished as advertisements urged consumers to "buy now and pay later." During the period from 1921 to 1929, America's gross national product soared from $74 billion to $104.4 billion. The unprecedented prosperity seemed to offer a glittering future that would continue to offer endless enjoyment.

8. The GREAT MIGRATION of African Americans from the rural South to industrial cities in the North and Midwest continued during the 1920s. Harlem emerged as a vibrant center of African American culture. During the 1920s a new generation of black writers and artists created an outpouring of work known as the HARLEM RENAISSANCE. Many embraced the term

"New Negro" as a proud assertion of their African American heritage and culture.

9. A group of writers and poets known as the Lost Generation became disillusioned with America's frivolous mass culture. Lost Generation writers such as Sinclair Lewis, F. Scott Fitzgerald, and T. S. Eliot criticized shallow middle-class materialism and mindless conformity.

10. The 1920s marked the appearance of America's first youth culture, in which a generation of under-25-year-olds deliberately flaunted a new set of styles, attitudes, and ways of behaving. Young women known as FLAPPERS became the most publicized and controversial representatives of both rebellious youth and the new American woman. Flappers defied conventional standards by wearing short skirts and makeup, dancing to jazz, and enjoying wild parties. Print magazines, Hollywood films, and radio advertisements all glamorized the flapper's carefree and often shocking lifestyle.

TOPIC 23.2
THE 1950s

1. On February 9, 1950, Senator Joseph R. McCarthy told an audience in Wheeling, West Virginia, "I have in my hand a list of 205 names known to the Secretary of State as being members of the Communist Party and who nevertheless are still working and shaping the policy of the State Department." Although never substantiated, McCarthy's accusations touched a particularly sensitive public nerve. During the early 1950s McCARTHYISM became associated with a new Red Scare. The political climate of the McCarthy era resembled the attacks on radicals following the First World War. McCarthy's campaign of innuendo and half-truths finally turned public sentiment against him. In December 1954, the full Senate formally censured McCarthy for his dishonorable conduct. Flashing his famous grin, President Eisenhower asked his cabinet, "Have you heard the latest? McCarthyism is McCarthywasm."

2. Although McCarthy's wild accusations lacked substance, the public's fear of Communist aggression was grounded in a harsh reality. During the 1950s the United States and the Soviet Union remained locked in a prolonged period of economic and political rivalry known as the COLD WAR. By 1954 both superpowers had exploded hydrogen bombs. What Winston Churchill called "a balance of terror" seemed frighteningly real. Worries about the threat of a Soviet nuclear attack prompted the construction of well-marked fallout shelters in public buildings. Anxious school officials ordered

elementary students to practice hiding under desks as part of Duck and Cover drills.

3. The fall of McCarthyism corresponded with a period of unprecedented prosperity. The gross national product soared from $200 billion in 1945 to $500 billion in 1960. With just six percent of the world's population, Americans drove 75 percent of the world's automobiles, consumed half of its energy, and produced almost half of its manufactured products.

4. America's robust economic growth sparked a strong demand for new homes in the suburbs. Builders met the demand by using assembly-line production techniques pioneered by William J. Levitt. Of the 13 million new homes constructed in the 1950s, 11 million sprang up in the suburbs. New interstate highways enabled suburbanites to commute from their homes to jobs in the cities. Much of the suburban growth occurred in an arc of states stretching from the Carolinas to Florida and on to Texas and Southern California. Known as the SUNBELT, this region steadily gained political, economic, and cultural influence.

5. On January 19, 1953, a record audience turned on over 70 percent of America's television sets to watch an episode of *I Love Lucy*, featuring the birth of Lucy's son Little Ricky. The overwhelming popularity of this program provided a vivid example of the explosive growth of television. In 1946 there were just 7,000 TV sets and six TV stations in the entire country. By 1953 half of all homes had a TV set, and the average family spent five hours a day gathered around it. Like radio in the 1920s, television played an increasingly important role in shaping popular opinions and stimulating consumer demand for new products.

6. Economic prosperity and suburban growth did not encourage a renewal of women's rights activism. Instead magazines, movies, and television programs all glamorized romantic love and celebrated marriage. The marriage boom triggered a postwar baby boom. The 1950s witnessed a tidal wave of 40 million births. The young families populated suburbs that became known for a revival of the CULT OF DOMESTICITY. The mass media reinforced and idealized traditional gender roles, in which men commuted to work while their wives stayed home and raised their children.

7. Not all Americans hailed the rapid suburbanization of American life. In her song "Little Boxes," Malvina Reynolds decried the homogenized suburbs where everyone lived in "little boxes" that "all look just the same." A group of writers and poets known as BEATS shared Reynolds's disdain for middle-class culture. Like the Lost Generation writers of the 1920s, Beat writers felt

alienated from America's excessive materialism and constant pressure to get along.

8. In the Spring of 1953 a poor truck driver walked into Sun Records in Memphis and politely introduced himself: "My name is Elvis Presley and I want to make a record." The head of the studio, Sam Philips, soon realized that Elvis was "a white man who had the Negro sound and the Negro feel." Elvis quickly became the best-selling recording artist in America. His rock and roll songs proved to be more than just a passing fad. Like Beat writers, rock and roll singers challenged accepted beliefs about sex, race, and work. Rock and roll soon became the sound that helped shape and define the new teenage culture.

9. The Supreme Court ruling in *Brown v. Board of Education of Topeka* overturned the "separate but equal" doctrine established in *Plessy v. Ferguson*. The decision opened a new era in the African American struggle for equal rights. The unanimous *Brown* decision placed the Supreme Court on the side of racial justice. Galvanized by the Court's ruling, America's 15 million black citizens began to demand, "Freedom Now!"

10. The next step on the road to freedom began on a bus in Montgomery, Alabama. On December 1, 1955, a weary black seamstress named Rosa Parks defied local segregation laws and refused to give up her bus seat to a white man. Her arrest outraged Parks's 26-year-old minister, Dr. Martin Luther King, Jr. Dr. King mobilized Montgomery's black community by organizing a boycott of the city buses. His leadership in the Montgomery Bus Boycott transformed him from an unknown local minister into America's foremost civil rights leader. Within a short time Dr. King founded the Southern Christian Leadership Council (SCLC) to apply the principles of nonviolent civil disobedience to test cases across the South.

CHAPTER 24
THE KOREAN WAR AND THE VIETNAM WAR

LOCATION AND STRATEGIC IMPORTANCE

The Korean War and the Vietnam War both occurred during Period 8 (1945–1980). This chapter can stand alone as part of a topical review. Another option would be a to use it after Chapters 10 and 21 as part of a chronological review.

The information in Chapter 22 has generated a significant number of multiple-choice and short-answer questions. Test writers often use political cartoons to generate multiple-choice questions on the Vietnam War. In addition, both wars have been central parts of short-answer questions.

TOPIC 24.1
THE KOREAN WAR

1. The Korean peninsula shares a long border with China and extends to a point just 100 miles northwest of Japan. At the end of World War II, American and Soviet troops arbitrarily divided the Korean peninsula at the 38th parallel. Although this began as a temporary arrangement, the chill of the Cold War soon froze the boundary, thus creating two rival Korean states—a Soviet-sponsored Communist government in the north and an American-supported pro-Western government in the south.

2. The Korean War began when a powerful North Korean army invaded South Korea on June 25, 1950. Within days, the North Korean forces overran Seoul, the South Korean capital, and seemed certain to conquer the entire Korean peninsula.

3. The Truman administration viewed the invasion as a test of CONTAINMENT and thus America's position as leader of the Free World. Truman did not ask Congress for a declaration of war. Instead, he called upon the United Nations to intervene. Taking advantage of a temporary Soviet boycott, the UN Security Council voted unanimously to send troops to South Korea. This

marked the first time in history that a world organization mobilized to stop aggression.

4. The Korean War's first year of combat featured astonishing and rapid reversals of fortune. Led by Douglas MacArthur, American forces reversed the North Korean invasion and then attempted to reunify the peninsula. However, the Chinese army intervened and forced the U.S. and its allies to retreat. The next two years settled into a bloody stalemate near the original border along the 38th parallel. In fighting reminiscent of the trench warfare in World War I, American soldiers lost their lives fighting dangerous patrols and repelling enemy raids.

5. Prior to the Korean War, American soldiers fought in segregated units. In July 1948, President Truman ordered the racial desegregation of the U.S. armed forces. The Korean War marked the first time American soldiers fought in integrated combat units.

6. Peace talks began in July 1951. While the talks dragged on, the fighting continued. After 25 months and 158 separate meetings, the warring sides finally signed an armistice or cease-fire agreement. Although the armistice established a truce, it was not a peace treaty.

7. The Korean War has cast a long shadow over events in Asia. The conflict left the Korean peninsula permanently divided between a brutal dictatorship in North Korea and a prosperous democracy in South Korea. A heavily fortified, 160-mile-long and 2.5-mile-wide Demilitarized Zone (DMZ) separates the two Koreas. About 28,000 American soldiers remain stationed along the DMZ. Backed by America's overwhelming military power, these troops help deter North Korean aggression while reassuring South Korea that America will stand by its ally.

8. The Korean War ended any chance that the United States would recognize the People's Republic of China. As relations with China deteriorated, the United States pledged to protect Taiwan. This commitment enabled Taiwan to survive and prosper.

9. The Korean War's seesaw battles and long stalemate took place in a period just before television became a ubiquitous part of American life. The Korean War failed to generate either ardent supporters or outraged protestors. Instead, the costly limited war provided a source of frustration that contributed to a period of paranoia and unsubstantiated accusations of disloyalty known as McCARTHYISM.

10. The Korean War provided the justification for a massive American military build-up. Defense spending rose from $13 billion in 1949 to $50 billion in 1953. These expenditures helped fuel a period of sustained economic

growth. Defense spending played a role in spurring economic growth in parts of the South and West Coast.

TOPIC 24.2
THE VIETNAM WAR

1. Vietnam forms a long curving S on the eastern side of the Indochina peninsula. Although ranging from 33 to 300 miles wide, Vietnam stretches almost 1,400 miles in length from the Chinese border to the Gulf of Thailand. Despite its strategic location, most Americans knew very little about Vietnam's struggle struggle for independence.

2. France conquered Vietnam during the late 1800s. By the 1930s, Vietnam became a prized colonial possession that produced all of France's raw rubber and much of its imported rice. Following World War II, communist forces led by Ho Chi Minh declared Vietnam an independent country. However, the French refused to accept the loss of their valuable colony. Supported by generous American aid, the French soon became entangled in a costly war with Ho's guerilla forces. The war ended in a disastrous French defeat that left Vietnam divided at the 17th parallel. Ho Chi Minh and his communist government ruled north of the parallel, while a French-backed government ruled south of the parallel.

3. The French defeat forced President Eisenhower to make a crucial decision. The U.S. experience in Korea seemed to validate the belief that American power could be effectively used to contain Communism in Asia. Ike refused to abandon Vietnam. At a news conference he explained that "When you have a row of dominoes set up, you knock over the first one, and what happens to the last one is the certainty that it will go over very quickly." The president's message was clear—the United States would not allow Ho Chi Minh to take over South Vietnam. According to Ike's DOMINO THEORY, the fall of South Vietnam would inevitably lead to Communist expansion throughout the rest of Southeast Asia.

4. During his inaugural address, President Kennedy pledged that the United States would "pay any price, bear any burden, meet any hardship...to assure the survival and the success of liberty." At the time he made this pledge, South Vietnamese communists called Viet Cong began to fight a guerilla war to overthrow the American-backed government. Kennedy responded by ordering over 16,000 American military advisors to help train the South Vietnamese army.

5. President Johnson inherited a dangerously deteriorating situation in South Vietnam. Bombings by Viet Cong terrorists became an almost

daily occurrence as rural roads became death traps for government soldiers. Sensing that South Vietnam was on the verge of collapse, the North Vietnamese sent more aid to reinforce the Viet Cong. On August 4, 1964, President Johnson received unsubstantiated reports that North Vietnamese gunboats had fired on two American destroyers patrolling the Gulf of Tonkin. The next day, Johnson asked Congress to pass a resolution authorizing him to take "all necessary measures to repel any armed attack against the forces of the United States and to prevent further aggression." Passed with almost unanimous Congressional support, the Gulf of Tonkin Resolution gave President Johnson a blank check to escalate the American war effort in Vietnam.

6. In March 1965, President Johnson took the fateful step of ordering a massive escalation of U.S. forces in Vietnam. But the Viet Cong's refusal to fight large-scale battles turned the war into an endless series of small but terrifying clashes. Still convinced that American power would prevail, Johnson poured additional men and money into the war effort. By the end of 1967, almost 500,000 American soldiers guarded South Vietnam's cities and towns. At the same time, American warplanes sprayed the countryside with deadly herbicides such as Agent Orange.

7. When the war did not end quickly, a growing number of alarmed citizens began to question America's involvement in Vietnam. Unlike the "silent generation" of the 1950s, college students became particularly vocal leaders of the antiwar protest movement. Television brought both the war and the protests into the nation's living rooms. Scenes of young soldiers dying in faraway jungle villages and of protestors shouting antiwar slogans angered and confused many Americans. By the end of 1967, the war polarized Americans into "hawks" who supported the war effort and "doves" who opposed it. The high cost of the war crippled Johnson's Great Society programs and eroded his popularity.

8. On January 31, 1968, Viet Cong and North Vietnamese forces launched a surprise attack on over one hundred cities, villages, and military bases across South Vietnam. The Tet Offensive marked a turning point in the Vietnam War. Although U.S. forces regained the initiative and won a military victory, the heavy fighting undermined Johnson's confident prediction that "victory was just around the corner." Faced with plummeting public approval, Johnson told a nationally televised audience that he would not seek re-election.

9. Richard Nixon won the presidency in 1968 with a promise to achieve "peace with honor" in Vietnam. He announced a policy called Vietnamization that called for training South Vietnamese soldiers to take the place of

withdrawing American forces. After five more years of bloody fighting and intense U.S. bombing, Nixon signed an agreement that called for the release of American prisoners of war and the withdrawal of the remaining U.S. troops and advisors.

10. The Vietnam War finally ended in 1975 when the North Vietnamese captured Saigon and unified all of Vietnam. Unlike the armistice that ended fighting in Korea, the fall of Saigon resulted in a defeat for the United States policy of containment.

CHAPTER 25
ENVIRONMENTAL ATTITUDES AND POLICIES

LOCATION AND STRATEGIC IMPORTANCE

Geography and the environment form an important APUSH theme. This chapter can stand alone as part of a chronological review of this theme. The information in Chapter 25 has generated a number of multiple-choice and short-answer questions. Exam writers have paid particular attention to the similarities and differences between the preservation and conservation movements.

25.1
EXPLOITING A NEW LAND

1. Native Americans viewed the earth, sky, and water as communal possessions that could not be owned by individuals. In contrast, the English settlers viewed land as a commodity that could be exploited to achieve power and wealth.

2. The settlers believed that America provided a vast new world that contained a limitless supply of forests, minerals, and wildlife. Convinced that they had a manifest destiny to exploit the environment, American settlers advanced across the continent ignoring the environmental costs of their shortsighted emphasis upon unimpeded growth.

3. The market revolution accelerated the unchecked assault on the environment. Settlers cut forests, cleared fields, built dams, and dug mines. They exploited each natural resource until it either ran out or was no longer economically profitable.

4. The three decades following the end of the Civil War witnessed a period of unprecedented industrial growth and expansion. Timber companies cut the best trees and then moved on without reforestation. Hunters slaughtered the buffalo herds and decimated bird populations to harvest feathers for women's hats. At the same time, steel and chemical companies polluted rivers, lakes, and the atmosphere.

5. In 1865, wood supplied 90 percent of the nation's fuel. It provided the fuel for stoves, boilers, and steam engines on ships and trains. However, coal proved to be a superior fuel that burned longer and hotter than wood. By 1900, coal supplied three-fourths of America's energy. But coal mines left permanent scars on the land while polluting the air in industrial towns and cities across the nation.

25.2
PRESERVATION

1. The wanton waste of forest and wildlife resources sparked a growing public awareness that strong measures had to be taken to protect America's endangered forests, wildlife and scenic wonders. Congress took the first step when it created Yellowstone National Park in 1872. Presidents Harrison, Cleveland, and McKinley used the Forest Reserve Act of 1891 to preserve 45 million acres of timberland.

2. The appalling exploitation of America's wilderness areas outraged President Theodore Roosevelt. As a dedicated outdoorsman he sympathized with the viewpoint of preservationists, a naturalist group that advocated a strict "hands-off" approach to nature. Preservationists believed that people can have access to the land, but should only utilize it for beauty and inspiration.

3. John Muir was America's foremost advocate of the preservationist viewpoint. He wrote 10 books and over 300 articles warning that without strong actions much of America's natural beauty would be lost. He urged his readers to "Keep close to Nature's heart….Everybody needs beauty as well as bread, places to play in and pray in, where nature may heal and give strength to body and soul."

4. John Muir played a key role in convincing many Americans that immediate actions had to be taken to preserve the land in its natural state. His determined campaign contributed to the establishment of Yosemite Park and the founding of the Sierra Club, an organization committed to the enjoyment and protection of mountain regions along the Pacific Coast.

5. Roosevelt and Muir spent four days camping together in Yosemite Valley. Inspired by the experience and by Muir's eloquent writings, Roosevelt fulfilled many preservationist goals by adding 5 national parks, 4 national game preserves, 51 federal bird preserves, and 18 national monuments.

25.3
CONSERVATION

1. Roosevelt also sympathized with leaders of the conservation movement. Conservationists believed that the environment and its resources should be managed in a responsible and sustainable manner.

2. Gifford Pinchot, TR's first head of the National Forest Service, endorsed the conservationist perspective. With Roosevelt's enthusiastic support, the federal government tripled the number of acres in its forest preserves.

3. A clash between the conservations and preservationists erupted in a dispute over the Hetch Hetchy Valley in Yosemite National Park. The name Hetch Hetchy derives from a local Indian term meaning "grassy meadows." Pinchot and the conservationists viewed the valley as an ideal location for a dam to supply water for San Francisco. Muir and the preservationists viewed the spectacular high-walled valley as a sacred site that "ought to be faithfully guarded."

4. The dispute between the conservationists and preservationists left TR with divided loyalties. After some indecision, he turned the issue to Pinchot who approved construction of the dam. Finally completed in 1934, the Hetch Hetchy Project involves a dam, reservoir, and a series of aqueducts that supply San Francisco with 80 percent of its water.

5. The conservationist viewpoint continued to have a significant impact on America's land use policy. The Hoover Dam, Tennessee Valley Authority (TVA) and Civilian Conservation Corp (CCC) are all examples of managed land use projects.

25.4
THE ENVIRONMENTAL MOVEMENT

1. In just one generation, the American people moved from the depths of the Great Depression to enjoy the highest standard of living the world had ever known. But, the unparalleled growth came with an environmental price. In 1959, industrial and private sources of pollution emitted 24.9 million tons of soot into the air. Frequent smog alerts became a worrying part of daily life in Los Angeles, New York City, and other metropolitan centers across America.

2. Chemical companies hailed DDT as a miracle synthetic pesticide that would eradicate mosquitoes and other harmful insect pests. However, an American marine biologist named Rachel Carson conducted research

indicating that DDT and other chemicals were in fact killing beneficial insects, bees, livestock, and birds. Carson published her findings in *Silent Spring*, a groundbreaking book that helped launch an environmental movement based upon the ecological principle that all life is part of an integrated web. Carson issued an ominous warning that, "Our heedless and destructive acts enter into the vast cycles of the earth and in time return to bring hazard to ourselves."

3. Two environmental disasters further alarmed the public. In January 1969, an oil rig explosion in the Santa Barbara Channel turned miles of pristine Southern California beaches into an environmental nightmare. Within two days, a black tide 6 inches thick covered 800 miles of ocean and 35 miles of coast. The disaster killed thousands of seabirds and marine animals. Just six months later a second environmental disaster struck the Cuyahoga River in Cleveland, Ohio. For years, steel mills, oil refineries, chemical companies, and people dumped waste including raw sewage, acid, and floating debris into the river. On June 22, 1969 sparks from a train ignited a fire that damaged two bridges. Pictures of a river on fire became a symbol of environmental degradation.

4. The Santa Barbara oil spill and the Cuyahoga River fire appalled the public and helped spur widespread protests. On April 22, 1970, over 20 million concerned citizens participated in America's first annual Earth Day. Fully 70 percent of the public ranked the environment as the nation's most pressing problem.

5. Congress responded to the public outcry by enacting a far-reaching program of environmental legislation. The Clean Air Act set strict standards to reduce automobile and factory emissions. The Water Pollution Control Act provided funds to protect America's sea coasts and clean up its neglected rivers and lakes. The Endangered Species Act protected rare plants and animals from extinction. In addition to these measures the Nixon administration banned the use of DDT and created the Environmental Protection Agency (EPA) to enforce a range of environmental guidelines.

.

PART VI

TEST-TAKING STRATEGIES

CHAPTER 26
MASTERING THE MULTIPLE–CHOICE QUESTIONS

TOPIC 26.1
BASIC INFORMATION

A. NUMBER AND IMPORTANCE

Your APUSH exam will begin with a 55-minute section that contains 55 multiple-choice questions. Each question is worth one point. Taken together, the 55 multiple-choice questions comprise 40 percent of the 140 points on an APUSH exam. There is no guessing penalty, so be sure to answer each question.

It is important to remember that the APUSH exam scoring scale is much more lenient than the grading systems used by most high schools. In a typical high school, you would have to correctly answer 50 of the 55 multiple-choice questions to earn an A, 49 to earn a B, and 39 to earn a C. Relax! On the APUSH exam, correctly answering 29-32 multiple-choice questions will put you on pace to earn a three! You can earn a four by correctly answering 35-37 questions, and a five by correctly answering 43-45 questions.

B. QUESTION SETS

Each multiple-choice question is part of a set located under a stimulus prompt. Most prompts feature a brief passage drawn from an important historic document or written by a professional historian. Political cartoons, graphs, and maps can also serve as prompts. The 2018 APUSH exam contained 16 prompts drawn from written sources, two political cartoons, and one graph.

Each APUSH exam contains 18-20 prompts. These prompts generate sets of two to four multiple-choice questions. On the 2018 exam, four prompts generated two questions, 13 generated three questions, and two generated four questions.

TOPIC 26.2
CONTENT AND REASONING SKILLS

A. BIG-PICTURE CONTENT

More good news! The multiple-choice questions are not designed to test your ability to recall information from a long list of facts. APUSH test writers will not ask you to remember an obscure fact, a specific date, or a remote geographic location.

So what will test writers expect you to know? Multiple-choice questions focus on big-picture content. Test writers craft questions that ask you to demonstrate your understanding of the causes and consequences of important historic trends and influential ideas. For example, a typical test question might ask you to connect the decline of manufacturing employment from 1980 to 2010 with a simultaneous decline in union membership.

B. ESSENTIAL HISTORICAL REASONING SKILLS

Historians do more than study big-picture trends and ideas. As part of their research, they strive to apply historical ways of thinking to the documentary evidence. The APUSH test committee has identified contextualization, causation, continuity and change over time, comparison, and analysis of primary and secondary sources as five key historical reasoning skills. Each multiple-choice question is designed to test your ability to apply one of these skills to a source document.

TOPIC 26.3
HISTORICAL REASONING SKILLS

A. CONTEXTUALIZATION

Historical events do not occur in a vacuum. Contextualization is the ability to connect historical events to a broader setting. Here are five frequently used contextual questions. Note that each question asks you to link the prompt to important contemporary developments.

- The excerpt best reflects which of the following?

- The image was created most directly in response to which of the following?

- Which of the following most directly contributes to the sentiments expressed in the excerpt?

- The ideas expressed in the excerpt are most closely connected with which of the following broader historic developments?

- Which of the following most directly affected the lives of colonial women?

Contextual questions typically comprise about one-third of the 55 multiple-choice questions on an APUSH exam.

B. CAUSATION

Historians take great pride in their professional curiosity. They strive to identify, analyze, and evaluate the causes and consequences of events and social movements. Historians understand that no single cause can adequately explain a historical episode. Instead, events have multiple causes and effects. Here are five frequently used causation questions:

- Which of the following most directly contributed to the conflict referenced in the excerpt?

- Which of the following most directly led to the change described in the excerpt?

- Which of the following was a widespread effect of the market revolution?

- The ideas described in the excerpt contributed most directly to which of the following?

- Which of the following was the most significant impact of the Seneca Falls Convention?

Causation questions typically comprise about 30 percent of the 55 multiple-choice questions on an APUSH exam.

C. CONTINUITY AND CHANGE OVER TIME

Humans live a relatively short time. In contrast, ideas and institutions can endure for centuries. As a result, all periods of American history exhibit some degree of continuity. However, historians also recognize that powerful social forces can produce momentous changes. Historians thus attempt to identify, analyze, and evaluate the dynamics of historical continuity and change over time. Here are five frequently used continuity and change over time questions:

- Which of the following was an important continuity in immigration life throughout the nineteenth century?

- By the 1930s, the conditions described in the excerpt were addressed by which of the following?

- Which of the following events best represents continuity of the sentiment expressed by President Washington in his Farewell Address?

- Which of the following best represents a logical extension of the ideas expressed in the excerpt?

- Arguments similar to those expressed in the excerpt were later employed to justify which of the following?

Continuity and change over time typically comprises about 12 percent of the 55 multiple-choice questions on an APUSH exam.

D. COMPARISON

Historians recognize that history does not repeat itself. However, as the novelist and social critic Mark Twain observed, "History doesn't repeat itself but it does rhyme." APUSH comparison questions ask students to look for those historic rhymes by comparing related historical developments and processes that occur across time or in different societies. Here are five frequently used comparison questions:

- Which of the following developments from the 1900s emerged from ideas most similar to those in the excerpt?

- The conflict described in the excerpt is most similar to conflict in which other period?

- Populism, as described in the excerpt, has the most in common with which of the following later domestic reform movements?

- Which of the following later trends was most similar to the pattern described in the excerpt?

- The ideas in the excerpt have the most in common with which earlier idea about women's roles in society?

Comparison questions typically comprise about 12 percent of the 55 multiple-choice questions on an APUSH exam.

E. ANALYSIS OF PRIMARY AND SECONDARY SOURCES

Historians make an important distinction between primary and secondary sources. A primary source is a document, speech, or other type of evidence written or produced during the time under study. For example, Carl Schurz's *Report on the Condition of the South* is a primary source description of the South immediately after the Civil War. In contrast, a secondary source provides an interpretation or analysis of primary sources. Secondary sources are thus one step removed from the original event. For example, Kenneth Stampp's *The Era of Reconstruction, 1865–1877* is a secondary source interpretation published a century after the Civil War.

The multiple-choice section of the APUSH exam utilizes a variety of prompts drawn from primary and secondary sources. Here are five frequently used questions that test your ability to analyze primary and secondary sources:

- The excerpt most directly expresses a political perspective that…

- Dr. King's main purpose in the excerpt was to…

- Based upon the excerpt, President Wilson would be most likely to support which of the following?

- Based on the excerpt, the Great Migration of African Americans to the North was most likely motivated by…

- Which of the following could best be used as evidence to support the argument in the excerpt that…

Analyzing primary and secondary source questions typically comprise about 12 percent of the 55 multiple-choice questions on an APUSH exam.

TOPIC 26.4
ANSWERING MULTIPLE-CHOICE QUESTIONS

A. STEP 1—READ THE SOURCE LINE

Most students begin by carefully reading the passage. Resist this temptation. Instead, begin by focusing on the information in the source line at the end of the passage. Although it is short, the source line provides valuable contextual information.

The information contained in the source line can often enable you to answer many questions without first reading the passage. For example, closely examine the following source line: Bartolomé de Las Casas, *A Short Account of the Destruction of the Indies*, 1552. What comes to your mind when you think of Bartolomé de Las Casas? Hopefully, you will recall from Chapter 1 that Las Casas was an outspoken critic of the *encomienda* system. The Spanish used this labor system to force Native Americans to harvest sugar cane on West Indian plantations. This cruel system combined with epidemic diseases to decimate the Native American population in this region. As a result, the Spanish began to import enslaved Africans.

Now take a look at the questions. Your knowledge of Las Casas and the *encomienda* system may enable you to answer one or more of the questions! If so, this will save you time and mental energy.

B. STEP 2—READ THE PASSAGE

The passage is called a stimulus for a reason. Don't overanalyze the passage. Instead, read the excerpt and note how the author uses key phrases and evidence to support a main idea. For example, in his speech entitled "The Conquest of Mexico," John C. Calhoun adamantly declared, "Ours, sir, is the Government of a white race." This key idea leads to the logical conclusion that Calhoun would endorse proslavery arguments.

C. STEP 3—USE THE PROCESS OF ELIMINATION

Many times your knowledge of the topic will enable you to quickly spot the correct answer. However, there are questions in which the correct answer will not jump out and say, "Here I am!" When this happens, don't panic! APUSH wrong answers are not designed to be tricky. Instead, they fall into three easily indentifiable categories.

First and foremost, many answer choices can be eliminated because they are factually incorrect. For example, Lincoln's main purpose in his Gettysburg Address was not to support racial equality. Similarly, Andrew Carnegie's main purpose in his essay on "Wealth" was not to advocate using federal power to redistribute wealth.

Second, many answer choices are true statements that are chronologically out of place. For example, Marcus Garvey's views on black pride were not influenced by Truman's decision to integrate the armed forces. Similarly, President Kennedy's 1963 speech at the Berlin Wall was not influenced by Richard Nixon's 1972 strategy of détente.

And finally, many answer choices contain accurate information that is unrelated to the question. For example, Rachel Carson's *Silent Spring* was unrelated to the growing number of Baby Boomers enrolled in college. Similarly, Phyllis Schlafly's argument against the Equal Rights Amendment (ERA) was not related to the growing influence of computers.

TOPIC 26.5
PRACTICE QUESTIONS

The following five sets will give you an opportunity to practice your APUSH multiple-choice test-taking skills:

Questions 1–2 refer to the excerpt below.

"In your hands, my dissatisfied fellow-countrymen, and not in mine, is the momentous issue of civil war. The Government will not assail you. You can have no conflict without being yourselves the aggressors...We are not enemies, but friends. We must not be enemies. Though passion may have strained, it must not break our bonds of affection. The mystic chords of memory, stretching back from every battlefield and patriot grave to every living heart and hearthstone call over this broad land, will yet swell the chorus of the Union, when again touched, as surely they will be, by the better angels of our nature."

Abraham Lincoln, First Inaugural Address, March 4, 1861

1. **Which of the following issues of the period was Lincoln most likely concerned with in the excerpt?**

    A. The secession of seven Southern states
    B. The imminent threat of foreign invasion
    C. The unchallenged growth of slave labor
    D. The emergence of a new political party centered in the South

2. **President Lincoln's main purpose in the excerpt was to**

    A. reassess President Jackson's nullification proclamation
    B. advocate the expansion of slavery to the western territories
    C. reduce tensions between the North and South
    D. declare a national commitment to build a transcontinental railroad

Questions 3–4 refer to the following excerpt.

"For the past 15 years, we have been occupied with the very real problem of jobs leaving this country...One example of this is American Airlines, which historically used keypunch operators earning between $8 and $10 an hour to process the previous day's used tickets and handle the billings and record-keeping. This is now done in Barbados for $2 an hour. Each day an American Airlines aircraft flies to Barbados and deposits the tickets which are keypunched at one-fourth or one-fifth the U.S. wage level, and then transmitted back to the United States via satellite in finished form."

    Speech by an unidentified unionist, 1987

3. **Which of the following most directly led to the changes described in the excerpt?**

    A. The increasing sophistication of new consumer products
    B. The dramatic increase in air travel
    C. The increase in immigration from the West Indies
    D. The increasing integration of the U.S. into the global economy

4. **The conditions described in the excerpt most directly led to**

    A. a boon for U.S. financial and stock markets
    B. a decline in union membership
    C. the implementation of tariffs to protect American workers
    D. the continued migration of American workers to the Sunbelt

Questions 5–6 refer to the following excerpt.

"The white race deems itself to be the dominant race in this country…But in view of the Constitution, in the eye of the law, there is in this country no superior, dominant, ruling class of citizens. There is no caste here. Our Constitution is color blind, and neither knows nor tolerates classes among citizens. In respect of civil rights, all citizens are equal before the law. The humblest is the peer of the most powerful. The law regards man as man, and takes no account of his surroundings or his color when his civil rights as guaranteed by the supreme law of the land are involved. It is, therefore, to be regretted that this high tribunal, the final expositor of the fundamental law of the land, has reached the conclusion that it is competent for a State to regulate the enjoyment by citizens of their civil rights solely upon the basis of race."

John Marshall Harlan, Dissent in *Plessy v. Ferguson*, 1896

5. **Which of the following was the most immediate result of the *Plessy v. Ferguson* decision?**
   A. Segregationists in several Southern states temporarily closed many public schools in an effort to resist the decision.
   B. Sharecropping continued to entrap many black and white tenant farmers in an endless cycle of debt and poverty.
   C. The "New South" became less dependent upon agriculture and more committed to industrialization.
   D. Jim Crow segregation laws spread across the South.

6. **Which of the following best represents a continuity with the sentiments expressed by Justice Harlan?**
   A. The Supreme Court decision in *Worcester v. Georgia*
   B. The Supreme Court decision in *Dred Scott v. Sandford*
   C. The Supreme Court decision in *Korematsu v. United States*
   D. The Supreme Court decision in *Brown v. Board of Education*

Questions 7–8 refer to the following excerpt.

"The National Progressive Party, committed to the principle of government by a self-controlled democracy expressing its will through the representatives of the people, pledges itself to secure such alterations in the fundamental law of the several states and of the United States as shall insure the representative character of the government."

Progressive Party Platform, 1912

7. **The ideas of the Progressive Party, as expressed in the excerpt, had the most in common with the ideas of the**
   A. Federalist Party
   B. Whig Party
   C. Populist Party
   D. Know-Nothing Party

8. **Activists formed the Progressive Party most directly in response to the**
   A. abuses of powerful corporations and urban political machines
   B. exploitative practices by railroads
   C. formation of new labor unions to confront managerial power
   D. emergence of the Civil Rights movement

Questions 9–10 refer to the following excerpt.

"Lincoln did not live to preside over Reconstruction. That task fell to his successor, Andrew Johnson. Once lionized as a heroic defender of the Constitution against Radical Republicans, Johnson today is viewed by historians as one of the worst presidents to occupy the White House. He was incorrigibly racist, unwilling to listen to criticism, and unable to work with Congress. Johnson set up new Southern governments controlled by ex-Confederates. They quickly enacted Black Codes, laws that severely limited the freed people's rights."

Eric Foner, historian, "Why Reconstruction Matters," *New York Times*, March 29, 2015

9. **Which of the following could be used as evidence to support Foner's argument that Johnson was "unable to work with Congress?"**

   A. Johnson toured the country to arouse popular support for the Fourteenth Amendment
   B. Johnson pardoned thousands of former Confederate senior officials
   C. Johnson repeatedly vetoed legislation favored by the Radical Republicans
   D. Johnson agreed to readmit Southern states that revoked their ordinances of secession and ratified the Fifteenth Amendment

10. **Based upon the excerpt, Foner would most likely approve the goals of**

   A. Southern Redeemers
   B. Radical Republicans
   C. Northern carpetbaggers
   D. Northern industrialists

ANSWER KEY

1. A - Contextualization

2. C - Analyzing a primary source

3. D - Causation

4. B - Causation

5. D - Causation

6. D - Continuity and Change over Time

7. C - Comparison

8. A - Causation

9. C - Analyzing a secondary source

10. B - Contextualization

CHAPTER 27

MASTERING THE SHORT–ANSWER QUESTIONS

TOPIC 27.1
BASIC INFORMATION

A. FORMAT

Your APUSH exam will continue with a 40-minute section containing four short-answer questions. Don't panic! You are only required to answer three of these questions. So that means you have about 13 minutes for each question. Furthermore, short really does mean short. You are allocated one 23-line page for each question.

The questions will include topics covering material from pre-Columbian North America to events and trends in the early twenty-first century. You are required to answer the first two questions. They will both cover material from Periods 3–8. You then have a choice between Question 3, which covers Periods 1–5, and Question 4, which covers Periods 6–9. Take a minute to determine which of these two questions covers a topic you feel most confident answering.

B. IMPORTANCE

The three short-answer questions are worth 20 percent of your total exam score. Since the APUSH exam contains 140 points, the three short-answer questions are worth 28 points. Remember, you only need about 75 points for a three. You will need 95 points for a four, and 110 points for a five.

C. IT'S AS EASY AS A, B, C

Each short-answer question contains three sub-parts labeled (a),(b), and (c). Readers will assign each sub-part a score of either zero or one. Each of the nine sub-parts is worth 3.1 points toward your total APUSH score. So correctly answering five of the nine sub-parts will increase your total APUSH score by 15.5 points.

The three sub-parts are scored independently of one another. If you ace part (a) and (b), but miss part (c), you will receive a two. Since a blank space will receive a zero, always try to write a plausible answer.

TOPIC 27.2
THREE TYPES OF QUESTIONS

A. DUELING HISTORIANS/CONTRASTING CONTEMPORARIES
The first short-answer question features a pair of paragraph-length sources. In some questions, two historians present different perspectives on an event or time period. In other questions, two contemporaries present contrasting views of an important event, movement, or trend.

B. PRIMARY SOURCE IMAGE
The second short-answer question features a visual image. Typical examples include political cartoons, advertisements, posters, graphs, or maps.

C. DIFFERENCES AND SIMILARITIES
The third and fourth short-answer questions will ask you to describe specific historical differences and similarities between major trends, events, or ideas. For example, you might be asked to briefly describe the differences and similarities between the Korean War and the Vietnam War.

TOPIC 27.3
SIX IMPORTANT DO'S AND DON'TS

1. Time and space are limited. Remember, you have a total of 40 minutes and a 23-line page for each question. So get right to the point. Don't attempt to write an introduction or a thesis statement. Each sub-part can be answered in two to four sentences.

2. Devote a separate paragraph to each sub-point. Write complete sentences. Don't use bullet points or sentence fragments.

3. Provide brief but specific examples that illustrate your key points. Briefly explain why each example is relevant to the question. Don't write general statements or just mention an event.

4. Use your own words to fully answer each question. Don't repeat the question or use excessive quotes from the sources.

5. Strive to provide accurate information. However, don't stress over minor errors. Readers are trained to ignore errors that do not detract from your overall argument.

6. Readers are on your side. They view each response as a first draft written under great time pressure. Grammatical errors and misspellings will not be counted against you unless they obscure your answer.

TOPIC 27.4
PRACTICE—CONTRASTING CONTEMPORARIES

"If a wrong step be now made, the republic may be lost forever....And here I would make this inquiry of those worthy characters who composed a part of the late federal convention....What right had they to say, We, the people, instead of, We, the states?...The federal Convention ought to have amended the old system; for this purpose they were solely delegated; the object of their mission extended to no other consideration."

>   Patrick Henry, Virginia ratifying convention, 1788

"An objection is made to the form: the expression, We, the people, is thought improper. Permit me to ask the gentleman who made this objection, who but the people can delegate powers? Who but the people have a right to form government?...But the power of the Convention is doubted. What is the power? To propose, not to determine. This power of proposing was very broad; it extended to remove all defects in government: the members of that Convention, who were to consider all the defects in our general government, were not confined to any particular plan....Then the question must be between this government and the Confederation. The latter is no government at all."

>   Edmund Pendleton, Virginia ratifying convention, 1788

Using the excerpts above, answer (a), (b), and (c).

A. Briefly describe ONE major difference between Henry's and Pendleton's views of the proposed Constitution.

Henry argued that the proposed Constitution ignored the states. He further maintained that the "old system" had flaws that could be corrected. In contrast, Pendleton argued that true power derived from the people and not the states. He further argued that the "general government" had too many defects and served no useful purpose.

COMMENTARY: The response to A would receive one point because it addresses both Henry's and Pendleton's arguments and describes differences between the their views. Note the use of the transitional phrase "in contrast" to signal that the answer will address the two contrasting viewpoints.

B.   Briefly explain how ONE specific historical event or development from the period 1776–1788 that is not explicitly mentioned in the excerpts could be used to support Henry's argument.

The states sent 55 delegates to the Constitutional Convention for the sole purpose of revising the Articles of Confederation. This would support Henry's argument that the Convention had no right to say "We, the people." Indeed, the delegates who sat in the Philadelphia State House all represented the interests of specific states. For example, delegates from large states such as Virginia argued that representation should be based upon population, while delegates from small states such as New Jersey argued that each state should receive the same number of representatives.

COMMENTARY: The response to B would earn one point because it uses the historic fact that states and not the amorphous "people" sent delegates to the Constitutional Convention. The specific example about the argument between the populous states and the small states connects to Henry's argument.

C.   Briefly explain how ONE specific historical event or development from the period 1776–1788 that is not explicitly mentioned in the excerpts could be used to support Pendleton's argument.

The Articles of Confederation contained a number of defects. For example, the Confederation Congress lacked the power to regulate interstate commerce. This deficiency left the states free to establish different and often conflicting laws regulating tariffs and navigation. This defect provides evidence for Pendleton's contention that the Confederation "is no government at all."

COMMENTARY: The response to C would receive one point because it uses the historic fact that the Confederation government lacked the power to regulate interstate commerce. This specific example supports Pendleton's argument that the Confederation was "no government at all."

TOPIC 27.5
PRACTICE—ANALYZING A POSTER

The World War II poster above depicts Rosie the Riveter. Using the image, answer A, B, and C

A. Briefly describe ONE perspective about women's role during World War II expressed through the image.

The Rosie the Riveter poster encouraged women to replace millions of male workers who joined the armed forces. The famous "We Can Do It" slogan expressed the confidence that American women could leave their homes, join the labor force, and make a positive contribution to the war effort.

COMMENTARY: The response to part A would earn one point because it describes the image's perspective that women could and should make a valuable contribution to the war effort.

B. Briefly describe ONE specific historic development or circumstance that led to the change suggested by the image.

World War II forced the United States to wage a total war to defeat the Axis powers. Faced with a pressing shortage of workers in defense plants, the government launched a propaganda campaign to encourage women to volunteer for work previously performed by men.

COMMENTARY: The response to B would earn one point because it describes a specific historic circumstance that necessitated the government to commission posters that encouraged women to volunteer for wartime service in munitions factories and shipyards.

C.   Briefly explain ONE specific historical change suggested by the image.

Although the Rosie the Riveter poster became a cultural icon, World War II did not alter the widespread belief that women should only play a temporary role in the defense industry. However, the poster contributed to the ongoing trend of increasing female participation in the labor force.

COMMENTARY: The response to C would earn one point because it describes a significant historic change suggested by the poster.

TOPIC 27.6
PRACTICE

Answer A, B, and C.

A.   Briefly describe ONE specific historical difference between Southern attitudes towards slavery in the period 1790–1820 and in the period 1830–1850.

During the late 1700s and early 1800s, many Southern leaders described slavery as a "necessary evil" inherited from their colonial past. In contrast, during the 1830s and 1840s, slaveholders such as John C. Calhoun articulated a systematic argument to justify slavery as a "peculiar institution" that they defended as an essential part of the Southern way of life.

COMMENTARY: The response to A would receive one point because it describes specific differences in Southern attitudes towards slavery that characterized the two required time periods. Note the use of the transitional phrase "in contrast" to signal that the answer describes contrasting viewpoints.

B.   Briefly describe ONE specific historic similarity between Southern attitudes towards slavery in the period 1790–1820 and in the period 1830–1850.

The defenders of slavery as a "necessary evil" and as a "positive good" both recognized slavery's paramount importance for the Southern economy.

Regardless of the nuances of their arguments, almost all Southern slave owners resisted any outside attempt to interfere with their "peculiar institution."

COMMENTARY: The response to B would receive one point because it describes a specific historic similarity in Southern attitudes towards slavery in the two required time periods.

C. Briefly explain ONE specific historical impact of the Southern attitudes toward slavery in either period.

The "necessary evil" argument encouraged a movement to gradually emancipate a growing number of slaves. These freed slaves became an important group living on the margins of Southern society. Their ability to perform skilled work served as a highly visible refutation of the racist image of enslaved Africans as an inferior people only fit to work on plantations.

COMMENTARY: The response to C would receive one point because it uses the growing number of freed slaves as a specific historical impact of the "necessary evil" argument.

CHAPTER 28

MASTERING THE DOCUMENT–BASED QUESTION (DBQ)

TOPIC 28.1
BASIC INFORMATION

A. FORMAT

After completing the short-answer questions, you will have a well-deserved ten-minute break. When you return to your desk, your exam will resume with the document-based question (DBQ).

The DBQ is an essay question requiring you to analyze and interpret seven primary source documents. The documents are taken from letters, newspaper articles, speeches, diaries, and official decrees. In addition, the DBQ can include a political cartoon, map, or graph.

The College Board recommends that you begin your DBQ by devoting about 15 minutes to reading the documents, organizing your thoughts, crafting a thesis, and creating a topical outline. Once you have completed these tasks you should begin writing your essay. The College Board recommends that you devote about 45 minutes to writing your DBQ.

B. IMPORTANCE

The DBQ can earn up to seven rubric points. Each rubric point is worth five exam points. So a perfect score of seven is worth 35 points, or 25 percent of your total exam score. It is important to remember that earning three of the seven possible rubric points well keep you on pace to score a three. Scoring four of the seven possible points will keep you close to the pace you need to score a four. And finally, scoring five of the seven possible points will keep you on pace to earn a five.

TOPIC 28.2
THE DBQ SCORING RUBRIC

A. THE ALL-IMPORTANT THESIS—1 POINT

1. Everyone agrees that a well-constructed thesis is essential for a strong essay. Don't be intimidated by the word "thesis." A thesis is the position or argument you are advancing to answer the DBQ prompt.

2. Your thesis must consist of one or more sentences located in one place. College Board readers strongly recommend that you place your thesis in your opening paragraph.

3. Your thesis should clearly state the arguments your essay will support.

D. CONTEXTUALIZATION—1 POINT

1. History is not a series of unconnected events. Like the experiences in your life, historical events occur in a setting. Contextualization refers to the broader historical context that is relevant to your DBQ prompt.

2. The historical setting establishes the stage for your DBQ essay. Readers expect your contextualization paragraph to follow your thesis statement.

3. Avoid a "Star Wars" opening statement in which you take your readers on a journey to a historic event that took place in the distant past. Instead, pick a historic turning point closest to the starting date in your prompt and use it as an entry point.

4. Your contextualization statement should focus on the big themes and ideas that have influenced the issue in the DBQ prompt.

E. DOCUMENT USE—FIRST POINT

6. The first document use point is a gift from the College Board. Don't refuse it. All you have to do is accurately describe the contents of THREE documents and relate them to the topic posed by the DBQ prompt.

7. You can do it! Remember, a thesis statement followed by a contextualization paragraph is worth ten exam points. The first document use point will add five points to your total. Fifteen points is 20 percent of the 75 points you need to score a three!

H. DOCUMENT USE—SECOND POINT

1. The DBQ rubric awards a second document use point for using the contents of six of the seven documents. However, there is a catch. If you simply quote a document or summarize its contents, you won't receive the second point.

2. So how do you earn the second document use point? The test writers selected each of the seven documents for a reason. To earn the second

point you must use the contents of six of the seven documents to support your thesis.

3. Many graders recommend that you use all seven documents. There is no penalty for misusing a document. If you misuse one document but correctly use six documents, you will receive the second document use point.

D. EVIDENCE BEYOND THE DOCUMENTS—1 POINT

1. The seven documents do not cover all the possible relevant events, ideas, trends, and perspectives. The DBQ rubric will reward you with a point for including evidence that is not found in the documents.

2. The evidence cannot be a random fact that you "drop" into your essay. Instead, the evidence must advance your argument.

3. College Board readers recommend that you do not rely on a single example of outside evidence. Instead they recommend that you "flood your essay with historical evidence."

4. Your outside evidence must be relevant. That is, it must fall within the chronological period established by your DBQ prompt.

E. ANALYSIS OF SOURCES—1 POINT

1. Each of your documents can be analyzed in four ways. First, by establishing its historic setting. Second, by determining the author's point of view. Third, by identifying the document's purpose. And finally, by pinpointing the document's intended audience.

2. The DBQ rubric awards one point for correctly identifying and analyzing the historic situation, point of view, purpose, OR intended audience for THREE of the documents. It is very important to remember the capitalized words OR and THREE!

3. College Board readers believe that identifying the historic setting is the most straightforward and therefore the easiest of the four document characteristics. You should be able to explain the historic setting for each document in a sentence or two.

D. COMPLEX UNDERSTANDING—1 POINT

1. The complexity point is by far the most difficult rubric point to earn. In 2018, College Board readers awarded this point to less than five percent of the 501,530 DBQ essays.

2. The complexity point is awarded to essays that demonstrate a complex understanding of the historical development that is the focus of the DBQ prompt.

3. DBQ questions are written to invite sophisticated responses. A sophisticated response would examine more than one cause or consequence of an event. It would also recognize the presence of both continuity and change in a historic era.

4. DBQ readers are especially looking for your ability to see relationships among the seven documents. For example, try to group documents that have similar viewpoints. Also be on the lookout for documents that corroborate, qualify, or modify your argument.

5. The complexity point does require thoughtful analysis. Don't give up. The complexity point may be elusive, but it is not impossible!

TOPIC 28.3
SIX IMPORTANT DO'S AND DON'TS

1. Use the reading period to carefully evaluate the prompt and each of the seven documents. Don't begin your essay until you have a historically defensible thesis. Remember, no wind favors a ship without a destination. The thesis statement is the wind powering your essay!

2. Use short quotes from your documents to illustrate key points. Don't use long quotes.

3. Always strive to analyze and evaluate the documents. Don't summarize the documents.

4. Try to provide evidence beyond the documents that develops a key point that is not contained in the seven documents. Don't "drop in" a name or event.

5. Use documentary evidence in your body paragraphs. Avoid using documents in your thesis statement.

6. Do write a clear and concise thesis. Don't underline your thesis. Readers are trained to look for it in your opening paragraph. Many readers recommend that you also write a concluding paragraph that briefly restates your thesis. A concise conclusion ties your essay together by providing a clear statement of your thesis.

TOPIC 28.4
SAMPLE DBQ—CAUSATION

Prompt
Analyze the causes of the development of the institution of slavery in Virginia in the period from 1607 to 1750.

Document 1
This is to let you understand that I your child am in a most heavy case by reason of the country, is such that it causeth much sickness, as the scurvy and the bloody flux and diverse other diseases which maketh the body very poor and weak....I have nothing to comfort me, nor is there nothing to be gotten here but sickness and death, except [in the event] that one had money to layout in some things for profit. But I have nothing at all—no, not a shirt to my back but two rags, nor no clothes but one poor suit, nor but one pair of shoes, but one pair of stockings, but one cap. My cloak is stolen by one of my fellows, and to his dying hour would not tell me what he did with it; but some of my fellows saw him have butter and beef out of a ship, which my cloak I no doubt, paid for....I am not half a quarter so strong as I was in England, and it is for want of victuals; for I do protest unto you that I have eaten more in a day at home than I have allowed me here for a week....Good father, do not forget me, but have mercy and pity my miserable case.

> Richard Frethorne, indentured servant, letter to his mother and Father, March 1623

Document 2
Whereas some doubts have risen whether children that are slaves by birth, and by the charity and piety of their owners made partakers of the blessed sacrament of baptism, should by virtue of their baptism be made free, it is enacted and declared by this Grand Assembly, and the authority thereof, that the conferring of baptism does not alter the condition of the person as to his bondage or freedom; the diverse masters, freed from this doubt, may more carefully endeavor the propagation of Christianity by permitting children, though slaves, to be admitted to that sacrament.

> Virginia General Assembly, 1667

Document 3
One Mr. Nathaniel Bacon, a person of little experience and but of two years continuance in this country, thinking himself wiser than the Law, hath stirred up a great number of indigent and dissatisfied persons to obstruct the proceedings

upon the acts of Assembly, raising forces by beat of drum marching in a warlike posture, in terror of his Majesty's good subjects the intent of which...is the subversion of the Laws and to level all, this Mr. Bacon being styled by the Rabble their General (and indeed so he hath been in the loss of more men than ever was in all rights with the Indians) he having entered into oaths to stand by him and not withstanding the great care of our Governor and his several proclamations, refusing to surrender himself, which caused great fear to his Majesty's loyal subjects and is of most dangerous consequence in this time of war with the Indians and this hopeful Country which hath for many years past been under a quiet Government having Justice equally distributed to all men, is now in a languishing condition, the Rabble giving out they will have their own Laws...

> Letter from William Sherwood, a member of the Virginia House of Burgesses, to Sir Joseph Williamson, a member of the King's Privy Council in London, June 1, 1676

Document 4

Population of Virginia, 1630–1750

Year	Total	White	African	Percentage African
1630	2,500	2,450	50	0.02
1640	10,442	10,292	150	0.01
1660	27,020	26,070	950	0.03
1680	43,596	40,596	3,000	0.06
1700	58,560	42,170	16,390	0.27
1720	87,757	61,198	26,559	0.30
1740	180,440	120,440	60,000	0.33
1750	231,033	129,581	101,452	0.43

> Source: *The Statistical History of the United States*, U.S. Bureau of the Census, Population of Virginia, 1630–1750

Document 5

Chapter XXII. An act declaring the Negro, Mulatto, and Indian slaves within this dominion, to be real estate

Be it enacted, by the governor, council and burgesses of this present general assembly...that from and after the passing of this act, all Negro, mulatto, and

Indian slaves…shall be held, taken, and adjudged, to be real estate…and shall descend unto the heirs and widows of persons departing this life, according to the manner and custom of land and inheritance….

Chapter XLIX. An act concerning Servants and Slaves

And be it further enacted, that no minister of the church of England, or other minister, or person whatsoever, within this colony and dominion, shall hereafter wittingly presume to marry a white man with a Negro or mulatto woman; or to marry a white woman with a Negro or mulatto man, upon pain of forfeiting and paying, for every such marriage the sum of ten thousand pounds of tobacco.

Virginia General Assembly, October 1705

Document 6
February 22, 1709: I rose at 7 o'clock and read a chapter in Hebrew and 200 verses in Homer's Odyssey. I said my prayers and ate milk for breakfast, I threatened Anaka with a whipping if she did not confess the intrigue between Daniel and Nurse, but she prevented by a confession.

June 10, 1709: I rose at 5 o'clock this morning but could not read anything because of Captain Keeling, but I played billiards with him and won half a crown of him and the Doctor. George B-th brought home my boy Eugene…In the evening I took a walk about the plantation. Eugene was whipped for running away and had the [bit] put on him. I said my prayers and had good health, good thought, and good humor, thanks be to God Almighty….

William Byrd, *The Secret Diary of William Byrd of Westover*, 1709–1712

Document 7
Ran away from the Subscriber's in Prince George County, 14 or 15 weeks ago, a Mulatto Man Slave, named Tom, 25 years old, about 5 feet 8 or 9 inches high, thin faced, and bushy hair, if not cut off, he is very apt to grin when he speaks, or is spoken to; had on an old dark Fustian Coat, with plain yellow metal buttons; Hath been several times taken up and escaped again before he could be deliver'd to the Quarter whereunto he belon'd; and the last time shackled, handcuffed, and an iron collar about his neck…Whoever will deliver him to me shall have a Pistole Reward, besides what the law allow, paid by John Stith

Advertisement, *Virginia Gazette*, May 5, 1738

TOPIC 28.5
SAMPLE DBQ ESSAY—CAUSATION

The Virginia Company founded the Jamestown colony to make a profit for its investors. Tobacco provided a valuable cash crop that saved the colony. As demand for tobacco steadily increased, profits soared, creating an ever-increasing need for inexpensive labor. The institution of slavery developed in the period from 1607 to 1750 because of the pressing need for a stable labor force, the legal sanction provided by slave codes, and the social and moral support provided by white Virginians.

Rapidly rising tobacco profits created a demand for inexpensive labor. At first Virginia planters relied upon indentured servants from England. Document 1 provides a vivid account of the hardships endured by Richard Frethorne. Like other indentured servants, Frethorne suffered from a lack of food, inadequate clothing, and debilitating diseases. Frethorne's poignant story about his stolen cloak underscores his desperate situation and helps explain his urgent plea to his parents for "mercy and pity."

Very few tobacco planters treated their indentured servants with compassion. After surviving four to seven years without wages, indentured servants earned their freedom. However, a combination of falling tobacco prices, rising taxes, and dwindling opportunities to purchase fertile land caused bitter feelings of frustration and resentment. Long-simmering grievances fueled a rebellion against the arbitrary rule of Governor Berkley and the arrogant class of wealthy planters he represented.

Document 3 provides a contemporary but biased description of Bacon's Rebellion. Written by William Sherwood, a wealthy member of Virginia's House of Burgesses, the letter blames the violence on Nathanial Bacon and a "Rabble" composed of "a great number of indigent and dissatisfied persons." As an established landowner, Sherwood opposed policies that would favor the interests of former indentured servants. He feared that Bacon and his followers would enact "their own laws" and upend Virginia's existing social order. Sherwood's fears did not materialize. Although the rebels successfully captured and burned down Jamestown, Bacon's sudden death from dysentery enabled Governor Berkley to gain the upper hand and crush the leaderless rebels.

Bacon's Rebellion marked a significant turning point in the development of slavery in Virginia. Frightened planters began to replace troublesome indentured servants with more easily controlled enslaved Africans. Document 4 reveals that Africans comprised less than six percent of Virginia's total population prior to Bacon's Rebellion in 1676. However, within two decades the percentage of enslaved Africans soared to 27 percent of Virginia's total population. This percentage continued to steadily increase throughout the first half of the eighteenth century.

Documents 2 and 5 mark defined legal milestones in the development of the institution of slavery in Virginia. In Document 2, the Virginia General Assembly decreed that "the conferring of baptism does not alter the condition of the person as to his bondage or freedom." This released slave owners from the longstanding British Common Law tradition that Christians could not legally own other Christians as slaves. In 1705, the Virginia General Assembly codified slavery as a system of race-based, inherited, and perpetual bondage (Doc 5). The law further established a system of harsh punishments designed to enforce strict racial boundaries. Virginia thus developed a rigid racial system that contrasted with the racially mixed society that evolved in New Spain.

The majority of white families in Virginia did not own slaves. However, few if any questioned human bondage as morally unacceptable. This widespread social support began with members of the planter elite. Document 6 provides an insight into the daily life of William Byrd, one of Virginia's wealthiest and most influential landowners. Byrd's diary reveals that he is a devout, well-educated man who began his day by praying and then reading "a chapter in Hebrew and 200 verses in Homer's Odyssey." But Byrd's devotion to God and classical learning did not prevent him from severely punishing slaves he viewed as little more than property.

The lack of moral outrage enabled the institution of slavery to grow and endure. Document 7 further clarifies the legal identify of enslaved Africans as property. The document quotes a newspaper advertisement describing an escaped slave and offering a reward for his return. The ad is directed at a morally insensitive population of readers who could be persuaded to capture a human being in exchange for a pistol. Slavery and racism thus became inseparably intertwined in Virginia. Impoverished farmers and wealthy planters found a shared identity in a rigid social order in which every white person was superior to every black person.

Documents 6 and 7 illustrate the results of a process whereby Virginia planters responded to economic necessities while drawing upon widespread social support for the creation of a legally sanctioned institution of slavery.

TOPIC 28.6
SCORING COMMENTARY

A. THESIS—1 POINT

The response earned a point for the following thesis statement: "The institution of slavery developed in the period from 1607 to 1750 because of the pressing need for a stable labor force, the legal sanction provided by slave codes, and the social and moral support provided by white Virginians." It is very important to note that the prompt for this DBQ asks for "causes" and not just one cause. Historians believe that no single causal factor can fully explain a major historical development. The thesis clearly identifies three significant causal factors responsible for the development of the institution of slavery in the required period from 1607 to 1750.

B. CONTEXTUALIZATION—1 POINT

The response earned a point for contextualization. The opening three sentences in the first paragraph describe a broad historic context by briefly explaining the importance of tobacco and the link between this vital cash crop and Virginia's need for a source of inexpensive labor.

C. DOCUMENT USE—2 POINTS

The response earned a point for using at least three documents to address the topic of the prompt. Indeed, the response successfully used all seven documents to address the prompt.

The response also earned a point for using the content of at least six documents to support an argument in response to the prompt. The responses provide specific information that explains the meaning of each document. This information supports the essay's overall argument.

D. EVIDENCE BEYOND THE DOCUMENTS—1 POINT

The response earned a point for using at least one additional piece of specific evidence that relates to an argument about the prompt. For example, the third paragraph explains the grievances that sparked Bacon's Rebellion. The detail about the destruction of Jamestown in paragraph 4 helps explain the alarm felt by William Sherman (Doc 3) and other planters.

E. ANALYSIS OF SOURCES—1 POINT

The response earned a point for explaining the relevance of sourcing to the argument for at least three documents. For example, the response identifies the purpose of Document 2, the point of view for Document 3, and the historic setting for Document 6.

F. COMPLEX UNDERSTANDING—1 POINT

The response earned a point for demonstrating a complex understanding of the historical development that is the focus of the prompt. The response expressed the nuances of the issue by describing the relationship between three causal factors responsible for the development of the institution of slavery in Virginia. The response also made a relevant and insightful connection by pointing out that Virginia "developed a rigid racial system that contrasted with the racially mixed society that evolved in New Spain."

TOPIC 28.7
SAMPLE DBQ—CONTINUITY CHANGE OVER TIME

Prompt

Evaluate the extent of change in ideas about American independence from 1763 to 1776.

Document 1

We, the Commissioners of your Majesty's Treasury, beg leave humbly to represent to your Majesty that having taken into consideration the present state of the duties of customs imposed on your Majesty's subjects in America and the West Indies, we find that the revenue arising therefrom is very small and inconsiderable,…and is not yet sufficient to defray a fourth part of the expense necessary for collecting it. We observe with concern that through neglect, connivance, and fraud, not only is revenue impaired, but the commerce of the colonies diverted from its natural course…[This revenue] is more indispensable when the military establishment necessary for maintaining these colonies requires a large revenue to support it, and when their vast increase in territory and population makes the proper regulation of their trade of immediate necessity.

     British Order in Council, 1763.

Document 2

Resolved, that the taxation of the people by themselves, or by persons chosen by themselves to represent them, who can only know what taxes the people are able to bear, or the easiest method of raising them, and must themselves be affected by every tax laid on the people, is the only security against burdensome taxation, and the distinguishing characteristic of British freedom, without which the ancient constitution cannot exist.

Resolved, that his Majesty's liege people of this ancient colony have enjoyed the right of being thus governed by their own Assembly in the article of taxes and internal police, and that the same have never been forfeited, or any other way yielded up, but have been constantly recognized by the king and people of Great Britain.

> Source: The Virginia House of Burgesses, The Virginia Resolutions on the Stamp Act, 1765.

Document 3

They call me a brainless Tory; but tell me, my young friend: Which is better—to be ruled by one tyrant three thousand miles away or by three thousand tyrants not a mile away?

> Source: Mather Byles, renowned Boston Loyalist minister, question posed March 1770.

Document 4

All men have a right to remain in a state of nature as long as they please; and in case of intolerable oppression, civil or religious, to leave the society they belong to, and enter into another. When men enter into society, it is by voluntary consent; and they have a right to demand and insist upon the performance of such conditions and previous limitations as form an equitable original compact....

The natural liberty of man is to be free from any superior power on earth, and not to be under the will or legislative authority of man, but only to have the law of nature for his rule.

> Source: Samuel Adams, *The Rights of the Colonists*, 1772.

Document 5

That a British and American legislature, for regulating the administration of the general affairs of America, be proposed and established in America, including all the said colonies; within, and under which government, each colony shall retain its present constitution, and powers of regulating and governing its own internal police, in all cases whatsoever.

That the said government be administered by a President General, to be appointed by the King and a Grand Council, to be chosen by the representatives of the people of the several colonies, in their respective assemblies, once in every three years.

Source: Joseph Galloway, "A Plan of a Proposed Union Between Great Britain and the Colonies," proposal debated and then rejected by the First Continental Congress, 1774.

Document 6

Some of these people, who from a sense of their duty to the king, and a reverence for his laws, have behaved quietly and peaceably; and for which reason they have been deprived of their liberty, abused in their persons, and suffered such barbarous cruelties, insults, and indignities, besides the loss of their property, by the hands of lawless mobs and riots, as would have been disgraceful even for savages to have committed. The courts of justice being shut up in most parts of the province [Massachusetts], and the justices of those courts compelled by armed force, headed by some of your Congress, to refrain from doing their duties, at present it is rendered impracticable for those sufferers to obtain redress....

Source: In "Plain English," a Loyalist describes the reign of "lawless mobs," 1775.

Document 7

The hopes of reconciliation, which were fondly entertained by multitudes of honest and well meaning, though weak and mistaken people, have been gradually and, at last, totally extinguished. Time has been given for the whole people maturely to consider the great question of independence, and to ripen their judgment, dissipate their fears, and allure their hopes, by discussing it in newspapers and pamphlets, by debating it in assemblies, conventions, committees of safety and inspection, in town and county meetings, as well as in private conversations, so that the whole people, in every colony of the thirteen, have now adopted it as their own act....

I am well aware of the toil, and blood, and treasure, that it will cost us to maintain this Declaration, and support and defend these States. Yes, through all the gloom, I can see the rays of ravishing light and glory. I can see that the end is more than worth all the means. And that posterity will triumph in that day's transaction.

Source: John Adams, *Letters of John Adams, Addressed to his Wife*, July 3, 1776

TOPIC 28.8

SAMPLE DBQ ESSAY—CONTINUITY AND CHANGE OVER TIME

The period from 1763 to 1776 witnessed a dramatic change in colonial ideas about independence. When the period began, the colonists were proud subjects of a British king who ruled by divine right. However, a divisive dispute over a change in British taxation policies began the process of straining long-standing ties between the colonies and their mother country. At the same time, a growing commitment to republican values caused many colonists to support self-government. Although some colonists remained loyal to the Crown, by July 1776 a determined group of Patriots overcame their opposition and declared independence from Great Britain.

The French and Indian War climaxed the long struggle between Great Britain and France for control over North America. The war left Britain with a great empire and a mounting national debt. The financial burden forced Britain's young and untested monarch, George III, and his first minister, George Grenville, to end the period of salutary neglect, enforce the Navigation Acts, and raise revenue from their North American colonies.

The financial crisis prompted the Commissioners of the King's Treasury to evaluate Britain's colonial trade and taxation policies (Doc 1). The Commissioners discovered that revenue from customs duties was "very small and inconsiderable." They therefore issued an Order in Council urging George III and Lord Grenville to make the "proper regulation" of trade an "immediate necessity."

Grenville reviewed the report and persuaded Parliament to enact a Stamp Act to raise revenue. Instead, the act raised questions about Parliament's right to tax the colonies. In 1765, the Virginia House of Burgesses passed a series of Resolutions on the Stamp Act (Doc 2). The resolutions directly challenged Parliament's authority to tax the colonies. While continuing to express loyalty to the king, the Resolutions insisted that local control over taxation represented a "distinguishing characteristic of British freedom." As intended by the House of Burgesses, copies of the Virginia Resolutions quickly spread to other colonial assemblies. The Resolutions thus marked the beginning of a shift in colonial ideas about the need for American independence.

The economic dispute over taxes quickly ignited a political movement inspired by republican values. Republicanism is the belief that government should be based upon the consent of the governed. The trans-Atlantic exchange of Enlightenment ideas familiarized Samuel Adams and other colonial leaders with John Locke's theory of natural rights. In *The Rights of the Colonists* (Doc 4), Adams asserted that "the natural liberty of man is to be free from any superior power on earth." Adams thus turned to Enlightenment ideas of natural rights to undermine the existing belief in the divine right of kings. This marked an important change from accepting the divine right of a distant ruler to a system based upon the will of the people.

The growing calls for independence alarmed Loyalists who valued tradition, law and order, and allegiance to the Crown. They pointed to escalating acts of violence, such as the Boston Massacre and the Boston Tea Party, as examples of the actions of lawless mobs that proclaimed liberty for themselves while denying it to others. In Document 6 a Loyalist decries the "barbarous cruelties, insults, and indignities" inflicted on peaceful citizens. The violence in Boston particularly distressed Mather Byles. In Document 3 Byles poses as a "brainless Tory," who asks why the rule of one tyrant reigning three thousand miles across the Atlantic Ocean is worse than the rule of "three thousand tyrants not a mile away." His insightful question challenged Samuel Adams's (Doc 4) assumption that the will of the people will always be constructive.

Byles's question underscored the possible dangers posed by the shifting ideas about American independence. Moderates tried to find a compromise between submission to British authority and the unknown perils of independence. Like other Loyalists, Joseph Galloway (Doc 5) hoped to resolve the crisis by creating an "American legislature." The elected body would be responsible for the "general affairs of America." Galloway's plan was thus consistent with the goals stated in the Virginia Resolves (Doc 2). However, the First Continental Congress defeated Galloway's plan by one vote. The outcome provided a striking indication of the growing support for Patriots like Samuel Adams who demanded full independence from Great Britain.

A Second Continental Congress convened in Philadelphia in 1775. The delegates faced a deepening crisis as reports of bloody battles between colonial militia and British soldiers swept across the colonies. As hopes for reconciliation faded, the Congress authorized a committee to write a Declaration of Independence. John Adams served as one of the five members of the committee. Doc 7 is from a letter Adams wrote to his wife on July 3rd, the day before the Second Continental Congress officially declared American independence.

Adams begins Document 7 by dismissing Galloway and other Loyalists (Document 5) as "honest and well meaning, though weak and mistaken people." He proudly notes that the "whole people" had considered and approved "the grand question of independence." Although aware that the struggle for independence would require great sacrifice, Adams confidently predicted that the rewards of freedom would be more than worth the cost.

The Patriots successfully overcame the objections of Loyalists and issued the Declaration of Independence the day after Adams penned Document 7. The Declaration of Independence documented the dramatic shift from colonists loyal to a monarch ruling by divine right to an independent people committed to the republican principle of self-rule.

TOPIC 28.9
SCORING COMMENTARY

A. THESIS—1 POINT

The response earned a point for the following thesis statement: "A divisive dispute over a change in British taxation policies began the process of straining long-standing ties between the colonies and their mother country. At the same tine, a growing commitment to republican values caused many colonists to support self-government. Although some colonists remained loyal to the Crown, by July 1776 a determined group of Patriots overcame their opposition and declared independence from Great Britain." This thesis responds to the prompt with a historically defensible claim that establishes a sophisticated line of reasoning. Note that the thesis establishes a level of complexity by identifying British taxation policies and a growing colonial commitment to republican values as causes of the dramatic change in ideas about independence. The thesis also qualifies its argument by noting that the Patriots had to overcome the opposition of Loyalists. The essay's final sentence provides a succinct restatement of the thesis.

B. CONTEXTUALIZATION—1 POINT

The response earned a point for contextualization. Paragraph 2 describes the broader historic context by summarizing the economic crisis triggered by the French and Indian War and the end of Britain's policy of salutary neglect.

C. DOCUMENT USE—2 POINTS

The response earned a point for using at least three documents to address the topic of the prompt. Indeed, the response successfully used all seven documents to address the prompt.

The response also earned a point for using the content of at least six documents to support an argument in response to the prompt. The responses provide specific information that explains the meaning of each document. This information supports the essay's overall argument.

D. EVIDENCE BEYOND THE DOCUMENTS—1 POINT

The response earned a point for using at least one additional piece of specific historical evidence that relates to an argument about the prompt. For example, paragraph 5 amplifies Document 4 by defining republicanism and explaining how the trans-Atlantic exchange of information enabled Samuel Adams to learn about John Locke's theory of natural rights.

E. ANALYSIS OF SOURCES—1 POINT

The response earned a point for explaining the relevance of sourcing to the argument for at least three documents. For example, the response explains the historic setting for all seven documents. In addition, the response explains the purpose and audience for Document 2.

F. COMPLEX UNDERSTANDING—1 POINT

The response earned a point for demonstrating a complex understanding of the historical development that is the focus of the prompt. The response expresses the nuance of the issue by describing the changes in colonial attitudes towards independence between 1763 and 1776. The response makes relevant and insightful connections between the documents. For example, the response uses Byles's question in Document 3 to challenge Henry's assumption in Document 4 about the will of the people. In addition, the response qualifies its argument by taking into consideration that some colonists remained loyal to the British Crown.

CHAPTER 29
MASTERING THE LONG-ESSAY QUESTION (LEQ)

TOPIC 29.1
BASIC INFORMATION

A. FORMAT

After completing the DBQ, you will yearn for a break to rest your tired writing hand. Unfortunately, there is no break. Instead, you must be resolute and focus on your next and final APUSH challenge—the long-essay question.

The long-essay section will ask you to examine three questions focusing on the same historical reasoning skill. The three questions are distributed across the entire course, with the first question addressing a topic from Periods 1–3, the second addressing a topic from Periods 4–6 and the final question addressing a topic from Periods 7–9.

Fortunately, you only have to answer ONE of the questions. You will have 40 minutes to write your essay. The College Board recommends that you devote five minutes to choosing a question and crafting a thesis. This will leave you 35 minutes to write your essay.

B. IMPORTANCE

The long-essay question can earn up to six rubric points. Each rubric point is worth 3.5 exam points. So a perfect score of six is worth 21 points or 15 percent of your total exam score. It is important to remember that earning three of the six possible rubric points will keep you on pace to score a three. Earning four of the six points will keep you safely on pace for a four. And finally, earning five of the six rubric points will exceed the level you need for a five.

TOPIC 29.2
THE LONG-ESSAY SCORING RUBRIC

A. THE ALL-IMPORTANT THESIS—1 POINT

1. Everyone agrees that a well-constructed thesis is essential for a strong long-essay score. Don't be intimidated by the word "thesis." A thesis is the position or argument you are advancing to answer the long-essay prompt.

2. Your thesis must consist of one or more sentences located in one place. College Board readers strongly recommend that you place your thesis in your opening paragraph.

3. Your thesis should clearly state the arguments your essay will support.

D. CONTEXTUALIZATION—1 POINT

1. History is not a series of unconnected events. Like the experiences in your life, historical events occur in a setting. Contextualization refers to the broader historical setting that is relevant to your long-essay prompt.

2. The historical setting establishes the stage for your long essay. Readers expect to find a contextualization paragraph located right after your thesis statement.

3. Avoid a "Star Wars" opening statement in which you take your readers on a journey to a historical event that took place in the distant past. Instead, pick a historic turning point closest to the starting date in your prompt and use it as an entry point.

4. Your contextualization statement should focus on the big themes and ideas that have influenced the issue in the long-essay prompt.

E. EVIDENCE—2 POINTS

1. The first evidence point is a gift from the College Board. Don't refuse it! All you have to do is accurately identify at least two specific historical examples of evidence that are relevant to the TOPIC of your prompt. For example, the refrigerated rail car and the telegraph both provide examples of new technology that fostered change in American industry between 1865 and 1900.

2. Earning a second point is not difficult. All you have to do is use your examples to support your ARGUMENT. For example, refrigerated rail cars can be used as evidence to support the argument that technology enabled the West to become an integral part of the U.S. economy.

C. ANALYSIS AND REASONING—1 POINT

1. The APUSH course focuses on causation, comparison, and continuity and change as key historical reasoning skills. See Chapter 23 for a detailed explanation of each of these three reasoning skills.

2. Each long-essay prompt will focus on a specific historical reasoning skill. The long-essay rubric awards one point for using this skill "to frame or structure" an argument.

3. What does it mean to "frame or structure" an argument? Framing and structuring are another way of saying organizing. For example, you would organize your response to a causation prompt by focusing on the relative importance of multiple causal factors. You would organize your response to a continuity and change prompt by focusing on the relative importance of both continuity and change. And finally, you would organize your response to a comparison prompt by focusing on the similarities and differences between two time periods, ideas, or social movements.

D. COMPLEX UNDERSTANDING—1 POINT

5. The complexity point is by far the most difficult rubric point to earn. In 2018, College Board readers awarded this point to less than five percent of the 501,530 long-essays.

6. The complexity point is awarded to essays that demonstrate a complex understanding of the historical development that is the focus of the long-essay prompt.

7. Long-essay prompts are written to invite sophisticated responses. For example, an essay on how new technology fostered change in American industry between 1865 and 1900 would earn the complexity point by exploring specific ways the new technologies affected industries such as steel and meatpacking.

TOPIC 29.3
SIX IMPORTANT DO'S AND DON'TS

1. Use the five-minute review period to carefully evaluate the prompt. Don't begin writing your long essay until you have a historically defensible thesis and strong list of the examples you plan to use as evidence.

2. Write a clear and concise thesis. Don't underline your thesis. Readers are trained to look for it in your opening paragraph.

3. Strive to use specific historical evidence to illustrate your key points. Be as analytical as possible. Don't write vague, overgeneralized points.

4. Strive to demonstrate complexity by analyzing multiple variables. Don't write a quick comparison to another time period. It will not earn a complexity point.

5. Write well-organized paragraphs. Don't use bullet points.

6. Always respond directly to the prompt. Don't digress to topics that are not required by the prompt.

TOPIC 29.4
SAMPLE LONG ESSAY—CAUSATION
PROMPT
Evaluate the extent to which the counterculture affected U.S. culture in the period between 1965 and 1980.

The counterculture erupted in the mid-1960s as millions of young, white Americans openly rejected the values and lifestyle of mainstream American culture. Although the counterculture's independent spirit faded a decade later, it left a lasting impact on American culture by encouraging a vision of freedom that fostered experimentation and inspired more permissive norms of behavior. However, the counterculture also sparked a backlash among evangelical Christians that contributed to the resurgence of the conservative movement.

Conformity and consensus dominated American life during the 1950s and early 1960s. Nevertheless, a small but culturally influential group of self-styled "Beats" rejected suburban America's carefree materialism and mindless conformity.

As the 1950s gave way to the 1960s, the civil rights sit-ins and protest marches inspired a new spirit of youthful activism At the same time, a new Baby Boom generation of college students began to bitterly criticize the sudden escalation of fighting in Vietnam. Disillusioned students argued that something was fundamentally wrong with a system that denied equal rights to African Americans while bombing innocent civilians in Vietnam.

A youthful rebellion spread across the United States during the late 1960s. A growing number of young people known as hippies challenged traditional values by following a distinctive lifestyle or counterculture. Hippies rejected the conventional values of hard work, neat appearance, and economic success taught by their parents. Instead, the new counterculture emphasized a more authentic "do your own thing" lifestyle. Hippies stressed creative experimentation by embracing long hair, colorful clothes, casual sex, and psychedelic drugs. They listened to rock music, purchased organic foods, and encouraged diversity.

Hippies believed they were leading America into a new age of harmony and understanding. A 1967 "Summer of Love" in San Francisco's Haight-Ashbury district attracted thousands of "flower children" to a "love-in" featuring sexual freedom, mind-altering drugs, psychedelic music, and communal living.

The counterculture reached its peak at the Woodstock Music Festival in August 1969. Over 400,000 young people enjoyed three days of rock music and protest songs. But the festival did not launch the dawning of a new age of peace and love. Instead, the de-escalation of fighting in Vietnam and the economic recession caused by the Arab oil embargo sapped the energy from the once-vibrant counterculture.

The counterculture did not dismantle America's political establishment or reform its capitalist economic system. However, it did play a significant role in reshaping American culture. The counterculture's tolerant view of sexual roles paved the way for the 1970s women's liberation movement. The hippies' penchant for natural foods helped promote co-op groceries and a more eco-friendly attitude toward the environment. And finally, the counterculture's rebellious disdain for the repressive norms of mainstream culture helped influence previously marginalized people such as gays and lesbians to launch movements for social acceptance and legal equality.

Cultural movements like the counterculture can have unintended consequences. The counterculture shocked and offended Americans who upheld the nation's traditional values. The hippies' experiments with drugs and their celebration of premarital sex outraged evangelical Christians. As a result, many devout Christians became part of a movement known as the Religious Right.

The Religious Right became a significant force in American politics when Jerry Falwell, a Baptist minister and popular religious broadcaster, formed the Moral Majority. Launched in 1979, the organization advanced a "pro-life, pro-family, pro-morality, and pro-America agenda."

The Moral Majority and other conservative Americans became part of a cultural backlash that rejected the counterculture and played a key role in the rise of Ronald Reagan. Reagan launched his political career in California in 1966 by targeting "spoiled" student protestors and hippies at the UC Berkeley campus. His promise "to clean up the mess at Berkeley" played a key role in his election as governor of California. The conservative backlash against the counterculture helped propel Reagan to a victorious presidential campaign in 1980.

The counterculture produced both intended and unintended cultural consequences. It advocated a liberated lifestyle that encouraged tolerance, eco-friendly attitudes, and social acceptance of marginalized groups. However, the counterculture unintentionally sparked a conservative backlash that helped elect Ronald Reagan in 1980.

TOPIC 29.5
SCORING COMMENTARY

A. THESIS—1 POINT

The response earned a point for its thesis: "Although the counterculture's independent spirit faded a decade later, it left a lasting impact on American culture by encouraging a vision of freedom that fostered experimentation and inspired more permissive norms of behavior. However, the counterculture also sparked a backlash among evangelical Christians that contributed to the resurgence of the conservative movement." This thesis responds to the question with a historically defensible claim that establishes a line of reasoning about the prompt.

B. CONTEXTUALIZATION—1 POINT

The response earned a point for contextualization. The references to the Beats, Baby Boomers, civil rights movement, and Vietnam War protests describe several broader historical contexts relevant to the question.

C. EVIDENCE—2 POINTS

The response earned a point for providing specific examples of evidence relevant to the question, as well as a point for using the evidence to support an argument about the question. Specifics included the counterculture's emphasis upon authentic lifestyles and creative experimentation in dress, sex, music, psychedelic drugs, and diversity. The response explained how these characteristics reshaped American culture by encouraging the women's liberation movement, environmentalism, and the gay rights movement.

D. ANALYSIS AND REASONING—1 POINT

The response earned a point for using causation to frame an argument that addresses the prompt. The response provided a detailed understanding of both the causes and the consequences of the counterculture.

E. COMPLEX UNDERSTANDING—1 POINT

The response demonstrated a detailed understanding of how the counterculture affected American culture in the period between 1965 and 1980. Its in-depth discussion of changes included an analysis of how the counterculture played an unintended role in the revival of the conservative movement and the rise of Ronald Reagan.

TOPIC 29.6

SAMPLE LONG ESSAY—CONTINUITY AND CHANGE OVER TIME

PROMPT

Evaluate the extent to which the Supreme Court decision in *Brown v. Board of Education* fostered changes in American society in the period from 1954 to 2010.

The Supreme Court decision in *Brown v. Board of Education* struck down *de jure* or legal segregation in the nation's public schools. This momentous decision placed the Supreme Court on the side of racial equality, thus helping to galvanize the Civil Rights Movement into launching a full attack on Jim Crow segregation. However, the *Brown* decision did not succeed in its mission to fully integrate public education in the United States.

In 1896 the Supreme Court ruled in *Plessy v. Ferguson* that racially "separate but equal" public facilities are constitutional. The "separate but equal" doctrine created separation, but it did not create equality. When the 1953–54 school year opened, 17 Southern and border states plus the District of Columbia required *de jure* segregation.

Led by Thurgood Marshall, the National Association for the Advancement of Colored People (NAACP) Legal Defense team argued that the facilities in an all-black elementary school in Topeka, Kansas, were not equal to those in a nearby white school. Even more importantly, Marshall argued that the idea of separating groups of people was inherently discriminatory and thus a violation of the equal protection clause of the Fourteenth Amendment. Speaking for a unanimous Court, Chief Justice Earl Warren agreed with Marshall, ruling "separate education facilities are inherently unequal."

The *Brown* decision opened a new chapter in the African American struggle for equal rights. It overturned *de jure* segregation, thus placing the Supreme Court's moral prestige and legal authority on the side of racial equality. The landmark ruling conferred legitimacy to the growing Civil Rights Movement. During the next decade a wave of sit-ins, freedom rides, voting registration drives, and mass marches swept across the South. These protests ultimately mobilized what Dr. King called a "coalition of conscience" that led to passage of the Civil Rights Act of 1964 banning segregation in public facilities.

The *Brown* decision played a key role in the overall success of the Civil Rights Movement. However, it did not fulfill its mission to desegregate America's public schools. One year after issuing the *Brown* decision, the Supreme Court directed the states to desegregate their public schools with "all deliberate speed." Instead of complying, Southern leaders called for "massive resistance" to the Court's ruling. By 1964, fewer than two percent of African American students attended multi-racial schools in the 11 states of the Old Confederacy.

Prompted by court-ordered busing, Southern states did begin to integrate their public schools during the 1970s and 1980s. However, the trend toward integration did not continue. As the 60th anniversary of the *Brown* decision approached, about three-fourths of African American children attended schools where the majority of students were not white.

The *Brown* decision successfully struck down *de jure* or legal segregation. However, it did not affect *de facto* or "by the fact" segregation. The trend toward re-segregation that began in the 1990s reflected continuity in patterns of residential segregation based upon income. Public schools continue to be segregated today because students live in segregated neighborhoods. Although school segregation is no longer a legal issue, it remains a socio-economic issue.

The *Brown v. Board of Education* decision marked a watershed event in American history. It reversed the "separate but equal" doctrine and helped accelerate the Civil Rights Movement. Although it struck down *de jure* segregation in the public schools, it failed to overcome continuing patterns of economic inequality and thus racial segregation. As a result, a majority of African American students continue to attend racially segregated public schools.

TOPIC 29.7
SCORING COMMENTARY

A. THESIS—1 POINT

The response earned a point for its thesis: "This momentous decision placed the Supreme Court on the side of racial equality, thus helping to galvanize the Civil Rights Movement into launching a full attack on Jim Crow segregation. However, the *Brown* decision did not succeed in its mission to fully integrate public education in the United States." This sophisticated thesis responds to the question with a historically defensible claim that establishes a line of reasoning that embraces both continuities and changes over time.

B. CONTEXTUALIZATION—1 POINT

The response earned a point for contextualization. The second paragraph references the *Plessy v. Ferguson* decision and establishes the extent of *de jure* segregation in the public schools on the eve of the *Brown* decision.

C. EVIDENCE—2 POINTS

The response earned a point for providing specific examples of evidence relevant to the question, as well as a point for using evidence to support an argument about the question. Specifics included the moral prestige given to the civil rights protests, the passage of the Civil Rights Act of 1964, and the impact of the "massive resistance" campaign. The response explained how these events produced both continuity and change in American society.

D. ANALYSIS AND REASONING—1 POINT

The response earned a point for using both continuity and change over time to frame an argument that addresses the prompt. The response provides a detailed understanding of how these historic processes affected American society.

E. COMPLEX UNDERSTANDING—1 POINT

The response demonstrated a detailed understanding of how the decision in *Brown v. Board of Education* affected American society in the period between 1954 and 2015. Its in-depth discussion included details about both how the decision sparked momentous social changes while at the same time failing to affect America's underlying economic inequalities and patterns of racial segregation.

PART VII

GLOSSARY

GLOSSARY

KEY TERMS AND HISTORIC GENERALIZATIONS

YOU ABSOLUTELY, POSITIVELY HAVE
TO KNOW

The glossaries in APUSH textbooks and prep books contain hundreds of vocabulary terms. If all of these words had an equal chance of appearing on your APUSH exam, studying would be very time-consuming and tedious.

Fortunately, the College Board provides APUSH students and teachers with a definitive course Framework. You can find this document at the AP Central website. The Framework provides a definitive presentation of the key terms and historic generalizations that form the backbone of the APUSH course. All of the questions on your APUSH exam are anchored in the course Framework.

The terms and generalizations featured in this Glossary are all derived from the APUSH Framework and are covered in Chapters 1–22. That is why you absolutely, positively have to know this essential content. It will make a significant contribution to your APUSH score!

PERIOD 1
1491–1607

1. COLUMBIAN EXCHANGE—The exchange of plants, animals, people, and germs between the New World and Europe following the discovery of America in 1492.

    Nutritious New World foods such as maize (corn) and potatoes improved the European diet, lengthened life spans, and stimulated a surge in economic activity that contributed to the ongoing shift from feudalism to capitalism in Western Europe.

    European diseases such as smallpox, measles, and influenza had a devastating impact on the Native American population. The sudden collapse of entire New World communities enabled European colonists to more easily gain control over Native American lands.

2. The *ENCOMIENDA* SYSTEM—The Spanish Crown rewarded important officials with an *encomienda*, a grant conferring the right to demand

tribute and labor from the local Native Americans. The Spanish used the encomienda system to organize and exploit Native American labor.

The *encomienda* system produced widespread abuses. In his *A Short History of the Destruction of the Indies*, Bartolomé de Las Casas described Spanish officials as "ravening wolves" who perpetrated unspeakable atrocities on Native Americans.

The abuses of the *encomienda* system played a key role in sparking the Pueblo Revolt in 1680.

PERIOD 2
1607–1754

3. INDENTURED SERVANTS—People who agreed to work for a set number of years in return for passage to the colonies. Indentured servants regained their status as free persons at the end of the contractual period.

   Virginia tobacco planters originally relied upon indentured servants from England. The number of indentured servants originally exceeded the number of enslaved Africans. The shift to enslaved Africans began in the years following Bacon's Rebellion in 1676.

4. ATLANTIC SLAVE TRADE—An inhuman commerce that uprooted more than ten million Africans from their homes and loved ones.

   Portugal initiated the Atlantic slave trade in the second half of the fifteenth century. European nations continued and expanded the slave trade to include colonies in the New World.

   Enslaved Africans replaced indigenous laborers and indentured servants on West Indian sugar plantations and Chesapeake tobacco plantations.

   The overwhelming majority of enslaved Africans worked on plantations in the Caribbean and Brazil. The British North American colonies had a lower demand for slaves than did the colonies of other European nations.

5. TRANS-ATLANTIC TRADE—The exchange of goods and labor between Africa, the Americas, and Europe. The complex web of trade routes led to the emergence of a thriving trans-Atlantic economy.

   West Indian sugar, Chesapeake tobacco, British manufactured goods, and West African slaves dominated trans-Atlantic trade. At the same time, many ships also carried books, newspapers, pamphlets, and letters.This trans-Atlantic print network spread Enlightenment ideas to influential colonial leaders.

6. MERCANTILISM—An economic policy followed by Great Britain and other European nations from the sixteenth to the eighteenth century.

    Under the mercantile system, Great Britain attempted to achieve a favorable balance of trade by purchasing raw materials from its North American colonies and then selling them more expensive manufactured goods.

    The British enacted a series of Navigation Acts to regulate commerce with her colonies. However, the British failed to enforce these regulations during a period known as "salutary neglect."

7. FIRST GREAT AWAKENING—A period of intense religious revival that began in New England in the mid-1730s and then spread across all the colonies by the 1740s.

    The First Great Awakening stressed emotion as a way to achieve personal salvation. Its emphasis upon personal salvation undermined the authority of established Congregational and Episcopalian ministers. The emergence of new Protestant denominations contributed to a spirit of independence and to a greater diversity of thought.

PERIOD 3
1754–1800

8. ENLIGHTENMENT—An eighteenth-century philosophical movement that emphasized the use of reason to question previously accepted doctrines and traditions.

    Leading Enlightenment thinkers such as John Locke stressed that all people have natural rights to life, liberty, and property. Locke's ideas prompted colonial leaders such as Tom Paine and Thomas Jefferson to rethink their rights as British subjects.

9. REPUBLICANISM—The belief that government derives its power from the people. This belief was a key part of the revolutionary spirit that motivated resistance to Britain's arbitrary taxation.

10. REPUBLICAN MOTHERHOOD—The idea that the primary political role of American women was to instill a sense of patriotic duty and republican virtue in their children.

    Republican motherhood enabled middle-class and upper-class women the opportunity to play an important role in shaping America's moral and political character. This role placed a new emphasis upon increasing educational opportunities for women.

11. ANTI-FEDERALISTS—Opponents of the proposed Constitution who favored strong state governments and a limited national government.

Anti-Federalists drew support from state officials, small farmers, debtors, and shopkeepers. They warned that the proposed Constitution failed to include a Bill of Rights to safeguard essential individual liberties.

PERIOD 4
1800–1848

12. JUDICIAL REVIEW—The power of the Supreme Court to strike down an act of Congress as unconstitutional. Established by the Marshall Court in *Marbury v. Madison*.

13. JUDICIAL NATIONALISM—The Supreme Court practice of rendering decisions that increase the power of the federal government.

The Marshall Court (1801–1835) issued a number of landmark decisions that illustrate judicial nationalism. For example, *McCulloch v. Maryland* declared the national bank constitutional and denied the right of a state to tax the legal activities of the federal government.

14. JACKSONIAN DEMOCRACY—A set of political beliefs associated with Andrew Jackson and his supporters. Jacksonian democracy included the appointment of political supporters to government offices and opposition to privileged Eastern financial elites.

15. AMERICAN SYSTEM—A legislative program promoted by Henry Clay. The American System included the following three major provisions. First, a tariff to protect American industries and raise revenue to finance internal improvements. Second, a national bank to promote financial stability. And finally, a network of federally financed roads and canals to facilitate commerce.

16. NULLIFICATION—John C. Calhoun argued that a state legislature or convention could void, or nullify, a law passed by Congress. The idea of nullification emerged from a larger intellectual debate over the relationship between the federal government and the states.

Nullification prioritized state and regional interests over national interests. Southern secessionists later used the doctrine of nullification as part of their legal justification for leaving the Union.

17. MARKET REVOLUTION—The term Market Revolution refers to the creation of a national economy between 1820 and 1860.

During the early 1800s, most Americans bought goods from friends and neighbors in a local economy. A growing network of roads, canals, steam ship lines and rail lines linked consumers and producers in regional and even national markets.

The creation of large profitable markets led to an American system of manufacturing that utilized machines with interchangeable parts to mass produce standardized low-cost goods.

The Market Revolution accelerated the rate of industrial growth in the Northeast. It also accelerated the migration of settlers into the Midwest. Canals, roads, and rail lines linked the economies of the Northeast and Midwest. However, the South failed to keep up with the pace of industrial and urban growth in the Northeast and Midwest. It remained an agricultural economy dominated by an elite group of wealthy planters.

18. CULT OF DOMESTICITY—The Cult of Domesticity is the idealization of women in their roles as wives and mothers. As a nurturing mother and faithful spouse, the wife had a special responsibility to create a home that was a "haven in a heartless world."

As the Market Revolution gained momentum, it encouraged a division of labor between home and work. While men held jobs in a competitive market economy, the home became the special "sphere" for women.

The Cult of Domesticity embodied a cultural ideal that best applied to middle-class families who could afford to maintain separate spheres for their work and home lives. However, a wide gap separated these privileged women from mill women working in factories, frontier women working on isolated farms, and enslaved African women working on cotton plantations.

19. SECOND GREAT AWAKENING—A wave of religious fervor that swept across America between 1800 and the early 1830s.

Leading Second Great Awakening ministers such as Charles Grandison Finney delivered inspiring sermons stressing that Christians are not doomed by original sin. Instead, Finney insisted that people are "moral free agents" who could achieve personal salvation and thus spiritual rebirth.

It was a short step from the Second Great Awakening's emphasis upon spiritual progress to a belief in social progress. The optimistic belief that Christians have an obligation to improve their society generated a number of reform movements, ranging from temperance to abolitionism.

Middle-class women played an especially important role in the Second Great Awakening. They boosted church membership and also spearheaded a number of reform movements.

20. PERFECTIONISM—Belief that people can achieve a moral perfection in their earthly lives. Perfectionism led to an optimistic faith in the human ability to build a just society.

PERIOD 5
1844–1877

21. MANIFEST DESTINY—Nineteenth-century belief that the United States was destined to spread democratic institutions and the blessings of liberty across the North American continent.

   The ideology of Manifest Destiny contributed to the U.S. decision to fight the Mexican-American War. Manifest Destiny is similar to the ideology that supported American involvement in the Spanish-American War.

22. NATIVISM—Anti-foreign sentiment among native-born Americans. It was originally triggered by the wave of Irish Catholic immigrants in the 1840s and 1850s.

   Anti-Catholic and anti-immigrant passions sparked the formation of the Know-Nothing Party. Although the Know-Nothings soon disappeared, the party marked the beginning of a recurring pattern of nativist backlash against immigrants.

23. POPULAR SOVEREIGNTY—Belief that the settlers in a given territory have the right to decide whether or not to accept slavery.

   Kansas marked the first important test of popular sovereignty. Within a short time, proslavery and antislavery groups streamed into Kansas to influence the elections. A civil war erupted, claiming almost 200 lives. The violence gave the territory the nickname "Bleeding Kansas."

24. BLACK CODES—Laws passed by Southern states after the Civil War denying ex-slaves the civil rights enjoyed by whites. The codes punished "crimes" such as failing to have a labor contract or travelling outside a plantation without a pass.

   President Johnson did not object to the Black Codes. His lenient view of Reconstruction placed him on a collision course with a Congress dominated by Radical Republicans who wanted to transform the South by extending civil and political rights to African Americans.

25. SHARECROPPING—Following the Civil War, Southern planters adopted a labor system in which newly freed slaves became sharecroppers who exchanged their labor for the use of land, tools, and seed.

Sharecroppers typically gave the landowners half of their crop. The system trapped African Americans in a seemingly endless cycle of poverty and debt.

26. FOURTEENTH AMENDMENT—This landmark amendment granted African Americans citizenship, thus overturning the *Dred Scott* decision and the Three-Fifths Compromise.

    In addition, the Fourteenth Amendment prohibited states from depriving "any person of life, liberty, or property, without due process of law; nor deny to any person within its jurisdiction equal protection of the laws." The full force of the "equal protection" clause would not be felt until the watershed *Brown v. Board of Education* decision in 1954.

27. FIFTEENTH AMENDMENT—Ratified in 1870, the Fifteenth Amendment stated that male voting rights could not be denied based on "race, color, or previous condition of servitude."

    Southern states successfully used grandfather clauses, poll taxes, and literacy tests to circumvent the amendment and disenfranchise African Americans.

    The Fifteenth Amendment left women's rights activists feeling outraged and abandoned. Women did not receive the right to vote until the passage of the Nineteenth Amendment in 1920.

28. THE END OF RECONSTRUCTION—Reconstruction officially ended in 1877 when President Hays removed the last remaining federal troops from the South.

    The end of Reconstruction was not a surprise. Republicans had been growing weary of pressing their reform agenda in a hostile region. Efforts to change Southern racial attitudes and culture faltered because of the South's determined resistance and the North's waning resolve.

29. REDEEMERS—White Southern political leaders who claimed to "redeem" the South from Republican domination. Redeemers supported a "New South" based on diversified economic growth and white supremacy.

PERIOD 6
1865–1898

30. FORCED ASSIMILATION—Policy pursued by the Bureau of Indian Affairs to "Americanize" Native American children.

    The Dawes Act attempted to "civilize" the Plains Indians by turning them into individual homeowners and farmers.

Reform groups and churches launched an all-out campaign on Indian children by isolating them in a network of boarding schools. School officials attempted to "Americanize" Native American children by teaching them about American culture while simultaneously forcing the students to give up their indigenous culture, language, spiritual beliefs, and tribal names.

31. THE DOCTRINE OF "SEPARATE BUT EQUAL"—The "separate but equal" doctrine emerged from the Supreme Court decision in *Plessy v. Ferguson*. The Court ruled that racial segregation did not violate the equal protection clause of the Fourteenth Amendment.

    The doctrine of "separate but equal" led to the end of most of the political gains African Americans made during Reconstruction. It also marked the beginning of a long era of Jim Crow segregation in the South.

32. SOCIAL DARWINISM—The belief that there is a natural evolutionary process by which the fittest will survive and prosper. During the Gilded Age, wealthy business and industrial leaders used Social Darwinism to justify their success as both appropriate and inevitable.

    Social Darwinism provided a convenient explanation for the growing disparity of wealth between the rich and poor during the late nineteenth century.

33. GOSPEL OF WEALTH—View advanced by Andrew Carnegie that the wealthy have a moral obligation to help the less fortunate and improve society. Carnegie believed that the rich could best serve society by funding institutions such as colleges and public libraries that created "ladders of success."

34. SOCIAL GOSPEL—Late nineteenth-century reform movement based on the belief that Christians have a moral responsibility to actively confront poverty and other social problems. Led by Christian ministers, advocates of the Social Gospel argued that real social change would result from dedication to both religious practice and social reform.

35. NEW IMMIGRANTS—The massive wave of immigrants from Southern and Eastern Europe who came to America between 1890 and 1924. Booming industrial growth provided plentiful jobs, while America's constitutional freedoms offered hope for new lives.

36. URBAN POLITICAL MACHINES—Organization of professional politicians that dominated government in many American cities. Machine politicians established a personal relationship with working-class immigrants by providing social services in exchange for votes.

PERIOD 7
1890–1945

37. IMPERIALISM—The policy of extending a nation's power through military conquest, economic domination, and/or annexation.

    The United States undertook an expansionist foreign policy to locate sources of raw materials, open new markets for American goods, compete with European powers for colonies, and spread the ideals of liberty and democracy to nations in Latin America and Asia.

    The U.S. victory in the Spanish-American War transformed America into an imperial power. It also sparked debates about the wisdom of acquiring overseas territories. The acquisition of the Philippine Islands ignited a controversial debate over the merits of America's new interventionist foreign policy.

38. POPULIST PARTY—A third party that emerged during the early 1890s. The growth of corporate power in agriculture and discriminatory freight rates fueled the rise of the Populist Party.

    The Populist Platform called for a strong government role in the nation's economic system. Specific Populist demands included government control of the railroads, free coinage of silver, a graduated income tax, and the direct election of U.S. senators.

39. MUCKRAKERS—Progressive Era journalists who exposed illegal business practices, social injustices, and corrupt urban political bosses. Leading muckrakers included Upton Sinclair, Jacob Riis, and Ida Tarbell.

40. PROGRESSIVES—Predominantly well-educated, middle-class reformers who lived in urban areas. Middle-class women played a leading role in the Progressive movement.

    Progressives focused on a broad range of problems caused by industrialization, urbanization, and immigration. Progressives wanted government to play an active role in eliminating industrial abuses, expanding democratic practices, and supporting moral reform. However, Progressives devoted little attention to the plight of African Americans.

    Progressives supported constitutional amendments for women's suffrage, temperance, a graduated income tax, and the popular election of U.S. senators.

41. PRESERVATIONISTS/CONSERVATIONISTS—Both environmental movements responded to the wanton exploitation of western forests, wildlife, and scenic areas. Preservationists believed that government

policies should preserve wilderness areas in their natural state. In contrast, Conservationists believed that government policies should promote the management of environmental resources in a responsible and sustained manner.

42. RED SCARE—The wave of anticommunist hysteria that swept across the United States after World War I.

In November 1917, Bolsheviks led by Vladimir Lenin seized power in Russia and promptly created a communist dictatorship. The unexpected upheaval in Russia alarmed many Americans who believed that communist sympathizers and other radicals were secretly planning to undermine the United States government.

The public's anxiety about radicals led to a Red Scare that swept across the United States after World War I. The Red Scare's worst abuses included a series of government raids on alleged subversives and a suppression of civil liberties.

43. IMMIGRATION QUOTAS—The National Origins Act of 1924 established quotas that limited immigration to two percent of a country's population in the United States at the time of the 1890 census.

During the early 1920s, a combination of religious prejudice, economic competition, and scientific racism fueled a revival of nativist sentiment directed at the New Immigrants. The Red Scare also contributed to public fear of radicals who allegedly sought to overthrow the government.

Congress responded to the fear that immigrants were dangerous radicals by passing the National Origins Act of 1924.

44. THE GREAT MIGRATION—The mass movement of African Americans from the rural South to cities in the Northeast and Midwest is known as the Great Migration. The push of discrimination in the South and the pull of a booming Northern job market convinced about 1.5 million African Americans to migrate to the North in the years between 1910 and 1930.

World War II ignited a second phase of the Great Migration. During the 1940s, a massive wave of about one million Southern blacks boarded "liberty trains" heading for urban areas in the Northeast, Midwest, and Pacific coast.

In the quarter-century following World War II, more than five million African Americans left the South to search for better jobs, higher wages, and greater social equality. By 1970, about 80 percent of African Americans lived in urban areas.

45. HARLEM RENAISSANCE—A flowering of African American artists, writers, and intellectuals during the 1920s. Harlem Renaissance writers used the term "New Negro" as a proud assertion of African American culture.

46. FLAPPERS—Young women in the 1920s who defied conventional standards of conduct by wearing short skirts and makeup, dancing to jazz, and flaunting a liberated lifestyle.

    Women of the 1920s were able to take more active roles than had previous generations. Print magazines, moving pictures, and radio advertisements all glamorized the flapper's independent lifestyle.

47. NEW DEAL—A legislative response to the economic crisis caused by the Great Depression. New Deal relief programs provided direct federal assistance to unemployed Americans. New Deal recovery programs used deficit spending for public works projects to revive the economy. And finally, New Deal reform programs created regulatory agencies to address instability in the stock market and banking system.

    The New Deal did not end the Depression. However, it did leave a legacy of reforms such as Social Security and important accomplishments such as the Tennessee Valley Authority (TVA).

    New Deal programs helped African Americans survive some of the worst hardships of the Great Depression. However, the New Deal did not directly confront racial segregation. As a result, the New Deal did not include major civil rights legislation.

    African Americans became part of the New Deal coalition of voters. The coalition also included labor unions, ethnic minorities, and white Southerners.

PERIOD 8
1945–1980

48. COLD WAR—A prolonged period of economic and political rivalry between the United States and the Soviet Union. The Cold War began with the announcement of the Truman Doctrine in 1947 and ended with the fall of the Berlin Wall in 1989 and the collapse of the Soviet Union in 1991.

49. CONTAINMENT—America's Cold War strategy of blocking the expansion of Soviet influence. The Truman Doctrine committed the United States to use its military and economic strength to contain the expansion of Soviet influence.

    The Marshall Plan committed the United States to provide a massive program of economic assistance to help the nations of Western Europe recover from the devastation caused by World War II.

The United States, Canada, and ten Western European nations formed the North Atlantic Treaty Organization (NATO) as a military alliance to block Soviet expansion. NATO operates on the principle of COLLECTIVE SECURITY, in which member nations pledge to consider an attack on one as an attack on all.

50. DÉTENTE—A policy advocated by President Nixon and his national security advisor Henry Kissinger to relax tensions between the United States and the Soviet Union. Examples of détente include Nixon's trip to Moscow, the signing of a Strategic Arms Limitation Treaty, expanded trade with the Russia, and joint U.S. and Soviet space missions.

51. DECOLONIZATION—The emergence of nationalist movements in Asia, Africa, and the Middle East in the years following World War II. The United States and the Soviet Union competed for influence in the newly independent nations. Dr. King urged America to "get on the right side of the world revolution."

52. McCARTHYISM—Term associated with Senator Joseph McCarthy's anti-Communist crusade during the early 1950s.

McCarthy's unsubstantiated accusations that communists had infiltrated the U.S. State Department and other federal agencies reflected popular anxieties about Soviet influence at home and abroad. The political climate of the McCarthy era resembled the attacks on radicals and immigrants following the First World War.

53. BEATS—A small but influential group of literary figures based in New York City and San Francisco in the 1950s. Led by Jack Kerouac and Allan Ginsburg, the Beats rejected mainstream America's carefree consumption and mindless conformity.

54. DOMINO THEORY—Geopolitical belief that the fall of one nation to Communism would inevitably lead to the fall of other nearby countries. The domino theory played a key role in President Johnson's decision to escalate the Vietnam War.

55. BLACK POWER—The Black Power movement of the 1960s advocated that African Americans establish control of their economic and political lives.

Malcolm X and Stokely Carmichael stressed the importance of black racial pride. They viewed the American Black Power movement as a part of a global revolution by newly independent African nations.

56. COUNTERCULTURE—A cultural movement during the late 1960s associated with an alternative lifestyle based upon peace, love, and "doing your own thing."

The counterculture's independent spirit faded within a decade. It nonetheless left a lasting impact on American culture by encouraging a vision of freedom that fostered experimentation and more permissive norms of behavior.

The excesses of the counterculture sparked a backlash among outraged evangelical Christians that contributed to the resurgence of the conservative movement during the 1970s.

57. RIGHTS REVOLUTION—Between 1954 and 1969 the Warren Court issued a series of decisions that expanded civil rights and individual liberties. These decisions and the ongoing Civil Rights movement played an important role in encouraging a Rights Revolution among newly energized minority groups. For example, feminists, Latinos, American Indians, and gays and lesbians all organized mass movements that focused on issues of identity and social justice.

58. RADICAL FEMINISTS—A feminist movement that emerged in the late 1960s. Radical feminists focused on personal issues such as reproductive rights, domestic violence, and the objectification of women as sexual objects.

59. SUNBELT—A booming region of 14 states, stretching from North Carolina through Florida and Texas to Arizona and California. Sunbelt conservatives formed an important part of the conservative coalition that elected Ronald Reagan president in 1980.

60. RELIGIOUS RIGHT—Conservative Christians who opposed sexual permissiveness, the Equal Rights Amendment, and abortion.

The Religious Right became a significant force in American politics when Jerry Falwell founded the Moral Majority in 1979. The Religious Right became an important part of the conservative coalition that elected Ronald Reagan president in 1980.

PERIOD 9
1980–PRESENT

61. REAGANOMICS—Term used by the press to describe President Reagan's SUPPLY-SIDE economic policies. Reagan's program attempted to promote growth and investment by deregulating business, reducing corporate taxes rates, and lowering federal taxes for upper-income and middle-income Americans.

Reagan's economic proposals helped stimulate the economy and promote a period of sustained growth and prosperity. However, liberals and many senior citizens resisted his efforts to reduce popular programs such as Social Security and Medicare.

62. DIGITAL REVOLUTION—The microprocessor helped launch a Digital Revolution that included innovations such as personal computers, the Internet, and smartphones. These devices facilitated a new Digital Age, characterized by instantaneous communication and constant connectivity.

63. GLOBALIZATION—The process by which technological, economic, political, and cultural exchanges are making the world more interconnected and interdependent. As a result, the United States is now part of an integrated global economy.

   Globalization has intensified worldwide competition for low-cost labor. The lure of cheap labor encouraged American companies to relocate their production facilities in countries such as China and Mexico. This has caused a loss of well-paying manufacturing jobs and a sharp decline in union membership.

64. WAR ON TERROR—The 9/11 attacks on the World Trade Tower and the Pentagon prompted President Bush to launch a concerted campaign to destroy international terrorist groups. The War on Terror began with military campaigns in Afghanistan and Iraq.

   The War on Terror also sought to improve security within the United States. However, critics raised questions about how new security measures posed a threat to long-standing protections for civil and human rights.

Made in the USA
Coppell, TX
13 November 2020